NEVER SAY DIE

GEORGE PIGGINS

NEVER SAY DIE

THE FIGHT TO SAVE THE RABBITOHS

As told to Ian Heads

MACMILLAN
Pan Macmillan Australia

First published 2002 in Macmillan
by Pan Macmillan Australia Pty Limited
St Martins Tower, 31 Market Street, Sydney

National Library of Australia
Cataloguing-in-Publication data:

Piggins, George.
Never say die.

ISBN 0 7329 1105 2.

1. Piggins, George. 2. South Sydney District Rugby League
Football Club. 3. Rugby League football players –
Australia – Biography. 4. Rugby League football – New
South Wales. I. Heads, Ian. II. Title.

796.3338092

Typeset in 12.5/14 pt Bembo by Post Pre-press Group
Printed in Australia by McPherson's Printing Group

Lines from 'We Told You So' by Nancy Keesing
reproduced with permission of the estate of Nancy Keesing.

This book is dedicated to the people of Australia, those ordinary folk who gave all they had to fight for a poor, working-class sporting club . . . and a principle. To those wonderful human beings who proved the invincibility of People Power – thank you!

Contents

Acknowledgements   ix
A Few Words About George   x
Preface by Ian Heads   xv
Introduction: Final Judgment   1

PART ONE   17
1   Dog Days   19
2   The Wonderful World of Mascot   25
3   The Team in the Red and Green   36
4   Truckin'   54
5   Bloody Battles . . . and a Man Named Churchill   69
6   Blood 'n' Thunder Days: Playing the Game   80
7   The Coaching Caper: Simple Truths   94
8   Tea at Kerry's Place   115

PART TWO   125
9   Super League: The Monster that Ate Rugby League   127
10 The Day the ARL Threw in the Towel   161
11 Bali to Dubbo: A Bad News Odyssey   178
12 Into the Trenches   188
13 My Best Mate   220
14 Rabbit Cull   226
15 Our Day in Court: Round One   252
16 Our Day in Court: Round Two   273
17 The Longest Wait   293

Acknowledgements

There are many individuals to whom Souths owes an enormous debt and I am unable to name them all. But I would like to single out broadcaster and personal friend Alan Jones, whose moral and financial support, as well as his many deeds, kept our club afloat in its darkest hours.

I thank my good mate Norm Lipson, whose support and assistance throughout all of this was enormous. His loyalty to this cause was only matched by his great fighting spirit.

I thank the ethnic communities who came out in force, the wonderful Lebanese and Greek Australians who rallied and raised desperately needed funds.

I thank the various churches and religious organisations that stood by us and inspired us.

I thank the Construction, Forestry, Mining and Energy Union (CFMEU), whose leaders and members stood stead-fastly with us and took up the fight for the rights of ordinary people.

Lastly, to my wife Nolene, because it was your determination, energy and loyalty that played a major role in Souths' victory.

A Few Words About George

George is the exceptional character. I don't know whether he served in any conflict, but better than most in the classic struggle of 'David and Goliath', he understood that this was a war, a war to the great game of rugby league. There are no winners, only survivors.

He has single-handedly endowed the game with a new sense of moral capacity, not just for what it can earn but for what it represents: the ordinary person doing extraordinary things and rising above Goliath.

Perseverance, determination and the power of the people is what got this conflict across the line. And as God would want it, even now, Goliath will wear the colours of the mighty red and green!

Senator Aden Ridgeway

The fight for South Sydney's survival was about more than just sport. At stake were the rights of the little man versus the arrogant demands of big business. In a display of people power rarely seen in this country, tens of thousands of disenfranchised fans stood up and said 'No' to the most feared media monolith in the world. At their centre stood George Piggins; perhaps the

most immovable object an irresistible force has ever met. In the
end, the irresistible force was broken – and sport took its first step
back to where it belongs: in the backyards of ordinary Australians, rather than in the boardrooms of multinationals.
Andrew Denton

George Piggins didn't just deliver a South Sydney victory. He
returned to ordinary Australians a faith and a belief in the
supremacy of simple values. He reaffirmed that loyalty, tradition,
history and personal identity still mean something in a world
dominated by corporate bullying, big bucks and often total indif-
ference to the sensitivities and concerns of the individual.

George Piggins became sport's, and not just rugby league's,
Everyman – simple, straightforward, uncomplicated, but equally
uncompromising. Souths as a result emerged a winner. But the
biggest winner was the fact that a sporting life, based on values
and loyalty, tradition and passion, was still capable of asserting
itself.
Alan Jones

George had it right from the start. Souths had been the 'Pride of
the League' for more than 70 years, and there was no way he was
going to let them be pushed into any merger, or lower division
competition. As far as George was concerned the red and green
belonged to the club and belonged in the district – and that was
the way it was going to be. And he never let up, despite all the
people trying to tell Souths they had to merge. I have known
George Piggins from when he was a kid – and he was the same
then: tough and dogged. He won a comp for Souths (1971). He's
a beauty. He stuck to what was right and fair . . . and he beat
them.
Albert Clift

I'm sure the other clubs who succumbed to pressure and merged
now wish they had a George Piggins in their ranks. I've heard
him called the greatest saviour since Jesus Christ! I toured with

him on the World Cup campaign of 1975 and liked him then. You've got to admire the bloke. He stuck to something he believed in, and showed what power strong belief can have. George is the sort of bloke you'd like to have on your side, whatever you were doing. I always thought that what was done to Souths was wrong, that the decision was unjust. Souths were lucky to have George to lead the way and stand against it. His rock solid belief that the club had every right to stand alone saved the Rabbitohs. He didn't flinch.
Michael Cronin

When George Piggins said he'd rather hang up the Souths jersey in a glass case than amalgamate, he had my total support. 'Let's hold the line and see what happens,' he said to me at the time. In the maniacal days of Super League, when untold millions in Monopoly money were being shovelled at players and clubs, George took Kerry Packer's hand and said Souths would hold the ARL line. And we did – even when deals and double-crosses were done around us. I sat with George as the second courtroom verdict went against us. He mumbled one expletive, took a deep breath and told the media pack outside that Souths would hold the line. And we did. Thanks George.
Ray Martin

What George did best was share his enthusiasm. On game day he was always ready. He had the opportunity to move on to other clubs, but stayed with the Rabbits, because that was what he wanted to do. George told me never argue with the boneheads. He said: 'They will drag you down to their level, then beat you with experience.' George has been with the Rabbits close to 40 seasons. In that time he's gone from sitting at the end of the bench in third grade to president, holding just about every title along the way. This bloke hasn't got a nickname – it's just George.
Jack Gibson

'I would rather die on my feet than live on my knees.' I don't know where I first read that quote, but I have never forgotten it. It springs to mind every time I think of George Piggins and the mighty South Sydney Rabbitohs. George's message has always been simple. When you are right and you have truth on your side never back down to anyone. While others now learn to cope with life on their knees, South Sydney marches on!
Phil Gould

I remember the first time I met George at the club. I'd been invited to join a group of people dedicated to helping save the Rabbitohs. I was amazed that a man so famous for his tough attitude, not only on the field but also later in the press, was so quietly spoken. Yet how in a room filled with people used to hearing the sound of their own voices – radio broadcasters, television personalties, lawyers and politicians and the like – a few quiet words from George could rise above any conversation going on. To have any understanding of the Souths struggle over the past few years you have to understand George and to a great extent Nolene. Not only did the two of them work tirelessly, they became a rallying point around which other people could gather. On days when we were doing it tough you knew no-one felt worse than George and that's why when victory came at last the joy on George's face could have lit up all of Redfern.
Mikey Robins

George Piggins knew that what was being done to Souths was wrong, and there was no way the people trying to kill Souths were ever going to get on top of him. He was up against one of the biggest blokes in the world but he hung in, and hung in, because he knew he was right. George was like that as a footballer; he probably wasn't blessed with the talent of a Coote, a McCarthy or a Gasnier, but he was hard and determined, and he did the work. And that's exactly the way he's been throughout this. One thing I know is that Souths couldn't have done it without him. There were those on the board who wavered, and were

ready to put up their hands in defeat. George never did. It has been a marvellous effort – one that has probably taken a lifetime's toll on him, given him a real flogging. He did it because he loves Souths.
John Sattler

If the rest of the rugby league world wants an example of leadership, we should take George Piggins as our inspiration. George fought for over two years to have South Sydney reinstalled to the competition. He did it because he believed that rugby league is a game of the people, of tribal and community loyalties, not a pawn for the 'men in suits' to mould as just another business decision. Souths have now got the reward their perseverance deserves. They, and George Piggins, should be an inspiration to every rugby league person.
Harry Edgar

The leadership of George Piggins was obviously instrumental in holding this club together. It was an outburst of community cohesion that you seldom see in Australia, and it really is rewarding to see something like that. My first reaction (on hearing the verdict) was I grinned and thought, they've done it!
Kerry Stokes

Preface by Ian Heads

SOMEWHERE IN RUGBY LEAGUE'S archives is film of the amazing try George Piggins scored for South Sydney against Western Suburbs on the afternoon of Sunday, May 2, 1976. Piggins, chunky, fierce and determined, somehow batters his way through a wall of black-and-white defenders on his way to a most unlikely touchdown. As Channel 7 commentator Rex 'the Moose' Mossop screams, 'George only knows one way – and that's *hard*.' The suspicion is that if News Limited heavies or NRL suits had viewed that film – or the one of Piggins's famous SCG fight with the equally ferocious Malcolm Reilly in '73 – they would surely have gulped at what might lie ahead if and when South Sydney was kicked out of the competition to compress rugby league into the 'magical' 14-team format.

The decision, on October 15, 1999, to axe Souths – the most famous and successful club in the league – unleashed the dogs of war. As Souths chairman, General George Piggins, just as fierce and determined as he was back in the '70s, strapped on the gloves and shaped up. No way was some corporate mob going to steal the heritage of his district, or take away the 92-year-old football club that the people of Redfern and surrounds had lived for, cheered for, and cried for. Adding a hard edge of anger was the belief of Piggins and those around him that Souths had been 'dudded', the victims of a predetermined three-card trick when the 14 premiership spots were handed out.

And so the fight began, with Piggins at the helm, flanked by his equally determined wife Nolene, an influential group of committed lieutenants, and backed by a swelling army of Souths fans. In the course of a long battle, George Piggins of Mascot grew into something approaching an Australian folk hero. For many people in profoundly changing times, George represents the common man, leading the fight against the forces of globalisation, economic rationalism and the crushing influence of multinational giants. The *Daily Telegraph*'s premier columnist Mike Gibson captured the spirit of the times:

> The local branch of the bank has either closed or else they don't want to know you. The post office is gone. The family who sold the corner shop have sold out because they couldn't compete with the multi-nationally-owned supermarket at the mall. The pub has become a mini-casino where sad, solitary figures in darkened corners pour their pay packets into poker machines.

This book, shaped in the period during and after Souths' third Federal Court challenge, tells two stories. The first is an uplifting Aussie tale of a kid born without a silver spoon in his mouth in post-war Sydney who, through the sweat of his own labour and the use of a creative mind, built himself up to a position of affluence and success in the community. The George Piggins of 2002 lives comfortably, in a beautiful house overlooking the ocean, and owns two fine country properties south of Sydney – at one of them he stands the stallion Pre-Catalan and indulges his passion for breeding and racing thoroughbreds. The first story tells too of Piggins the footballer – one of the most loyal, toughest, hardiest characters ever to pull on the famous cardinal and myrtle colours of the South Sydney Rabbitohs. The trials and successes of his working life and the enduring doggedness of his 15 seasons as a hooker with Souths – during which he went all the way to winning a premiership and a coveted Australian jersey – are powerful clues behind the second part of George's story, the unyielding fight Piggins waged for his club after the Rupert Murdoch–backed Super League war broke foully over the game in 1995.

What follows here is George Piggins's uniquely personal story, reflecting his own deeply held thoughts and beliefs. Inevitably there will be those who disagree strongly with aspects of that Piggins view. For a long period, for example, there were fierce opponents of Piggins's unflinching view that a merger with some other club was *not* the answer for Souths – a stance incidentally that looked more and more right with every passing day, and especially so when the Manly–Norths partnership (the 'Northern Eagles') collapsed disastrously. There are even those along the way who have seen Piggins as the Souths *problem*, a football man from another era, standing in the way of progress for the old club in football's 'new age'. That sort of view is encapsulated in the last paragraph of the *Daily Telegraph*'s editorial which followed Souths' axing in October '99: 'The reasons for this action [the axing] lay with their own club officials who were inactive – relying on tradition and Souths' record, while other clubs worked towards the future.' Indeed it could be said that Souths were slow to change, slow to react to the new demands that modern sport presented. But the fact is that they *did* respond – they bit the bullet and introduced new people and new ways.

The 1990s were certainly times of below-par achievement on the football field for the Rabbitohs. But that's something clubs go through. For a long period in the 1940s Souths struggled to win a single game, then from 1950 to 1955 they won five premierships in six years, and were runners-up in the other year. For 92 years Souths had always paid their way, always got robustly through their seasons, and built more success than any other club in rugby league. The old football saying still resonates: 'When Souths are going well, rugby league is going well.'

Those at the club say that Piggins, an intelligent businessman, gradually softened his theory that if you 'hadn't pulled on a boot' and 'didn't understand football' then you had no chance of properly running a football club. A strong figure in the Souths fight said: 'He understands it now – understands now that being a good footballer doesn't necessarily equate with being a good businessman, and that he is the exception, not the norm. And he is the exception. He has a very good business brain.' Even so, Piggins himself admitted that he had not been 'as comfortable' working with the high-profile Souths board of recent times as he was with the 'old' board of committed, dyed-in-the-wool footy men.

The fact is that George, being the sort of bloke he is, has stepped on a few toes along the way. The Piggins management style could fairly be described as autocratic . . . boots 'n' all. For Piggins as chairman, the task of being at the head of a group which included philosophically opposed members of the NSW Labor Party was never easy. There have been blow-ups and dis-agreements, the worst of them perhaps the regrettable falling-out in December 2000 between Piggins and his deputy chairman, Test cricketer and Souths 'tragic', Mike Whitney. The story is told in Chapter 17. It shows the anger that can boil over occasionally in George Piggins at a perceived slight or wrong-doing. But, probably more than anything else, that incident reflects the stress and tension that all at Souths were under after more than two years of backs-to-the-wall fighting. All those in the leadership team were affected in one way or another; in George Piggins's case, his health suffered. A brief, fierce eruption, and Whitney was gone from the club, although his lifetime support of the Rab-bitohs remains solidly in place. He still rings to see how things are going.

'He was a hero of mine,' says Whitney, still bruised, 'and I was hell bent on seeing Souths fight through to the very end. George had my total support.' Whitney has talked to friends of how his regard for Piggins is such that he would have his statue 'cast in bronze' to stand forever at Redfern Oval, and that the club should 'forever and a day' make sure Piggins was honoured for the work he had done in fighting to save the club. Plans were afoot to have George, on his eventual stand-down from the chairmanship, whenever that came, as permanent life-patron of the club, forever on a pedestal. Others at Souths saw the blow-up as greatly regrettable and viewed Whitney as a casualty of the enormous pressure that the board had been under, and especially so its leader, Piggins, heading every twist and turn of the fight.

There were those in the wings who along the way accused Piggins of being a grandstander, of revelling in the spotlight that illuminated the struggle, as he and Nolene, such a powerful 'second force', led the fight, side by side. But his supporters strongly disagree. 'In fact he hates being the focal point of it all,' said Dr Jim Lahood, a good mate and a strong campaigner for the Souths cause. 'For George there was no quest for self glory. He has done what he has done simply because he believes very deeply in what he has been fighting for.' Nolene, who has fought as fiercely as her man, has said of him: 'He is not a person who wants to be seen as anything other than a normal guy, and nothing will change that. In fact he probably feels he's not good enough. He's embarrassed when people suggest that he's some sort of martyr.'

The *Daily Telegraph* sports columnist Paul Kent called Piggins 'a throwback to better times, he takes us to a time when your word was bond, when a handshake meant something, when you could tell a man by the look in his eye.' George is indeed 'old style'. In the world of club land, where largesse is a way of life and especially so if you happen to be a director, George *always* pays his way.

In the early months of 2001, rumours did the rounds that News Limited wanted to find a way to get Souths back in the competition, but could not bring itself to do it with Piggins at the helm. Piggins answered publicly and effectively that if such an offer existed in written form, he would immediately step down. There is no doubt that News Limited itself was sorely damaged by the battle. Estimates of its exposure to the game of rugby league since 1995 stand at $750 million. The company's public standing – and possibly newspaper sales – suffered as 'ordinary' people threw their support behind the Rabbitohs. In speculation about the eventual outcome, News was likened to ancient Rome: it would only extend mercy when it had broken the opposition, flattened them. But, as the company found, it's impossible to 'break' a club when a man such as George Piggins holds the reins.

There is no doubt that the Souths fight provided embarrassment and deep discomfort for both News Limited and the NRL. The outcome of that, added to the further (and justified!) unease at the damage done to the game by the botched Super League takeover bid, has caused an invisible line to be drawn on the past. Rugby league had always robustly celebrated its heroes and its traditions, and that link – present to past – has given the game much of its rich flavour down the years. But, as the game moves into the new century, its focus has been shifted almost entirely onto the 'now'. Famous ex-players are rarely invited into today's scene and many have drifted from the game. Distinguished, retired media men such as Frank Hyde and Alan Clarkson, whose working lives were committed so enthusiastically to telling rugby league's stories over a period of decades, are, sadly, out of the loop, when both still have much to contribute. Souths are an integral part of rugby league's tradition. No club has a record (20 premierships), a history or an aura to match them. It makes sense that the men who attempted to chop such a rich seam of history and achievement from the competition would shy away from looking back.

On the day Souths were axed, the *Daily Telegraph*'s editorial expressed sympathy for South Sydney supporters. The editor referred to the club's 'proud history', then made the point: 'However tradition – because of its reliance on past values – often clouds contemporary issues, evoking passion instead of clear, forward thinking.' Interestingly, one of the paper's leading sports authorities, Phil Rothfield, had written in the *Telegraph*'s '2000 Official NRL Album' that the game of rugby league in fact could be encapsulated in the word 'passion'. The *Sydney Morning Herald*'s Malcolm Knox observed the axing of Souths and the huge backlash that followed, and wrote: 'Under its new management the game will prefer to look forward. Looking back would cause too much embarrassment.'

Kilometres of white post-and-rail fences at the Piggins' stud farm Cadwarri, west of Bowral in the Southern Highlands, provided a metaphor for both George's struggle and that of the club. Throughout the long period of the court cases, Piggins undertook the monumental task of painting the fencing, all 3000 panels, stretching as far as the eye can see across lush grasslands. He escaped Sydney whenever he could. It was a crushing task, with the hours of daylight allowing for about 40 panels to be painted each day. To look up would have been hugely demoralising. But George considered only the post immediately at hand, then moved on, dogged, determined, unstoppable, able to glimpse the job's end in his mind's eye. And so it was with the impasse: News Limited/NRL v. Piggins and Souths – the irresistible force v. the immovable object.

The George Piggins story that unfolds in these pages is a tough one, characteristically offering no apologies and at times blistering opinions. Progressively, the story grows to become just as much about the remarkable power a peoples' movement can muster when a strong man is at the helm. Up-front throughout the Souths' fight was this solid, blunt, unusual man, exuding his own aura of gruff strength and quiet inspiration. A genuine, tough-minded Aussie, fighting on and on for a cause he believed in very deeply. People close to the club say that Souths could not possibly have taken the fight as far as they did without the leadership strength and unbending determination that George Piggins showed. There was a certain rough-hewn nobility in it, and even his opponents nod in grudging admiration.

For fans and those who love him and what he stands for, the red-and-green bumper sticker says it all: 'In George We Trust'.

And when, on the morning of July 6, 2001 the full bench of the Federal Court announced in Sydney their stunning verdict that Souths had beaten City Hall (News Limited and the NRL) and thus were to be back in the rugby league competition, the radio station phonelines sang hymns of praise to the tough little bloke from Mascot. 'He should be knighted,' one caller put it simply that day. But George's place in the scheme of things, in leading his brave guerilla fighters against a seemingly over-whelming force of corporate power and money was long-since established. By then George Piggins was already an All-Australian Hero.

This is his story.

Ian Heads
December, 2001

Introduction:
Final Judgment

Never doubt that a small group of thoughtful, committed citizens can change the world. Indeed it is the only thing that ever has.

Margaret Mead

IT WAS LATE Thursday morning when the phone rang. I had a horse entered at the Hawkesbury gallops that afternoon and was somewhere on the freeway heading west from Sydney, bound for the racecourse. The message was brief: our lawyer, Nicholas Pappas, had called to say that the Federal Court decision that would determine the future of the South Sydney Rugby League Club – the most famous of all Australian Rugby League clubs – was being handed down the following morning.

It was early July 2001, mid winter, and the news came out of the blue. The speculation had been that it would be weeks yet before we learned our fate. It had been 21 months since

1

the National Rugby League had booted Souths out of the competition – a decision based on criteria that were supposed to represent a level playing field for all clubs but which on closer examination proved to be anything but. Twenty-one months then since this, the bloody and wearying last chapter in our fight, had begun in late 1999, although in all truth, Souths had been under threat ever since the arrival of the Rupert Murdoch–backed Super League in 1995, and probably before. Now, the bell had sounded for the last round.

I headed on to Clarendon Racecourse at the foot of the Blue Mountains and watched Vain Vigil race poorly. He jumped well, took up a position, but didn't give a yelp in the straight. The ground was shifty and the horse just didn't like it, the jockey told us. It wasn't a great omen but I wasn't worried. I rated it a 60–40 chance that the full bench of the Federal Court would administer justice and declare that Souths had been unlawfully excluded from the competition. After all, back in '96, Super League had beaten the ARL under section 45 of the *Trade Practices Act* – which was precisely what we were aiming to do to the NRL and News Limited.

At the time of writing, I'm 57 years old and I imagine that however long I live I will never forget the day that followed – Friday, July 6. It started as most of my days do, with me walking my two boxers down in the pre-dawn darkness at Coogee Beach, followed by some weight training in the gym at home. Nothing else about that Friday was ordinary, however. A big scrum of us – including my wife Nolene, Alan Jones, Deirdre Grusovin, Laurie Brereton, Henry Morris, Dominic Sullivan and Anthony Albanese – gathered at Nick Pappas's Bligh Street office in downtown Sydney. At 9.40 am we began the lengthy trek up to the law courts on the corner of Macquarie and King streets. It was a march we'd made twice before only to hear Federal Court judges Peter Hely and Paul Finn rule against Souths, but this time I sensed more of a collective spring in our step. This time I was confident. I really thought it would be our day.

In a crowded courtroom 21A high above the city, one of the

most important decisions relating to the game of rugby league was delivered, ironically, in a remote and impersonal way. I kept waiting for the judge to appear but instead the verdict came via a smallish television set, plonked in the middle of the court. The words were so brief: 'I would dismiss the appeal,' said Justice Heerey. 'I am authorised by Justice Moore to say he would allow the appeal.' Then, a second voice: 'I would also allow the appeal' (Justice Merkel). And that was it. You bloody beauty, I thought. The matter would go back to Justice Paul Finn for assessment of damages to be paid to Souths.

After almost two years of waiting, $2 million in expenses and more blood, sweat and tears than you could possibly believe, it was done. The correct weight flag wasn't yet raised, but the score was on the board – and we had won!

With a collective cheer, the gathering in the court took to its feet and the realisation of the outcome began to sink in. Norm Lipson, one of the most loyal and true of the Souths 'stickers', clenched his fists and punched the air, like a fighter who had just climbed off the canvas to win the championship. And we had – we'd belted them. People power had won. With a lack of fore-sight and without care for the grassroots people who follow clubs like South Sydney, an organisation (NRL) backed by a giant corporation (News Limited) had come close to destroying one of the most important community assets that a district can have. But we had stuck to our beliefs, knowing we were right, and now Souths were going to be back where they belonged.

I know that much of what followed that day will soon become for me a blur of handshakes and media interviews and happy faces. It's pretty much that way already. There were tears too – from people overcome with the joyous news that the foot-ball team that had meant so much in their lives was suddenly born again. For some, the club was a mother and father, the biggest thing in their lives. They were crying with happiness. And outside the court building there was dancing in the streets, car horns blowing and red-and-green flags waving. It was like the end of a war. And here I was right in the middle of it with people cheering, and I was thinking – God strike me dead – all I did was stand up for a principle. Later on, I was talking to a bloke who happened to be in a club in Ipswich when the verdict was announced, and he told me how people there had ripped off their caps and hats and hurled them into the air in jubilation at the news.

Downstairs in the court foyer, the sheriff called Nolene over. 'Can you keep these people quiet?' he asked, looking out over the hundreds of delirious supporters. 'They're disturbing the other courts.' Of course she couldn't. When we came down in the lift and stepped out into the foyer, the roar nearly lifted the roof off the building. I'm told that the press conference that followed at the court doors, with me in front of a barrage of cameras, trying to hear the questions that were shouted out above the din, was one of the biggest that veteran journalists had seen. It was also the easiest press conference to hold. It felt a bit like we had just won a grand final – after losing the semi and the final. I was almost a footballer again, enjoying a sweet victory. 'This is a people's game, not a business,' I said. 'They've got to get the passion back into the game. This has been a great day for rugby league and it's a great day for South Sydney. Let's just hope we can start healing the game and get back to playing football.'

It was entirely in line with the South Sydney way of doing things that if we got the nod that morning, we were going to win with grace and dignity. The verdict handed down by the court virtually smashed the NRL's 14-team competition since, as of 10.05 that morning, it was illegal. If we had wanted to stop the competition stone dead, no doubt we could have, but such a move was never a consideration. We didn't want to start looking at what we could do to hurt the code or the game – there'd been enough damage done in that department. We had fought our fight simply to overcome an injustice, to get Souths back to fielding a side in the competition. All we wanted to do now was to take our time and think about things – and equally to give News and the NRL some time to do the same. My view is that Murdoch and News and the NRL got lucky on that Friday, July 6.

Yes, a big decision had been handed down against them but now they have a second crack at rugby league – a chance to pull it all together properly. I don't know Murdoch's reaction but I know this: he should be very pleased.

Free of the court precinct, and for hopefully the last time, we regrouped at a Bligh Street hotel coffee shop and spent a happy, relaxed hour or so savouring the moment. On the car ride Nolene and I subsequently took with Alan Jones across town to the Souths Leagues Club, Alan spoke to News Limited chief executive John Hartigan on the phone. A few minutes later my own mobile rang and it was Hartigan, offering his congratulations and telling me that News accepted the decision and that it would be strongly encouraging the NRL to include Souths in the 2002 competition. I appreciated that. 'I wish you could do the same thing for my business as I'm doing for yours,' I told him. 'I've got so many enthusiastic customers who want to come along to your games now. I wish I had half that many standing outside my nursery this morning.' Before long, I took a call of congratulations from NRL boss David Moffett also.

It is only now that I can tell the story of a confidential meeting I had with Hartigan, organised by Norm Lipson, some 10 weeks before this. Hartigan came to my house at South Coogee and we talked for an hour or so over coffee. He seemed a decent bloke, and our conversation was an amicable one. His visit also flew in the face of rumours that News was prepared to do business with Souths – but only with me, as chairman, out of the equation. I have no doubt that his trip was a damage-control thing though, since, by April 2001, News Limited was hurting, for sure. Business had undoubtedly been damaged by the public backlash against the decision to dump Souths, and News was trying to put a stop to it. Adding to its woes, the football competition was labouring badly, lacking the sting that the traditional 'tribal' matches had always given it.

Hartigan asked me what was negotiable as far as us being back in the competition. I told him that the colours weren't negotiable and neither was the emblem, but that we'd look at a takeover. 'What's your description of "a takeover"?' he asked. I said that if some sort of deal was done with Cronulla, for example, the new club would still be the South Sydney Rabbitohs, although we'd look at having the other team's name somewhere on the jersey (as St George had done in its merger with Illawarra). I offered Hartigan some extra advice that day: 'John, you blokes have got to have the balls to police the finances of the game if you want to save it.' To me, that is so essential – to have a ruthless, independent checking process in place to save clubs from themselves, and, hopefully as a result, to save the game. 'Your people have gotta get in and check the books, go through them with a fine-tooth comb,' I told him.

I honestly think there was an inclination by Hartigan to extend Souths an olive branch *before* the court case. Whether he couldn't muster the numbers, or whether the NRL was so sure it was going to beat us in court that the hardliners demanded that it push on, I don't know. Still, we heard nothing more and so the fight went on, right down to the wire.

I like John Hartigan and I hope he takes the time out to read this book. Then he will see where Souths were coming from, and why we fought the way we did. And maybe then News Limited can take the final step in the healing process, and apologise and admit it was wrong in the path it took in 1995. With some reasonable commonsense negotiating around the table, the likes of Murdoch and Kerry Packer could surely have got everything they wanted out of the game – and rugby league could have benefited too. *Everyone* could have been a winner in fact, but only three groups were: players whose accident of birth pitched them into that era of bloated payments; player managers, who reaped a fortune; and legal eagles, ditto. As it was, the *game* did not gain a single worthwhile thing and News got stung very badly indeed.

The flood of letters and messages that followed a later ABC *Australian Story* program, put together by Helen Grasswill in August, showed what they had taken away from ordinary people and battling people – or in our case, tried to. I have kept a letter from a supporter of ours, Lee Whiteman, who told two poignant stories. Lee wrote to tell me of cancer sufferer Kim Porter who happened to visit her oncologist on the day of the decision to receive the results of her latest tests. Kim told the doctor: 'You can't give me any bad news today.' 'Why not?' the doctor asked. 'Because Souths are back in the comp,' said Kim. Lee also wrote of his brother-in-law Jimmy, a paraplegic, who with his pensioner wife Norelle took part in both our big rallies and who made their way to the club on the day we won the court case. Wrote Lee: 'They, like Kim, don't ask for much. They have been dealt a pretty shitty hand in life, but having their beloved Souths back in the competition is as good as it gets.'

Most of my Friday, July 6 was spent where it should have been – back at the South Sydney Leagues Club in Chalmers Street, Redfern, with the people of the district. I was there until 11 o'clock that night, and the beaming faces, the things people said and the wonderfully happy atmosphere in that ocean of red and green made all we had been through worthwhile. The bad times (and there were some of those) were forgotten. All branches of the Souths 'family' – the Greeks, the Lebanese, the local Aboriginal people – were there. One thing that this fight did for us was to unite all the different ethnic communities that supported Souths. For that reason, and a whole lot more to do with us becoming smarter, leaner and more determined because of our fight for life, Souths will be a stronger club as we head into the future.

That afternoon, Andrew Denton compered a boisterous press conference at which three documents were read out. I have included excerpts from all three here, to provide further insight into an amazing day. The first was a statement on behalf of News Limited by company CEO John Hartigan, who assured Souths that any decision to appeal against the Federal Court judgment would not affect an application from South Sydney to participate in the competition.

> We did not set out to target Souths or any particular club.
> All we sought to do was to create a viable competition.

I understand this has been a very difficult time for South Sydney fans. It's been a long hard road for everybody involved. We acknowledge the club's grit and determination and believe today's decision signals that it is now time for us all to move forward.

Next up was a letter I'd received by courier from the Sydney Cricket and Sports Ground Trust's Rodney Cavalier, who was away interstate at the time:

On the day of your great victory in court, the Sydney Cricket Ground Trust expresses its congratulations to you and your fellow directors for leading the fight for the return of Souths to the NRL competition. The Cricket Ground and the Football Stadium are now flying the Souths flag from several flag-poles. I am told that it is a beautiful sight.

Social historians will recall this day as one of the few occasions since the 1980s on which the administration of sport reflected a sport's popular base – rather than the corporate interests who have seized control. The Trust now looks forward to discussions about how we can make the first return game, hopefully at the SCG, one of the great events of the sporting calendar in 2002.

And lastly, the club's 'winning statement' was read to a cheering crowd:

In the interests of all Souths fans around the country and the game in general, it's time to call a halt to the bloody battle and work to repair the damage. Today's court decision acknowledges the injustice done to this club. It is now up to the NRL to right the wrong. Souths has had two seasons on the sidelines, barred from doing what we had done for 92 years. Now we are itching to play footie. We are ready, willing and able to rebuild our club . . .

let's unclench the fists, put what has happened behind us and all get back to playing rugby league. We are certainly ready. As the great man of rugby league, former player and commentator Frank Hyde has said on many occasions: 'Rugby league started with Souths . . . and it will end with Souths.'

It was Norm Lipson who wrote the press release and called on us all to 'unclench the fists' in the interests of the game healing itself. I think Norm has paid an awful price for his unswerving loyalty to the club. A journalist of many years' experience, he was cut off from a fair chunk of his livelihood because of his support for Souths. I would hope that our own grace in victory will be matched by an equal approach from the other side – that a line can now be drawn, old enmities forgotten and blokes like Norm Lipson not further penalised because they happened to believe in and support a cause.

There were minor disappointments on that Friday, although none of them tarnishing the bigger picture. To be honest, I would have liked to have seen more old Souths players joining the likes of Jack Rayner, Clem Kennedy, Phil Blake, Les Davidson and the others who popped in. It was, after all, one of the most exciting and important days in the history of the Rabbitohs. And, among the many phone calls I took, there wasn't a *single* one from an NRL club – not even from any of the 'loyal' ex-ARL clubs we had fought alongside in the depths of the Super League war. And d'you know, we didn't hear from the Australian Rugby League either. Now you would have thought that the proudest and the oldest club in the game could have been worth at least a brief message!

Maybe they all needed some time to come to terms with a decision which so dramatically changed the landscape. Significantly, a few days later, none of the clubs stood in the way when it was officially confirmed that Souths were back for 2002 – but none came to say 'well done' or 'good luck' either.

For me, the failure of the clubs to show us any signs of

mateship that day is a sign of how things have changed since News Limited became involved. Before 1995, league had always had scoundrels in the game, blokes prepared to stab each other in the back in the interests of pinching a player, but there was always a great loyalty to the game itself. The Super League war killed that; it became every man for himself – and bugger the rest. The old tradition died on the day that the clubs all signed 'loyalty' agreements with the NSWRL in '95, then promptly sneaked off, signed with News and deserted their 'mates'.

Friday, July 6 was both an ending and a beginning for Souths. After the worst period in the club's history we had won our legal fight by telling the truth. It cost the club and its many supporters around $2 million for the truth to eventually win out, and that's an awful lot of money. But there was no other choice – we *had* to fight. Ahead for coach Craig Coleman and the board lay the challenge of rebuilding a high-class competitive Souths side worthy of wearing the famous red and green. The process began almost immediately. Within days we appointed as our new chief executive ex–Test forward Paul Dunn, an impressive bloke who had pushed on with his education after finishing football. Dunn, with coach Craig Coleman, newly appointed football manager Sean Garlick, financial controller Brandon Punter and Phil Gould – a willing and expert volunteer – began the task of building our team for 2002. Ours will be a team built on youth; we will throw Souths open as a club of opportunity, and build our future. We will run on strict business lines; we will pay players only what we can afford; we will operate on a financial plan that guarantees we don't get into the sort of financial strife that has just about killed some of the other teams.

The on-field quest began the very next day with a game at Gosford's NorthPower Stadium against the Umina Bunnies – a triumphant day which drew almost 11,000 fans. Already there were firm plans for a celebratory South Sydney match at the Sydney Cricket Ground to kick off the 2002 premiership season, a game that would be a guaranteed sell-out and a fantastic new beginning for league. The NRL talked of a double-header. Pig's arse to that,

I said. Souths *alone* would fill that ground, reinforcing what we've been saying all along. For rugby league, there's a hell of a lot of winning back to be done. Life has moved on – and nothing is ever going to be the same in sport now that TV companies have their tentacles wrapped around everything. They have made it so easy for people *not* to go to games. Get a freezing cold afternoon and the choice of a warm lounge-room or a few hours shivering at the ground . . . I know which one most people would pick.

There was enormous interest in Souths. On the way to Gosford that Saturday morning 2GB called me just as I had pulled into a service station to get petrol. I was third in line and magging away on the phone when suddenly this road rage scene erupted. The bloke directly in front of me apparently wanted to back out, and went off his head. I'm sitting there thinking, what I have I done friggin' wrong? It wasn't as if I had *hit* him or anything. Anyhow, I'm answering questions about Souths and the future and all that, and suddenly the bloke is out of the car scowling, and advancing towards me. 'Hold on a minute,' I said. 'I've just got to fix this clown up.' So I put the phone down and opened the door, at which point the bloke reconsidered and got back into his car. 'How'd it go?' asked the 2GB boys. Talk about live radio! After the radio interview the mobile phone didn't stop ringing so Nolene took over the wheel and we were so distracted by the phone calls we overshot the Gosford turnoff by miles! We finally made it, to be greeted by a sea of red and green, the fact being that *both* sides wear the colours.

Our resident poet, Morry Anthony, had penned a special poem for Friday's courtroom victory. 'We're Back' captured the story perfectly, and received a huge reception from the crowd at Gosford:

> Since the year of 1908, we've played a lot of games,
> But none compare with the one we've played since that
> day of shame.
> We never got to make a break, we never got the ball,
> Everything was thrown at us, but they never cracked the
> wall.

'Barney' led us from the front, he wouldn't compromise,
And 'Nick the Greek', who coaches us through, had fire
in his eyes.
Each week our mighty army put their bodies on the line
Each time they charged, we pushed them back – every
bloody time.

Today we scored the winning try
As the final bell was rung,
And a roar was heard around the world,
The Rabbitohs have won!

The courtroom and the clubhouse erupted into cheers,
The emotions and the passions, ended up in tears.
In the art of 'never giving up' we've just raised the bar,
We are proud of what we've done, and proud of who
we are.

Today belongs to battlers, who know that they are right,
Today belongs to underdogs, who have to stand and
fight.
Today we showed tradition is something you can't buy,
Today we will remember, until the day we die.

We are all a part of this, it's the greatest game we've
played,
Today we scored for rugby league, and history was made.
The message comes through loud and clear, let this saga
close,
'We're back!' and we're back to say: 'UP THE
RABBITOHS!'

Incidentally, 'Barney' is myself and 'Nick the Greek' is Nick
Pappas, head of our legal team and one of the heroes in Souths'
struggle.

———•◦•———

It was apparent pretty quickly that the path back would not necessarily be a smooth one. St George–Illawarra CEO Peter Doust made an unsmiling public observation on the fact that it would now be a 15-team competition, when 14 had been the agreement. Yet Saints were still enthusiastic about opening the 2002 premiership with a game against Souths at the SCG. Only problem was they wanted it to be *their* home game, with them getting the gate. No way, we said. Before long, the NRL and News Limited announced they would be seeking leave to appeal to the High Court against the Federal Court judgment. In doing so, the NRL and News Limited are seeking to challenge the findings of the full bench of the Federal Court to the effect that they (News and the NRL) breached section 45 of the *Trade Practices Act* by entering into an arrangement in December 1997 which contained an exclusionary provision, or in other words a provision which sought to restrict competition. However, it was clear that the outcome of that appeal would have no bearing on our participation in the competition for the 2002 season. We were officially on board again, to be given the same four year premiership 'term' as the others. Meanwhile the Northern Eagles teetered on the brink with the likelihood of them falling over the cliff (which they subsequently did), and Norths and Manly angling to go their own separate ways. Debate raged. Should it be a 15-team competition . . . or 16? There was some shuffling on the Souths board. From my point of view there was only one need: that we were all pulling in the same direction. With so much going on, this turned out to be a stressful time in the wake of the court decision. The euphoria of that day quickly changed into something tougher as the hard work began. But the big picture hadn't changed. New club memberships and merchandising were booming. And we were back.

In the days that followed the court judgment, our sponsors came enthusiastically on board: Kerry Stokes (via Australian Capital Equity), RSL COM and ISC. The NRL gave us the nod for 2002, promising us the same grant as the other clubs, and the other 14 went along with the fact that the Rabbitohs were back.

They didn't really have a lot of choice. It would probably be a 15-team competition, we were told, although there was agitation for the more sensible 16 (the number we had fought for back in '99).

The News Limited newspapers took a realistic approach, and covered Souths' return to the fold generously and at great length. Maybe *that* was their way of saying sorry. 'Pure magic' was the front-page headline of the *Daily Telegraph* on Saturday, July 7. Can't get much more positive than that, I reckon. With some media people who had been against us throughout, you could almost hear the sound of them scrambling back over the fence in the wake of the court decision – and hopping on the bandwagon. Those in and around the game who did the wrong thing by Souths won't be forgotten. We'll do business with them if we have to . . . but we won't forget.

This first chapter in a book which tells of a life in rugby league and how a great football club was hounded to the point of extinction by the intrusion of big business, badly-advised, is offered in a spirit of conciliation and healing. My genuine hope now is that the great game of rugby league with its mix of brawn, bravery and skill will find its way back to full health – hopefully with South Sydney leading the way. At some time in the future when Souths are safely installed in the competition and on course, I plan to quietly step down as chairman of the club and become a football fan all over again. I'd like to see the two South Sydney boards (leagues club and football club) become one again, with the right people there, for the right reasons. The happy ending for the book is right here therefore, at the beginning, in the penultimate judicial throw of the dice which got us back into the game after a succession of bad decisions and bad years for rugby league.

There is a growing tendency in the media now to rewrite or ignore recent league history, the fact being that it is far too painful and too damaging to contemplate. In fact, the words 'Super League' rarely appear in the News Limited newspapers these days. The cry now, always, is 'We must move forward.' And I don't disagree with that in any way. Of course, there has to be a healing process and a building of the future. I'm certainly not going to be in there kicking the shit out of them (the NRL) at every opportunity, and carrying on. I just want to get on with us playing football. The game is in a lot of danger and it's going to require tough, smart management if it is to survive.

To deny history and the lessons to be learned from the past is bloody foolish, however, and so the full, grim story must be told – and told straight. The performance of some self-serving individuals in and around the game has been nothing less than shameful, and rugby league deserves better than what many of them have dished up. There is a lesson to be learned in the Super League affair: *the game must never be treated this way again.*

PART ONE

The challenge for all involved in sport is for the management and administration of sport to guard its principles and ideals from the evils of market forces, from voracious sponsors, from agents and managers who see sports as their cash cows and from media moguls who want its drama, brilliance and glory as their vehicle for programming and subscribers.

Ric Charlesworth, former Hockeyroos coach

1. Dog Days

Fight one more round. When your feet are so tired that you have to shuffle back to the centre of the ring, fight one more round. When your arms are so tired that you can hardly lift your hands to come on guard, fight one more round. When your nose is bleeding and your eyes are black and you are so tired you wish your opponent would crack you one on the jaw and put you to sleep, fight one more round. Remembering that the man who always fights one more round is never whipped.

James J. Corbett, boxer

ONE EARLY MORNING during the first of the court cases that would decide the future of one of the greatest sporting clubs in Australia – the South Sydney Rabbitohs – I headed out from home to walk my dogs, Sam and Sophie. It's the way I always start my days when I am in Sydney. I get up early, 4 am or so, clean the backyard, then pile the dogs into the back of the truck. That way we beat the peak-hour rush of the workers, although not always the left-overs of the nights before. I have seen some sights down at Coogee, I can tell you. On this particular morning I had decided to go over to Botany Bay to give the dogs a run on the long sandy beach there. As I drove, my mind was full of the Federal Court interlocutory hearing before Justice Peter Hely – the beginning of what was to become a no-holds-barred David and Goliath battle. We, the most successful club in football, Souths, were David, matched against one of the largest corporations in the world, Rupert Murdoch's News Limited – Goliath. It was November 1999, soon after News and the new rugby league organisation they had marshalled into being, the National Rugby League (NRL) had booted South Sydney out of the competition, after 92 seasons of competition, unleashing a storm of anger and protest on an already troubled game.

I parked in my usual spot near the quiet waterfront that morning and walked around the back to let the dogs out. Problem was there *were* no dogs. My first thought was that they must have jumped out on the drive over, and I turned the truck around and headed slowly back, re-tracing my steps. There was no sign of them in the still-dark streets. I got home and there they were, waiting, puzzled, wondering what the hell was going on. I realised then that I had been so consumed by this long and wearing fight to save my football team, my club, that I had left them behind. It really hit home to me then, the toll that our struggle in support of a great principle, and a great club, had taken on me. After all, it had been going on by then for almost six years, from its shameful beginning in early 1995 when News Limited, in dead-of-night raids, had tried to steal away the people's game of rugby league. The clock had been ticking for South Sydney from that moment. And as chairman of the club for which I had played for over 15 seasons, I had carried a fair load of the weight. And the stress.

I began writing this book as the fight for survival continued. The result of yet another court hearing was pending, and there was no guarantee that even that would be the end of it. As Elmer Fudd found with Bugs Bunny, an uppity, determined rabbit is not an easy critter to bump off. And so it proved for News Limited and the NRL when they took on the South Sydney Rabbitohs. The best estimate of News Limited's investment into the black hole of rugby league so far is $750 million; and I can't think of *one* positive thing that has come out of it for the game. In 1999 the NRL cut the number of teams in the premiership to 14. We ran 15th but refused to accept the verdict, on many grounds, not the least of them being the questionable, shifting criteria drawn up to judge the clubs. A level playing field, they reckoned. Well, it was a lot more level for some than for others. At Souths, we always battled uphill, while the News Limited–backed clubs ran downhill with the greatest of ease.

My health has suffered in the years of the battle. The stresses have changed me and I am not the person I was when it all started. The fight has drained me, physically and mentally. But as a footballer it was never my way to walk away from a challenge. Sometimes that got me into strife. To walk away from this one before we had shed the last drop of blood, explored the last possibility, was never an option. This has been a fight for a principle, for a great sporting institution . . . and for ordinary people shattered by their football club being taken away from them. People like the very old lady I met one day not long ago who took my hand and said to me: 'George, Souths are my side and that's all I've got in life. Don't let me down.' Then there was Roger Harvey, a blind man who loves the Rabbitohs and attends every home match to cheer for them, even though he can only imagine what might be going on. And eight-year-old Bradley Hunt who scraped together his pocket money and sent it to us to help the cause. And the car driver who rolled down his window outside Bowral one day during the court case and hollered across the traffic: 'I hope you give it to 'em tomorrow George!' And all the others who have fought, and fumed and marched in protest, and cried, in the interests of Souths. How could I have possibly walked away from all of them? I sat and thought of these people and I wondered: how can I save this bloody thing? And I decided, until it was final, I'd keep doing my utmost to save Souths. If that meant anybody getting hurt because of my actions, as long as I was within the law . . . I couldn't have given a shit.

The fight was about 'rights' – about the right of a community organisation like Souths to keep doing what it has done for 92 years. Souths has provided entertainment and a sense of belonging to the people of the district for all that time, and provided, too, an opportunity for its young men, a chance that football could be a stepping stone to a successful life, as it has been for so many of us over the years. Through good years and not-so-good, we paid our way. At Souths, players were always paid, and so were the bills. The formula worked and Souths became the most successful club in rugby league.

In recent seasons, the fight was increasingly about survival. And the doctors tell me that the biggest change in my own health is a result of the stresses caused by that never-ending battle to keep afloat a football club that is an Australian treasure against the weight of unlimited cash and influence of one of the most powerful companies in the world.

I am now a diabetic, at the age of 57. I realised I had a problem one early morning in January 2000 when I was out walking the dogs along the beachfront at Botany Bay, minding my own business. Up ahead of me a scuffle broke out between a little bloke who I had seen down there before and a much bigger and younger bloke who was walking his alsatian. The little bloke used to earn a few bob swimming greyhounds behind a small boat. I'm not exactly sure what had taken place but there had been some sort of disagreement concerning the dogs, and on a near-empty beach the big bloke probably reckoned the little bloke was an easy mark and was pushing him around. When I got up close they were still at it and I said, 'C'mon, leave him alone.' The big bloke turned and looked at me. 'And what are you going to do about it, Piggins?' he said.

With that he reached down quickly and picked up and threw a handful of sand, which hit me in the mouth. I grabbed him and flung him to the ground, and lobbed on top of him. But, all of a sudden, I felt as weak as a kitten. I couldn't even muster the energy to pop one on his chin. Fortunately the big bloke wasn't too willing at all and it became a bit of a Mexican standoff – and then he left.

Back from the beach, I rang my good friend Jimmy Lahood, a doctor who has been a terrific supporter of the Souths' cause, and he booked me in to see a specialist. I had all the tests done and the doc told me I had a sugar level of 22 when the normal reading is somewhere between four and five. I had a problem. I had had a symptom or two without realising it, such as now and then developing a tremendous thirst.

Diagnosed as a diabetic, I have been monitoring my sugar levels ever since. With difficulty I have got my weight down by 6 kilograms or so – but I like my tucker. I am now 84 kilograms – well under the playing weight of my football days. I watch my diet and do what I can to make my lifestyle a bit healthier. Long days of hard physical work on the farm are beneficial. But my mum, Minnie, is a worry. Whenever I take her and my father – both of them in their 80s now – on a run she never hops into the car without a big bag of jelly beans or chocolates. And when it comes to chocolate, I'm very weak.

I have always had a clear view of where I believed Souths belonged: in the premier competition, and flying the red-and-green flag alone. I certainly don't see myself as a 'saviour' or 'hero'. I'm like everyone, I make mistakes – and I'm sure I made some along the track of this thing. But I knew that a great football club and Aussie sporting institution had been wronged, and I fought to right that wrong.

This book is divided, roughly, into two parts. It tells my own story, the story of a kid growing up in an ordinary working class family in the Sydney suburb of Mascot, and becoming a football player with Souths. That part of it – the work ethic I inherited from my dad and others around, and the sense of district and club pride, and of loyalty to friends and family – goes a fair way to explaining my role in the second section of the book. Part Two tells of Souths' fight against the injustice that the corporate world brutally imposed on our club. The principles and the simple, real things that I learned as a youngster have underpinned everything I have done these last six years.

When you read of the earlier years, you will have a clearer understanding of why an old Souths hooker, who would *much* rather be down at the farm painting the fences and looking after the horses, felt obliged to fight for his club . . . and to keep fighting.

To begin . . . Let me now take you back to suburban Sydney the way it was 50 years ago – when the corner store was still the focal point of the neighbourhood, when the sound of horses clip-clopping up the street was a regular daily pleasure, when the milko still came calling early each morning, when kids still walked to school each day and rode horses or kicked a footy around in the afternoon in one of the many open spaces that still existed.

To a time when a man named Clive Churchill, 'The Little Master', played fullback for South Sydney in the cardinal and myrtle jumper; to a time when Souths, home ground Redfern Oval, were the Pride of the League. To a time when, for me, it all began.

2. The Wonderful World of Mascot

Suburbs are known only to dogs and children,
They sniff, circle, explore, trespass, uncover
Unguessed, circuitous byways and acquire
Bizarre acquaintances.

Nancy Keesing, 'We Told You So'

THE FIRST THING I remember as a child is a night of life
and death. The year was 1949, the month May, and at our family
home, 202 Gardeners Road, Rosebery, my mother Minnie went
into labour. When the ambulance arrived to take my mum to
hospital there were already other ambulances, lights flashing,
right out the front. And fire engines. Two young blokes zooming
along Gardeners Road on a motor bike, on their way to play
tennis, had hit a patch of oil and skidded at high speed into a
telegraph pole with a bus-stop sign painted on it. Both were crit-
ically injured. So while my mum was being eased into her
ambulance, the medicos were there in numbers, picking these
poor buggers off the road. Both of them died. Sometime later

that night Mum gave birth to Stan, the fifth Piggins boy and one of seven children born to Wally and Minnie Piggins of Rosebery, and, before long, Mascot.

I lived all my early life in that district – and Mum, originally from Botany, and Dad, a Mascot boy, are still in the house in which I grew up, in Linden Street, Mascot. It was built by my grandfather and my grandmother. My Uncle Jack and Uncle Stan had a wholesale nursery in Mascot. When Uncle Stan built a new house in King Street he took Nana to live with him and Dad rented the Linden Street house from her. I was five or six at the time we moved in there. I remember well the night and day of the big move from Gardeners Road. We stayed overnight at Nana's house so we'd be at our new place early to help unload the truck.

The next morning I was out on the street standing on the two brick pillars which dominated the front of the house, and these three kids came along: Ronnie Coleman, Alan McCauley and the boy Moles. They all had boxing gloves on. 'Wanna fight?' asked Ronnie. 'Yeah,' I said. 'I've got some gloves' – they were my older brother Jeff's – 'I'll go and get 'em.' Inside the house Jeff stopped me. 'What are you doing?' he asked. 'Aw, these kids out the front want to fight. I'm just getting my gloves,' I said. Jeff walked to the front door and had a look. When he spotted Ronnie, who was about 10 months older than me and would become a life-long friend, he said, 'He's too big for you.' So Jeff put the gloves on and went out instead. He and Ronnie shaped up and Jeff went *whack!* . . . and knocked Ronnie Coleman's two front teeth straight out. The other boys shot through.

After that, I generally did my own scrapping. Some people may say I've been scrapping all my life. And not the least of it in the years since 1995, when Rupert Murdoch and his fellow travellers, aided by some traitors within the ranks, tried to kidnap the old working man's game of rugby league. And, sadly, succeeded.

But way back then I was only a little fella, although I thickened up later. Although I did get into scraps, I wasn't a person who went around searching for fights. But, yeah, if I got hit . . . I'd have a go.

I was born on October 14, 1944, pretty close to the end of World War II, into a tight-knit family, and into an era that would provide wonderfully happy memories of childhood years growing up in Sydney. I was the third-born, and third boy; two girls and two boys followed me. When I got to England with the 1975 Australian World Cup side, I did some work tracing our family name. We're from English stock mainly, although a bit of a mixture, and I discovered that the family name originated from 'Pigeon'. Dad's background is from the north of England; there is some Irish and French in Mum's. Her grandparents came from Mauritius.

I faintly recall traces of the war from my very young years. In Gardeners Road, in a house we had shared with an uncle, Jeff Phillips, and his three daughters, we lived just across from Rosebery Racecourse – and I was taken over there by my uncle when the racecourse reopened after the war. There were still dummies and targets around the place, for during the war the racecourse had been used for training and for housing troops.

But my main early memories are of Linden Street, not so far from the big city, as the crow flies, but a wonderful world apart. The sound of Linden Street was the sound of horses up and down the road at just about any time of the day or night. Freddy Lonsdale, the trainer, would come clip-clopping up our street at 4.30 in the morning, heading for Rosebery Racecourse, riding a pony and leading four horses, two on either side. Just about everyone in the street had a horse, or horses, and traditional racing families lived there, such as the Browns, the O'Rourkes, the Nicholls and the Lonsdales. And there were stables every-where, five of them within a 200-metre radius. On a Sunday afternoon, we'd sit on the fence at Syd Nicholls's place and watch him break in the yearlings.

It was a rural pocket in the heart of Sydney really. Old Harry Lodge down the end of the street had a cow and pretty much a mini-farm on his small block. Harry looked the part in his bib and braces, pottering around behind the high fence, working on his 'farm'. And just about everyone had chooks. My father was a great poultry man – he'd have anything up to 50 chooks and

50 ducks in the yard at any one time. At Christmas in the '50s he'd sell the ducks at 22/6 a pair – and be down the backyard on Christmas Eve morning, lopping the heads off and dressing them.

Wartime had brought with it some good fortune for us kids of Linden Street and surrounds. In the area behind, where a school stands today, there had been an old nursery, with a bush house on it – on four hectares or more of ground. The story went that one day in the early '40s a plane from nearby Mascot Airport had done a loop overhead, then fallen out of the sky, flattening the house and badly damaging the nursery. The place was never rebuilt and the land was left to grow wild. It was a miniature forest in the middle of Mascot, and it became the place where we kids lived and played and dreamed our dreams.

It was a fantastic place, part of every waking day. When my brothers, Albert and Stan, and I had horses, we tethered them there. My other brothers, Wally and Jeff, were more inclined to want to *back* horses. The slow, reluctant walk to school each day inevitably took us through 'the back paddock'. At one stage, someone let a couple of wild pigs go there, and we were always on the lookout for them. A neighbour and, later, fellow rugby league man, Frank Cookson (currently chairman of Souths Juniors) was walking down Coward Street one morning on his way to work at Manufacturers' Mutual, and was chased by the pigs. Or so he reckons. This was Sydney back then . . . well, our corner of the world, anyway.

My lifelong love of the countryside no doubt came from those early days – the paddock, the horses, the rural 'feel' that existed around Linden Street in the 1950s. And there were nurseries everywhere. Ronnie Coleman and I used to go down to the Craigies – great nurserymen, and still going – and hitch a ride on the trucks heading out to places like Hoxton Park which were still 'bush' then; where Italian migrants were establishing their farms, growing tomatoes and capsicums and all sorts of vegetables.

Life was much simpler, and the 'neighbourhood' very different from today's suburbia. This was 'working class' in the true sense of the words. And Australian Labor Party. If you happened to favour the Liberals and lived in Mascot, well, you didn't let on. I remember a night, later on, at the Tennyson Hotel around election time when some Liberal blokes came in handing out pamphlets (or trying to). Jimmy Cookson, a good Labor man, suggested they leave, but they lingered. 'I told you to go,' said Jimmy, emptying a bucket of cold water over one bloke's head.

I could still tell you the name of every person who lived in Linden Street in my growing years. Maxie's corner store was a focal point of the district, run by Maxie Wiseman. If I happened to be first in the door after school, Mum would often send me off to Maxie's – where I'd pick up the butter or bread or whatever was needed – on 'tick'. After school there'd always be something to do – water Dad's garden, chop the wood. Or old Mrs Beaver from down the street would be out the front demanding that you pick up the manure that your horse had deposited.

Dad worked on the railways and then on the wharves. He had a rule for life: you *work* in my house – and I've adopted that rule in my own life. For Mum, raising a family of seven, life was hard. With Dad away working long hours, she did just about everything at home. Early on, she would boil water on an old chip heater down the back and carry it up for the bath. And there'd be a daily trek for her to the shop to pick up the tucker for the family. There was no car then, and I can picture her now heading up the street, laden with groceries.

My belief that work is an essential and fundamental part of human existence came from my parents. (And I'd say that one of modern professional football's problems is that very few players have a *job*.) I never knew my dad to be unemployed until the day he retired. And Mum – if you had 10 people working for you as good as her, you'd be a multi-millionaire. I've seen her chop wood, carry hot water, and endlessly make those bloody bunks – because there were too many kids in the house to have normal beds. And I can see her when I was 11 or 12, out with the two girls, holding one by the hand, wheeling one in the pram and carting big, heavy string bags full of groceries, which would be cutting the circulation to her hands. Some days she would come home loaded up like a packhorse, but uncomplaining.

My schooling, what there was of it, began at Gardeners Road Primary. From day one I didn't like it. School was a mile's walk from home. I made a lot of friends walking to school and home again – and I've got happy memories of that part of the daily routine, if not the school itself. I think how different things are today when I drive past a school and see the lines of flash cars and four-wheel-drives dropping off and picking up the kids.

School and I never got on. I hated the place, just didn't want to go. I had difficulties. I was a slow reader and a dreadful speller, and I had all sorts of trouble focusing on learning. I've always learned more by listening than by reading. I am not dumb, but I had this difficulty – and still have it to a degree. There was a time at school when I thought that my brother Wal, three years my junior, was going to go past me. In my brief school life I responded best to an old teacher named Mr Thompson, who did his teaching by talking and explaining things rather than writing them on the blackboard. I did plenty of jigging (wagging school) as the school years went on. I'd much rather be out riding a horse than cooped up in the classroom.

Not so long ago, I ran into one of my old teachers, Mr Elliott, at Hawkesbury Racecourse. I had my trainer's licence then and had a horse in that day. He walked up to me and said, 'You won't remember me.' And I said, 'Yes I do, Mr Elliott.' We got talking (and I told him to put a bet on my horse). He talked about how I'd done well in life and made something of myself; and I reminisced about what a dreadful student I had been. 'Yes, that's true to an extent,' he said. 'You couldn't spell, but you were good at maths.' And I was. I was in a restaurant with my wife Nolene one day and told her how I had got 100 (out of 100) in one yearly maths exam. She looked at me and said: 'You wouldn't get 100 out of 100 for *anything*.' A few months later my mum dug out an old report card, the one recording that I *had* in fact turned in a perfect score. I suppose that goes some way to explaining why I've always been good at handling money.

Horses have been part of my life from my very early years. There's nothing I love more than spending time working on the horse stud Nolene and I have in the NSW Southern Highlands. My first link with horses probably came when I was taken to my Uncle Vic's stables. And Gardeners Road Primary was not that far from the old Victoria Park Racecourse. Its days as a racetrack had already ended and it had fallen into disrepair, but stretches of the white paling rails still stood. On the open ground roamed a number of horses which we kids called 'the Vicky Herd'. In dry spells when the grass was short, the horses would wander up close to the school. It was then I really fell under the spell.

The Piggins boys got our first horse out of the Vicky Herd. One afternoon after school, I noticed a nice chestnut that was quite lame after being kicked in the knee. I managed to catch him and took him up to Harry Donnelly, the vet, who had a connection with my uncle's stables. The injury was serious and would require a fair bit of treatment. We tracked down the owner of the horse, a kid named Alan Scott from Botany, and told him the news. 'Gawd strike me dead . . . how much is it going to cost?' he said. 'Probably five or six quid,' my brother Albert told him. 'Do you want to sell it?' 'Yeah, give me two quid and you can have it,' said Alan. We went back to the vet and he asked us who owned the horse. 'We do now,' we said. Harry, being a mate of my uncle, did us a favour and treated the horse for nothing. And so we got 'Betts' for two quid.

It was the start of something. From that point, horses were always in our lives. We'd go riding after school and on Sundays there'd be a big ride to Brighton where we'd meet the Brighton kids. All the different bunches of kids around there had horses. The Waterloo kids kept their horses at Victoria Park, we had ours in The Paddock at Mascot, the Botany kids had theirs in the grounds at The Stacks (so named because it housed stacks of paper and pulp), and the Maroubra kids had their horses out at La Perouse. The local truant officer called the whole district 'Cowboy Territory'. The near certainty was that if any kid was jigging school he'd be out riding a horse somewhere. And there would always be stories circulating, yarns about a horse or horseman – like local identity Lance Orchard, known as 'Itchy', who would ride his pony down Botany Road when he finished work, then saddle him up the next morning and ride him to the stables where he did some work for Uncle Vic. Or the horse named Old Chips who got hit by the Botany tram and, as legend had it, needed five bullets from the copper's gun to put him finally to rest.

For me growing up, the attraction was always the horses, never the punt. Gambling gouged a deep, painful and permanent scar in the Piggins family, one that will never heal. My older brother Jeff, the second eldest, committed suicide because of it, at Christmas 1959. Jeff was probably the best educated of us all, a bright young bloke with plenty going for him. Unfortunately he was epileptic and if he fitted when he was in company or with a girl he would get dreadfully embarrassed. Increasingly, he buried himself in a solitary life and in gambling. He became a mad punter.

Mum used to send me to the races with Jeff now and then to keep an eye on him. One Saturday afternoon we were on the top of the old Leger stand at Randwick. 'Have you got any money?' he asked me late in the program. I had three bob (shillings) in my pocket and I said, 'Yeah, I've got two bob.' 'Well,' he said, 'they reckon Blaze Away can win this. Give me the two bob.' I protested that it was the bus fare home, but gave it to him anyway and he ran down and backed Blaze Away. The horse led over the rise, but was quickly run down. 'C'mon,' he said, 'we've got a long walk home.' Not until we got out of the course and down to Anzac Parade did I produce the shilling I had left – enough to get us both to Mascot on the bus.

He found trouble – once when he tried to help a mate who had been unfairly pinched by the police, and again when he had an accident in the car he had bought. Probably he should never have been driving because of the fits he took. I was 15 when he had the prang, which needed panel beating, and I happened to have some money at that time. 'I'll sell you the car,' Jeff said to me, 'but if I win at the races, can I buy it back?' 'Yeah, that's fine,' I told him. At 15, I already had plans for a kid named Jimmy Rootsie, who was a bit older and had his licence, to chauffeur me around in my new car.

Anyway, Jeff went to the races one Saturday and won enough money to repay his debt. But as a punter, he wanted to go one better. He went on to the dogs at Wentworth Park, and lost the lot. He came home that night, wrote my mum a letter and took an overdose of sleeping tablets. We found his body the next day. It was shattering and put a dampener on the family for a long, long while. Especially so with my mother. I saw her crying so many times.

The trams that were gone from Sydney life by 1961 were a big part of our young lives. My mates and I – Jimmy Cookson, Ronnie Gill, Bluey McGee and some others – were expert at 'scaling' the old toast-rack trams that snaked in all directions through Sydney. The conductor would swing down one side collecting the fares – and we'd be over the other side on the walkway, hanging off the rail, dodging the trams coming the other way *and* the bloke collecting the fares. One day a mate named Buffrey lost a leg scaling the trams. He missed his footing while hopping aboard at La Perouse, and one leg went straight under.

I remember a day when a few of us were scaling the back of the tram on the 'wrong' side, and heading out of Maroubra Junction. Suddenly a couple of blokes in suits and ties were running for the tram. One of them jumped on – and the other bloke jumped, missed his hold and went into this sort of windmilling effect. He was there half-balancing and desperately trying to stop himself from falling back off, and I grabbed him and pulled him on. And you know what? They were bloody tramway inspectors. Bastards. And they pinched us. I should have let him go . . .

It was a shame about the trams. They were great people-movers, and they add character to a city. I always reckoned that we got it wrong with the trams. For starters, they should have been left on the city's main arteries because of their ability to shift a large number of people quickly. But I always figured that traffic would have moved better if the trams had run on the gutter, with the middle of the road left to the cars, and not the other way around. That would have left the flow of traffic unaffected.

What with the horses, the trams, the beach and the trains, life was crowded with possibilities. We used to ride the coal trains out to the Bunnerong Powerhouse at Botany, and to the Enfield mar-shalling yards in the other direction. And hitchhiking from the Burma Road out to Maroubra Beach was a big attraction. No-one had swimming pools in their backyards in those days and on a Sunday arvo there'd be 20,000 or so people laid out on the Maroubra sands. On other summer days we'd go instead to Ramsgate Baths or down to an old waterhole at Mascot which we called 'Sixie', where the kids of the district had swum for donkey's years. Every afternoon in summer we'd take our horses down to Sixie, behind the old St Bernard's School, close to the railway track. For me the Aussie summer game of cricket was never a great attraction – the reality of standing out in the scorching sun all day just didn't appeal.

The old steam trains that chuffed along through Mascot carrying their cargoes to the big industries further out at Botany – to Kellogg's, ICI, Davis Gelatine and the Powerhouse – pro-vided endless fun. We had the grades all figured out and the spots where we could hop aboard, especially the intersection just off Wentworth Avenue where the heavy loaders would have to stop and wait for the bloke with the lantern to come down and halt the traffic; and on the hill just over the bridge where they'd be pulling hard, doing only 8–10 kilometres an hour, and where a bunch of energetic kids could easily hop aboard.

God, we got up to some tricks – even uncoupling the engine from the rest of the train on more than a few occasions. One afternoon I was with Jimmy Cookson and I'd pulled the pin, releasing the engine. My legs were both sides of the train wheel and the thought occurred that if I let go, or slipped, I'd be cut in half. Luckily Jimmy had me by the belt, and pulled me up. Unhooked, the engine would head on. We'd get on the carriages and gather corn for the horses – the corn intended for Kellogg's, for Australia's most famous breakfast cereal.

3. The Team in the Red and Green

The history of rugby league
Is dressed in red and green,
A thousand tales, a thousand tries
The greatest ever seen.

Morry Anthony, Souths' resident poet

I PLAYED RUGBY league from when I was about 11 years old. I was a member, first of all, of the Gardeners Road five-stone, seven-pound team. All the Piggins boys played rugby league. It was just something you did if you were a young bloke growing up around there. We played for Mascot, then four or five years later, when a couple of my close mates got barred by the coach for mucking around at training, we formed a new club, the Mascot Jets, and Souths Juniors accepted us. It was Olympic Games year, 1956, when I first played for the Mascot Club, wearing the light blue–dark blue jumper. We won the comp that season. I was a second rower when I started out but in 1957, in F grade, when our hooker got hurt in the semi final, they put me in there. I stayed a hooker for 20 seasons or more, although I played some prop for Souths very late in the piece, when I was old and struggling.

The funny thing about me and football – even though some outsiders thought it dominated my life – was that it was really just no more than one of many things I did in my growing-up years. I suppose when I was battling away in the '90s trying to turn back the Murdoch tide, fighting to save Souths because I believed in the club, the people who supported it and the principle involved, it must have appeared that my life was consumed by football. It was never that way. I liked the game, and enjoyed playing. As a teenager I would play three games of football a weekend. But I enjoyed a lot of other things, too, and the truth of it was that there was no great South Sydney or rugby league culture in the Piggins house.

Souths weren't a factor in my life until I started playing for the club. I didn't even see the first-grade side play until I was a Rabbitoh myself. Ronnie Coleman loved Souths, knew all about Clive Churchill and Jack Rayner and the rest. But I was happy with my lot as a football *player* and a kid who loved horses; I wasn't too interested in the love of the district club. Playing for Mascot was enough. I was selected for the Jersey Flegg (under 18s) trials with Souths and didn't bother to turn up. Even when I got picked later for the President's Cup (under 21s), which was a stepping stone to grade football and, perhaps, the big time, I wasn't all that keen. What I enjoyed was playing football for Mascot with my mates as I worked my way through the juniors, C, B and A grade. When I finally went up to the South Sydney senior-grade teams, it was only because I had the chance of earning a quid there. None of that means that the club didn't *grow* to mean a lot to me. It did, of course. I wouldn't have fought the fight if I hadn't cared deeply about Souths.

It was during those seasons with Mascot that I first met – and played against – players destined for Rabbitoh fame such as Bob McCarthy and Ron Coote. In '59 Mascot won the E grade Cup, beating favourites Moore Park (McCarthy was in their team) in the final, and Kensington (Coote was in theirs) in the grand final, by 4–3.

I juggled school and football until I left school at 14. I went to Gardeners Road Public School for primary and, briefly, secondary school and hated most of it (although I enjoyed woodwork). I jigged all the time. Towards the end of it they'd let me come to school just on Wednesdays, to play football. All I had to do was find out where they were playing . . . and turn up.

My last day at school was a football day, and I had ridden my horse to the match, against Maroubra, and hitched him to a tree. Not long into the game this big kid from the other mob and I locked horns. Our sports teacher, Mr Grosvenor, was refereeing the match and he spun around and said, 'If you two want to fight, get to the sideline!' With that the big kid said, 'Come on!' – and we were off the field, and into it. Anything went as we slugged it out, then suddenly someone grabbed me from behind and forced my arms up my back. I dragged him around to the front . . . and it was the teacher from Maroubra. 'What's your name, son?' he barked. 'Piggins,' I told him. 'How do you spell that?' he asked. 'Well, you're the teacher. You're supposed to teach *me* how to spell,' I shot back. At that moment I saw our teacher, Mr Grosvenor, heading across the field towards me at some speed, and looking far from happy. That'll do me, I thought. I pulled my horse's bridle from the tree and swung into the saddle in full football gear. We took off at a brisk canter, straight across the field and past the oncoming Grosvenor. 'See you later,' I shouted. I don't think I ever did.

The next day the local schools' inspector, 'Mousie' O'Brien, came down to see Mum. I had not gone back to school that day, and had decided I would never go back. 'Look, he can't go to work yet, he's too young,' Mousie told my mum. 'Just as long as you keep him off the streets, keep him at home.' It was the end of school and me. Later on in my life I regretted my lack of education and wondered whether I would have gone further if I had stuck with it. The fact was, with my learning difficulty I wasn't getting anything out of it.

Also, I had a job already – a darned good paper run that brought me in 12 quid a week, working out of Mr Cleary's newsagency down in King Street, Mascot. I was selling 600 papers a day – the *Sydney Morning Herald* and the *Daily Telegraph* in the morning, and the *Sun* and the *Daily Mirror* in the afternoon. The paper run was my second job. I had picked up some casual work around the stables now and then.

I always put my work ahead of my football. I figured that getting my living was always going to be more important than playing sport. But I plugged away as a footballer and was picked in Souths' President's Cup squad in 1964, when Ron Coote and Bob McCarthy were just graduating to grade ranks. I was working hard then, as a wharfie, and my inclination was not to bother about the President's Cup call-up, despite the prestige involved – the cup having traditionally been *the* stepping stone to grade football and bigger things for young players. But the coach, Clem Kennedy, a Souths international, had just come to live next door in Linden Street, and his persuasion, along with that of my father, convinced me to go to the trials. I made the team, and that year we won the President's Cup, the most coveted junior trophy on offer in rugby league.

It was the beginning of a long and winding road, although it seemed for a time that my football career might be over before it had begun. I was called into grade by Souths towards the end of 1964 and promptly cracked five vertebrae in my spine the first time I pulled on the red and green (or 'the cardinal and myrtle' if you want to be strictly accurate). It was a third-grade match against Western Suburbs at Pratten Park, Ashfield, and as I turned to pass the ball, a player ran in to tackle me and caught me in the middle of the back with the full force of his head. My left leg went numb. They took me off the paddock, and I showered and dressed with difficulty. Back in those days, no-one ever worried much about getting you to the doctor. The drive home was a nightmare. My leg had seized up completely and I couldn't use the clutch so I had to work the revs to go through the gears manually and get the car home.

I was seriously injured, and on the Monday they sent me down to see the NSW Rugby League doctor, Len Greenberg, who passed me on to the radiologist. Doc Greenberg scanned the x-rays. 'Look, you've cracked five vertebrae,' he said, and showed me the damage. 'And there's nothing much we can do for you, other than an operation, and I don't want to be doing that. What you are going to have to do is go home and put yourself to bed, and stay there for 16 weeks.' So I went home and did what he said — although I didn't stay horizontal for anything like 16 weeks. The damaged vertebrae eventually grew spurs and every now and then, even today, they hook a nerve and give me trouble. My first day in grade football gave me a bad back for life. The old Souths international hooker Ernie Hammerton took an interest in me at the time and sent me to see a Macquarie Street specialist. I was offered some advice which, basically, was the same as Doc Greenberg's: just wait for it to heal.

The circumstances soured me on football for a time. By then, I was a married bloke with one child and one on the way, and there was no decent worker's compensation then. The club gave me less than a tenner a week (£10) and there was never any undertaking on their part to look after my welfare.

But I must have liked the game a lot, deep down. I always enjoyed the physical challenge of rugby league and the balance that makes the game such a good one. The winning formula has never changed over the years: the necessary hard work, mixed with skills and backed by determination, commitment and the ability to take a knock and keep going. And I liked the mateship of the game, sharing the experience with your pals.

By early '65, I was pretty much mended. I had not long before landed a job down on the waterfront, and I played the trials at the start of the '65 football season. The first trial, at Redfern Oval, was against St George, who that year were bidding to win their tenth straight first-grade premiership. After my trial game that afternoon, Saints' famous secretary, Frank 'Fearless' Facer, came to see me out of the blue and asked, 'Son, do you want to play for St George?' Later in life I came to realise what a tremendous honour it was to be asked such a question by a man of Facer's standing – and to be invited to play for a club such as St George. I thanked him but told him no. 'I am a Souths player,' I said.

Yet, as I've said, I had never even seen Souths play until I was called into grade. My answer to Facer's question was to do with something very deep down in me, something that is still there today. I believed that football was *tribal*. If you were a Mascot bloke, in your genes, well then you were a *Mascot* bloke, and if it came to football at a higher level, you weren't going to play for anyone but Souths. The fundamental things remain. The loyalty I had to Mascot, to my childhood friends who will be my friends until the day I die, widened into the loyalty that grew in me for the South Sydney club. Souths provided me with some recognition, put money in my pocket and provided a standard of living which meant that I no longer had to give the local tailor 15 bob a week to pay off my clothes. I could go down with cash and buy myself a pair of trousers. And shoes. Added to that, back in '65 I could never have seen myself knocking off work and battling out along General Holmes Drive to get to Saints training.

Souths must have got wind of the approach from St George and they offered me £300 for the 1965 season, a deal I accepted. But when I started working on the wharves on Saturdays and Sundays it became difficult to get the time off to go to training and, sometimes, to matches. Suddenly, for all the effort involved, the 300 quid wasn't looking really worth it, especially when I could get 60 quid a week down on the wharves. It was better for me and my family financially if I went to work, and took the overtime that was on offer. So there came a day when I went along to the Rabbitohs president, Bill Fletcher, and told him I didn't want the contract. I explained my reasons. 'Well, what are you going to do?' he asked me. 'Nothing special,' I said, 'I'll go back and play with Mascot.'

The club was not too impressed, possibly thinking I was trying to hold them up for more money, and they came back to me with the message: 'You'll play with us or no-one, that's the way it is.' 'Okay, it's going to have to be no-one,' I said. 'It is not worth my while giving up Sunday work to play football. I can earn more money going to work.' The club dug its heels in. It was an era when officialdom was a bit stiff-shirt as far as handling players goes. 'You signed a contract to play with us,' they told me, 'and that's the way it will be – play and earn the £300, or sit on the sideline.'

Barred from playing with Mascot, I kept myself fit by training with my mates at the club. I was not bothered. I was working for fair money – and at least I was able to train with the club. Things changed when Souths realised I was sincere; that I needed the money and I wasn't just screwing them around, and that I wasn't going to play anywhere else. Eventually they sent me a letter and asked me to come back and play with them. 'What do you want?' they asked me. I told them £1000 for the season. They gave it to me.

My career as a professional footballer was on its way. The best contract I finished up with at Souths was $10,000 for a year, including everything. Though tiny when compared to the money the game foolishly lavishes on players today, it was a great supplement to what I was earning in my 'real' life outside.

I remember a year when I was working on the wharves and contract negotiations were due. Charlie Gibson, an ex–Souths player, was club secretary, and I worked with Charlie's father – and got on well with both of them. The going rate for Souths' international players at that time was about $4000 a season. Charlie called me in one day. 'How much do you want?' he asked me. I quoted him a figure that was very much in the ball-park of what the club's star players were getting. 'George, if I give that to you, you can't *ever* tell anyone what you're being paid,' Charlie said to me. Players always knew who was going for contract renewals, and when. A few days after that I was out on a road run, passing Resch's Brewery, and another first-grade player said to me, 'How did you go with the contract, George? What did you finish up getting?' 'Two thousand,' I said. 'Gee whiz,' he said, 'you did alright for yourself.' I just kept running. But it was swings and roundabouts. There was another year when I signed only for match money – but *big* money when we won. I think we only won a couple of games with me in the team that year.

Overall, I was probably paid about what I was worth through my career. Today, the game overpays virtually everyone, and because of that, it may well send itself down the gurgler unless someone comes along who is strong enough to put the brakes on. That seems a forlorn hope.

I had never been on a plane until I played President's Cup for Souths back in 1964. I had never tried lobster until I played first grade for the Rabbitohs. I had never seriously considered travelling to the northern hemisphere until I made the World Cup squad of 1975. Oh yes, football opened some doors alright. The '60s, when it all started for me, was a time when the spending of leagues clubs was a bit out of control. The blokes at the helm could do what they liked – and for a footballer making some progress there was the chance for the sort of luxury that ordinary working-class people just didn't experience then. If you happened to be on that particular gravy train, you were one of the lucky ones.

In 1965, Souths took us to Surfers Paradise for our end-of-season trip. We stayed two weeks and they gave us £8 a day spending money, at a time when breakfast was 2/6 and you couldn't pay more than 12/6 for a slap-up dinner. I spent my money carefully, and bought some things for my wife and the kids.

For a boy from Mascot, the trip to Papua New Guinea in 1964 was a real eye-opener. It was like going to another planet. That year we won the President's Cup. As a reward Souths

Juniors, cashed up and in a generous mood, shouted us the trip to Papua New Guinea. Blokes like Eric Simms and Gary Stevens, bound for stardom with Souths and their international careers ahead, were in the side. In Port Moresby a group of us stayed in the Commonwealth Bank building, looked after there by a good-natured local named Ambrose, who was a genius at getting into locked rooms to retrieve dirty clothes.

The first night there we decided we'd head into town to get something to eat, at the RSL, which was not far down the road from where we were staying. We could hear something of a hullabaloo going on, and we turned a corner to be confronted by the biggest street fight I've ever seen. There must have been 200 people in it, with blokes belting each other with big clubs. The Red Cross people were in the middle of it, dragging the fallen ones out. 'You'd better get the hell out of here,' a copper told us. We didn't wait for a second opinion.

Despite that, we had a good time in Moresby, and played and beat a mixed-race team before a big crowd. Inadvertently Gary Stevens and I became heroes in that match. On the other side was a big red-haired white bloke they called 'Superman', who fancied himself a bit. Well, Superman made the mistake of running at Gary a few times, and (as plenty of players were to find out to their discomfort over the years) Gary was better than anyone at upending an opponent and dumping him. He had an unbelievable knack. The mob loved that. Then, at one stage, there was a bit of a blow-up, and I finished up hitting the red-headed bloke on the chin. Afterwards the crowd streamed onto the ground and picked Gary and me up and chaired us around the oval. It was unbelievable – a bit frightening actually. You had the feeling that the New Guineans had been copping plenty from some of the whites over the years. Now we had given a bit back – and they loved it!

As I said, it was another world to a bunch of young blokes from suburban Sydney. They took us to an island about six kilometres off the coast, a place where the white women could don their bikinis and have a swim. We were water-skiing between the island and the mainland, towing one of our blokes, Aiden Smith, when Aiden hit a wave and fell off. The fellow skippering the boat checked his fuel gauge and declared, 'I'm running out of juice, we won't be able to get him. We'll head into Moresby and get some fuel, then come back and pick him up.' So he just off and left, with Aiden wallowing in the middle of a channel where there were sharks and crocodiles and all sorts of dangerous creatures. We made it back in 20 minutes or so and Aiden, thankfully, was still there and still intact. The skipper turned around to me. 'You're next on,' he said. 'You're kidding, mate,' I replied. 'There's no way in the world I would get behind you. I'd have killed you if you did to me what you have just done to him.'

We went up the Kokoda Trail one day, and we still laugh about what happened to one of our touring party, a lovely old bloke named Wally Stigg. You had to see Wally. He had the biggest head you could imagine and because the sun was so severe up there he had spent three days searching around Moresby for a hat that would fit him. Finally, he found one. Somewhere up there we went into a hotel, a bar at which there is a tradition that if you walk in with a group, and you happen to be the first one sporting a hat, they take it off you, everyone signs it, and the hat is hung on the wall. Well, you guessed it. Wally walked in first wearing the big hat it had taken three days to find – and the hat ended up as a trophy on the pub wall.

Our hosts transported us north to Lae in an old DC3, which they reckoned General Douglas MacArthur had flown in, a troop carrier in which you sat on the floor and looked out the open door. In Lae, an enormously pretty place with hibiscus growing everywhere, Ray Coward and I were billeted out at a high school right on the edge of the jungle. The 'sing-sings' were on, and for a whole week, 24 hours a day, there was dancing and the non-stop 'boom, boom, boom' of the drums.

While in Lae, we were invited out to a coffee plantation on the Bololo River, and four of us piled into a 1958 Chevrolet with our assigned driver. The dirt road more or less followed the river and you could see these bloody big crocodiles basking on the flats. All the way there the bloke driving us was really flying. Finally I said to him, 'Hey, slow down, mate. If we finish up in that friggin' river we're gonna get eaten!' It was a fair trip, 100 kilometres or more, and when we finally arrived, a bloke stopped our (black) driver at the front gate. 'The boss doesn't allow you on the property,' he said. So we went in for lunch, and Ray 'Gus' Coward, Gary Stevens and I piled a plate with food and took it back to the car and set it up on the boot for the driver. 'The boss isn't going to like him staying out here,' the bloke from the plantation said to us. 'As far as I'm concerned,' I told him, 'you can't travel with a bloke for 100 ks, then leave him at the gate without a drink or a feed.'

It really was a sensational trip. I was privileged to see a place like Port Moresby when it still had a real rough frontier edge to it. I remember seeing the Bird of Paradise men in their amazing headdresses; they would just appear out of the bush, and the others were petrified of them. 'If you happen to run over one of the locals, don't stop,' a policeman told us. 'Just drive straight to the police station. There is a payback system and if you stop, they'll stone you to death.' It was another world.

My memories of those junior days are very happy ones, of good football, good companionship and good times. And characters – there were plenty of them. As a young hooker, graduating from the Juniors to Souths in '65, I especially remember Freddy Anderson and John 'Bomber' Hynes. Freddy, a bulky hooker of the old style who could strike with lightning speed in the scrum, was the first-grade hooker and Bomber was hooker in the seconds. Bomber had a liking for cigars, and later when he was a first-grader with Cronulla, the press would now and then picture him lighting up. If you're talking 'tough' . . . well, he was probably the toughest man in the club, throw John Sattler and the lot of them in. I liked him a lot; he was a real hard bugger and you knew exactly where you stood with him.

I'll never forget a story that my old C grade coach at Mascot, Popeye Mackie, told me. Popeye happened to be heading home at around 4 one morning. As he approached a little laneway near the Quality Street Stores off Botany Road, Popeye could hear a raised and angry voice: 'Look, George . . . if you don't come, I'm going to break your friggin' neck!' This is nice, thought Popeye, I've run into a couple of drunks – the worry with that being that two drunks fighting will sometimes turn on an outsider. So Popeye very gingerly tiptoed past the lane entrance, and when he glanced down the alley, there was Bomber Hynes leading one of the trotters he trained. 'I'll friggin' belt you if you don't come, George,' Bomber was growling. Football used to be about characters like Bomber Hynes and good times and funny stories. Much of that has gone now that the game has become a 'business' and a 'product' and 'pay TV fodder'. And it's a bloody shame.

Looking back now, it occurs to me that a lot happened early in my life. I left school when I was 14 and went into the workforce; I had a car when I was 15, still way too young to have a licence; and I was married when I was 17, going on 18. My first wife was Nona McKay, a local girl I had met after my schooldays. We were married young, probably too young, but we had three kids, Karen, Michael and Kellie, who meant a whole lot to me then, and do now. I see them every week.

With teenage marriage came responsibilities. For a time we were living at the back of my mum's place, in a garage, and it became very important to me to save up enough money for a deposit on a house. I found my first house as I made my way home at the end of a midnight shift on the wharves in 1967, a year in which I played a lot of first grade for Souths. Because I had a car I used to drop everyone off from our gang in the morning. Jimmy Cookson was the last, and as I headed up King Street, Eastlakes, there was a bloke knocking in a For Sale sign at the front of a cottage. It was 7 am. I pulled over, and it turned out to be a fella I knew, Stacky Barlow. I had gone to school with Stacky's two daughters. 'How much do you want for it, Mr Barlow?' I asked. 'George, I want $14,500,' he answered.

'Okay. I'll buy it,' I said. 'You sure?' asked Stacky. 'Yeah, I'm sure. I'll just have to organise the money.' 'Righto,' said Stacky. 'I'll take the For Sale sign down and it's yours.'

So five minutes or so after he had knocked the sign into the front lawn, Stacky Barlow was taking it down again. The sun was just peeking over the horizon, and I had a house – or just about.

My marriage to Nona lasted eight years. In the end the football, the shift work on the wharves and an accumulation of other things finished it. It was just one of those things that happen in life. Sadly, Nona died several years ago.

It was very early in my life too that I made a decision about alcohol. Oh, I tried it, and I grew 10 feet tall and six feet wide. I quickly weighed up that me and drink were not a good mix. You hear so often of people being addicted to drink or drugs, and I think there's a warning bell that rings pretty early for some of us in our connection with these things. I jerried that the booze wasn't for me. It changed my personality and I decided it was not going to be part of my life.

Being married in my teenage years played a part in that too. The responsibilities of marriage and having kids took me out of the social life very early on. Instead of being out sowing my wild oats and all that I became a worker. I wanted to put a house together and to have a place for the kids to be brought up in. Life to me was about putting priorities in place. I have never regretted my decision not to have anything to do with alcohol, although I think for the people who can handle it, who can go out and really enjoy a drink socially without any problems, then it is probably more of an asset than a hindrance. My brothers, for example, can go up to the pub, have a couple of beers and enjoy themselves, then come home. The problem lies with the bloke who comes home drunk, sparks an argument and throws his dinner on the ceiling, and worse. For too many people it can be a nightmare.

Playing rugby league, I was involved in a culture of alcohol that has always been part of the game. I was probably seen as a bit of an oddity. A prominent footballer who didn't drink! But I knew what I wanted to do and didn't want to do, so it was never a problem for me.

On reflection though, being a non-drinker probably didn't help my football career, the culture being so deeply instilled. Not being a drinker pretty much excluded me from the social side of the operation. Maybe it didn't help in my battle for the top hooking job at Souths either. But there was never any element of bitterness in that. Elwyn 'Aubrey' Walters was the first-grade hooker, I was the second-grade hooker – and that's the way it was (mainly) for six years or so. I played 16 first-grade games as early as 1967, and probably if I'd been more 'socially' involved with the firsts it might have been harder to take when I lost my spot to Aub.

In our playing days at Souths, rather than going to the pub or the club after training, Gary Stevens and I used to go and have a milkshake together. There was one of those old-fashioned milk-bars on Anzac Parade at Kensington, where the bloke had 40 different flavours. We worked our way right through the list. I'd shout one night, Gary would shout the next.

Work has always underpinned my life. I have virtually never been unemployed since I was 15 years of age. Sure, I 'retired' young – and I'll tell you about that further along the track – but in reality I have never stopped working. I'm a pre-dawn to dusk bloke; up at 4 each morning and never happier than when I am working on something productive through the day. I've had a heap of jobs over the years and no doubt learned something from all of them.

And I have no doubt either that the work ethic that I acquired from my parents helped me greatly in my football career. If you're prepared to tackle the hard yakka in life, you've got a chance. To me the absence of that principle and life-necessity – of having a job outside sport – is one of the big problems and dangers of modern professional football. We are breeding a race of young full-time footballers, whose brief time in that uncertain pursuit will finish when they're 30 or so (if they're lucky enough to get that far), leaving them largely unprepared for life in the real world outside.

The game is doing its young men no favours these days – pampering, publicising and spoiling them, heaping them with obscene amounts of money which rugby league can't remotely afford, failing to educate them for the life that they will have to confront one day, and providing them with large slabs of unproductive free time, which leaves them prey to drugs, booze and gambling. No wonder some stumble off the tracks.

The problem is not just football's of course. We seem to have a society now where temptation is put in front of kids all the time, with the easy availability of drugs, and pubs that never close. Somewhere along the line we need to re-educate kids about 'balance' in life; about paying board, going out only a couple of days a week, and working. There is a growing lack of balance in our society, too, between the 'haves' and the 'have-nots' – as the former Governor-General William Deane pointed out many times. Somehow the incentive to work seems to have been gradually taken away – and that's a fundamental government obligation, to provide that basic need to its people.

I'll give you a potted history of my own early working life, which included some remarkably unflash jobs. As a younger teenager I graduated from paperboy to working with a wool-wash mob down Botany Road, Miller & Ryan. They gave me a job cleaning the scourers out – a stinking, dirty task. Strike me dead! If you ever saw slavery in action, then this was it. I didn't stay long.

I moved from there to pie-making, working as a pastry cook at a place in Wellington Street, Mascot. The 2 am start was the problem there. You'd be working away waiting for the sun to come up every day, and it always seemed painfully slow arriving. One cold winter's morning, Mum was up as I was getting ready to leave for work. 'Do you like this job?' she asked me. 'No', I said as I headed out the door. 'Well, tell the bloke you're leaving,' she called as I headed off. So I did.

I joined an old established firm, Gearin & O'Riordans, as off-sider on a bone wagon, doing daily runs that took me into the near and slightly further countryside. Headquarters was in O'Riordan Street, Mascot. I was working with some good blokes, and it was a job with a future, with a decent old-fashioned employer who looked after his workers and helped them make their way in life. Plenty of blokes had started there as wagon boys, as I did, and finished up with good jobs.

My run initially was to Mount Victoria and then, after I got into an argument with the driver, they put me on another run, which often involved going out to Bowral, Picton, Canberra and Queanbeyan. Being a city boy, I had never really been out in the country. I worked from 6 am to 6 pm five days a week, and earned 10 quid. It doesn't sound like much of a job, but I liked it a lot. The trade was in fat and bone, which was melted down to be used in such things as perfume and soap, and there was plenty of graft in it. The drivers would rob one butcher to give to another butcher and the second bloke would then pro-vide the driver with meat. I became part of this fringe-benefit arrangement and most weeks, along with me giving Mum my board, I'd hand over some sausages and steaks, and a leg of lamb. The year was 1959, and I was earning £10/10 shillings a week, and paying a fiver for board.

I stuck with Gearin's until I got my driver's licence at 16 years and 10 months. There was a progression at Gearin's that guaran-teed I would become a driver at some time, but the waiting list was four years and I was impatient. I was really chasing the quid then. So I moved on again, taking on a Crystal Soft Drink run and biding my time until I could get my heavy-vehicle licence and move on to light trucks. From there I joined RN & AJ Miller, a transport company that carted out of the Sydney Paper Mills. Every morning I would go to WD & HO Wills at Kens-ington and pick up the scrap cigarette cartons for delivery to the mills. I plugged away at that for a time then got offered a job at my uncle's Arcadia Nursery (which is still there) at King Street, Mascot, driving a truck and delivering plants and seedlings.

By 1965, after I had first, briefly, tasted grade football in the red and green, I was a wharfie, and earning pretty solid money. The conditions were good, the wages were good, but it was no easy job. Anyone who has ever loaded a shipful of wool or bagged wheat or hides can tell you that at the end of it you know you've done a day's work.

It was a job that was pretty sympathetic to footballers, though. I never ran into any difficulty about getting the time off that I needed to train and play for Souths. They were great. Your gang would 'carry' you, meaning that you didn't have to put yourself off the working roster, but it worked both ways. You had to fill some gaps for the other blokes too. Gang 26, it was, and all from Mascot, apart from 'Midget' Ambrose, who was from Waterloo. They were blokes I had played football with – Jimmy Cookson, Johnny McGee, Roy Pardie, Tommy Vose, Midget, Paul White, Brucie Dickens, Trevor Freeman, Billy Gammel and my brother Albert. I was number 6835 – I can still remember that – and you'd listen for the call on radio station 2KY in the morning. I enjoyed being a wharfie and met some great people – the seamen and the captains and the wharf labourers from all over the place. There was a spirit there that made the job special.

The former federal minister for Workplace Relations, Peter Reith, did his best to wreck that, and, in my view, he's a very average kettle of fish. That's an opinion from an old wharfie's perspective certainly, but the fact is, things were never as black on the wharves as Reith's side of politics tried to paint them. A great deal of the stuff that comes into this country comes via the Sydney waterfront and, over more years than any of us could remember, enough of it was getting through efficiently for this country to make huge progress. Governments made a sport out of flogging the wharf labourer – and Reith made an art form of that.

Granted, in any job you can name, there are blokes who 'work' the system. The thing is you don't get the system to work if *everyone* is a rorter, which is the picture the conservatives tried to paint, year after year, of the waterfront. And the system on the

Sydney waterfront *didn't* break down, as evidenced by the giant leap this country has taken. The waterfront has always looked after its workers, and that's the way it should be. For my money, you can't knock an industry that does that. I think if an average worker can retire with an income that allows them a little bit of dignity, then that's great.

I left the waterfront in the end because I could do better outside. If I'd believed a better financial future existed for me on the wharves, then I would have stayed and probably been a wharfie all my life. I enjoyed the job, and the camaraderie that existed there.

The thing was that I had always had this fascination for trucks. In early 1967, I went out and bought my own truck, an International bogie with a good big body on it. From memory, I paid about $3500. At that stage Nona and I still didn't have a house; I had stuck my neck out and bought a truck before taking that next step for the family. Down at the wharves I did some under-the-lap business, and offered my working 'brief' (ticket) to a mate. It was something you weren't supposed to do. 'If it doesn't work out, I want my brief back,' I told him. That was the deal. My plan was never to go back to the wharves, but that came unstuck when I experienced a 'mishap' with that first truck, which I'll discuss in the next chapter. With no choice, I finished up working on the wharves for a further period. Notwithstanding, the trucking business eventually provided me with the breakthrough opportunity in life that all of us seek. Although, all that was a fair way down the track.

4. Truckin'

Steady work gives a man a sane outlook on the world.

William S. Osler

THE FIRST TRUCK I ever bought provided an instant chapter of accidents that showed what a hand fate can play in a life. I bought it in early 1967 on the urging of a mate who had been in the business for a while, carting the ash from Balmain Powerhouse to Homebush Bay. He said he could get me steady work on the salt boats. At the time there happened to be a big salt boat in and work was available, so I thought, 'I'll do it.' Next day I went out and paid cash – and became the owner of this big green truck.

I went to see Ronnie Bell, a good mate from Souths, at No. 1 wharf, Balmain. Ron was a bloke who would always do what he could to help any Souths player looking for work, but he couldn't avoid the problem of my lack of insurance on the new vehicle. 'Look, George, I can't start you until you organise some insurance,' he told me. So I drove straight across to the

Government Insurance place at Zetland and told them I had just purchased the truck, but was a bit short on cash – would they give me a cover note for a month and take me on? Yes, that was okay, they said.

Armed with the contract number, I went back to Ronnie Bell at Balmain and they loaded me up, and off I went. About 10 minutes later, on the steep run up Gladesville Bridge, almost right at the peak, I blew the clutch. The accident was probably more to do with me being inexperienced than anything else. Instead of driving the truck around for a while, I had virtually gone straight to work, with a heavy load, and promptly dropped a clutch.

It was 5 in the afternoon. Peak hour. And I was stranded atop one of the busiest bridges in Australia, in a truck packed full of salt. This is lovely, I thought . . . What am I going to do? There wasn't a lot of choice really. I pulled the handbrake on, put her in gear and left my new truck sitting there. I hailed a passing van and the bloke gave me a lift to Gladesville Police Station. At the counter, I was just into my story: 'Mate, I'm broken down on the top of Gladesville Bridge with a full load of salt on board. Can you organise a tow for me? It's going to cause chaos.' I had barely got the words out when a bloke ran in from the street: 'There's been a bad smash on Gladesville Bridge,' he said. 'A big truck has overturned . . . it's gone.' The policeman on the desk asked him: 'What colour is the truck?' 'Red' was the answer. 'And what colour is yours?' he asked me. 'Green.' 'C'mon,' he said. 'We've got real effing trouble with the two of them up there!'

When we got to the bridge we were greeted by an amazing sight. In a little park at the bottom of the Parramatta side of the bridge there was a truck upside down, buried in salt and showing only the red underside. Around the upturned truck were 20 or 30 blokes digging away furiously with bare hands and shovels, looking for the driver they believed was buried deep beneath. It was my truck, the green duco hidden by the mountains of salt. 'Don't worry,' the copper called out. 'We've got the driver here!'

If I ever won Lotto in my life, it was that afternoon. In peak hour the truck had taken off from the top of the bridge, rolling forward, had not hit anything else and had tipped itself over into a vacant allotment. If it had gone the other way, back down the bridge, I still shudder to think what the outcome might have been. I could have been sitting here today telling my story, knowing that I had been responsible for killing six or seven people.

I organised for a tow, and that night went to see Jack Craig, my uncle, and borrowed enough money to pay for the insurance cover note. I wasn't going to give them any glimmer of opportunity to scrub that, I decided. Next morning I was a very early customer at the insurance office, and handed over the money for the premium. As soon as that was fixed I asked the bloke behind the counter, 'And can I have a claims form, please?' He just looked at me. 'You're kidding, aren't you?' he said. The manager was duly called and I explained what had happened and that he should check with Gladesville Police and so on. I was told later that with some insurance policies there is some sort of 'sunset clause' whereby if you take out the policy during the day you are not covered until the end of that day. The manager went away for a while to ponder it, then returned. 'Gee whiz, this is your lucky day,' he told me. 'He's covered,' he told the clerk. 'Give him a claims form.'

They sent an assessor down to see the truck and he deemed it a write-off. That night I had the worst night's sleep ever. The money I had paid out for the truck, after all, had been earmarked for a deposit on a house. Anyhow, next day a bloke from Flemington Spares came by and saw the wreck. 'Who owns the truck?' he asked. 'I do,' I said. He bought what was left of my first truck, and with that and the money I got back from the insurance policy I ended up making about $200 on the deal.

It was quite a year for me, 1967. You could win some money on what I did on the football field that year. Most people probably think of me as a lower-grade player at Souths at that time, but in '67 I got picked for 17 first-grade games and played 16 of them.

In 1966, the rough 'order' of hookers at the club was Freddy Anderson, 'Aubrey' Walters, then me – although I got picked for the '66 second-grade grand final and they shifted Aub into the second row. When the '67 season kicked off, Freddy and Aubrey were rated ahead of me, and got picked.

Walters broke his arm, and after Freddy, who was getting on a bit, had played three or four games, they retired him. I got the call, and went on to play the next 16 first-grade games straight, in a year in which Souths won the premiership. Against Norths three weeks out from the semi finals, I got sent off, then exonerated. But the old Norths hooker, Rossy Warner, who had been sent off with me, had kicked me in the calf muscle in that match and I had to miss the next game against Penrith. Walters, who had been picked in reserve grade, got the call-up, played the remaining few games, including the winning grand final, and went on to win a place on the Kangaroo tour of England and France. I didn't even get to play in the reserve-grade grand final, having failed to qualify under the rules of the time because I had been playing first grade exclusively. It was a dud ending to a good season. Souths won the comp, and I could so easily have been part of it. Should have been, I reckon. Not until 1973, six long seasons on, did I win back the first-grade hooking job on any sort of permanent basis, even though I had the honour and enjoyment of playing in the winning grand final side of 1971.

In the circumstances following the smashing-up of my first truck in 1967, I had no choice but to go back to the wharves for a while. As you can imagine, I copped plenty from my mates down there when they heard the story. But I had taken the first step in the trucking business and before long, this time with more success, I was heading back that way. I bought a tip truck, doing general excavation work, and then got a big contract out at Phillips Chemicals at Kurnell, carting carbon black up to the dump at Homebush Bay. (We dumped so much of the stuff up there I wonder how the hell they ever got to stage an Olympic Games on the site!)

I did that for a while, coming to realise that the costs of repairs on hard-working trucks were pretty horrific, and then hooked up as a contractor with Kelvinator, delivering fridges on a piece-rates basis of so much per fridge. I wore a few offsiders out along the way, but I made fair money at that caper. The best day I put in was 33 fridges – as you can imagine, it was a hard graft lifting 33 fridges on and off a truck, and sometimes carting them up three flights of stairs. That was a big day, finishing at 11 at night. The company drivers didn't want the North Shore, and they didn't want the apartment areas, so that was generally where I finished up.

One of my best offsiders, Jimmy Formica from Botany, finished up dead in a gutter with a handful of bullets in him. Jimmy was as strong as an ox: I saw him squat 500 pounds. When we were working together there was never a problem throwing fridges around. I was fit and playing football and pretty strong myself. Jimmy wasn't the quickest thinker around, and some pretty shady people harvested the wrong side of him. He was the sort of bloke who could be nice and quiet, or could be turned into a monster. Obviously he trod on some toes pretty badly and they gave it to him, and squared the account.

Working so hard on the truck, it was sometimes a rush to squeeze in training. Fortunately the reserves coach, Fred Nelson, was very understanding and, even if I was a bit late at times, there were never any dramas. Even when I was up in firsts, coach Clive Churchill was good and gave me some leeway. On plenty of occasions I'd park the truck outside Redfern Oval, run in and train, then hop back in the driver's seat and get back to work. It wasn't an easy time, but I wanted to better myself in life and it was the only way I knew how.

I stayed with Kelvinator until 1972, when my brother Stan asked me if I wanted to go into business with a semi-trailer, bringing up rock from Kiama on the south coast for the runway extension at Mascot Airport. At that time, Stan and a good mate of his, Claude Grande, were working the truck in 12-hour shifts.

I joined them, and I remember a night early on when we came down a hill off Mount Ousley and I couldn't believe that a loaded truck could go that bloody fast. 'We've got to do this to get up the next steep hill,' my brother explained. Halfway up the hill, and having slowed to a crawl, we passed a bloke who was blasting away on his air horns, his truck stranded on the roadside. 'This poor bastard's in trouble,' said Stan. Knowing that if we stopped to help, we'd burn out the clutch trying to re-start up the hill I hopped off to see what I could do. 'What's up?' I asked him. 'My air [for the brakes] is running out, can you get some of these big rocks off to chock me?' he asked. I was able to get some rocks down from the back of his truck and he rolled back until they took the weight of the truck and he could put it in gear and stop there. The job done, I had to sprint back to the top of the hill to catch up with my brother. Heavy trucking was hard work.

A bastard of an insurance assessor just about ruined us not long afterwards. Stan was out at the airport tipping a load one night when a big rock got caught in the hoist well, causing the trailer to snap off and doing the truck no good either. The damage was bad and we had the rig taken down to the truck and trailer yards at Lords Road, Botany, to get it fixed. The assessor turned up and Stan pegged him straightaway: 'This bloke is going to *do* us,' he said. I tried to be Mr Diplomatic with him, but he'd made up his mind after looking over the truck. 'That crack there caused it to tip,' he said. 'It's the result of neglect.' He refused us the insurance claim. I bit my tongue then, but subsequently I got a design engineer and a metallurgist to inspect the truck. They gave me a report which suggested that the insurance bloke hadn't had a clue what he was talking about. There was a clause in the policy that pointed any sort of dispute into the Equity Court and the design engineer said to me: 'George, it's not worth it. It's not a big enough claim. You could lose your house if you lose this. You're gonna to have to let it go – put it down to experience.'

It came at a time in my life when I had remarried, to Nolene Jones, whom I had known almost all my life. In fact Nolene and

I had gone to school together from the day we were five years old; there is a photograph of us at kindergarten. So, as I write this in the year 2001, we're talking 50 years or so. Nolene came from a staunch family of Rabbitoh supporters. She was smarter than me and went to the A classes whereas I was in the D classes. When we started high school we had a bit of a crush on each other. I know she liked me but I just didn't have much confidence in myself. Our friendship endured right through school and we used to ride horses, go to the beach and do things like that together. But what happened to us happens to a lot of people, I suppose. Your life zig-zags a particular way and you head off in a different direction. I was young and immature when I left school and I went out and did the boy thing. I don't think there's any doubt that the attraction between us was there all along, but life tends to twist and turn and I met someone else who I was in love with at the time. If anyone caused the troubles that brought my first marriage unstuck, it was me.

I was about 24 when Nolene and I picked up the threads of the friendship. We ran into each other one night at the club and we've virtually been together ever since. In 1972 we were married at the Wayside Chapel, Kings Cross. Nolene had been married young too, and had a daughter, Tracie, so we have a mixed family: my three – Karen, Michael and Kellie – and Trace.

She has been a great wife, and unflinching in sharing my belief that the South Sydney club was sorely wronged by the people running rugby league. She fought as hard as me for the cause, maybe harder. She was just relentless. She put every spare minute into the fight. Some nights she'd be up until 1 or 2 in the morning, working on things that had to be done. The big fund-raising social functions we have had – the balls and dinners and rallies – Nolene worked unbelievably hard on all of them. In many ways, she was the focal point of the fight to save South Sydney.

That first big investment in a big truck, back in '72, saw us do our money cold. I was so filthy on the assessor bloke, I felt like putting my hands around his throat and throttling him. I won't tell you what I said to him, but he was left in no doubt about how I felt. I still had my fridge truck, so I went back to Kelvinator for a while, before Stan and I headed back into the tip-truck business. We got an extension to the chassis of the original (now repaired) truck, sold the fridge truck and bought a new tipper. And that, really, was where it all started.

We worked on just about every big building in town – Centrepoint, the T&G building, Parliament House and the Eastern Suburbs Railway. Along the way I got to have a look at the old Tank Stream, to see the cobblestones numbered and taken away, and then put back in. Eventually Stan and I split up and headed in our own directions. Then one day at Parliament House, a bloke dropped a big rock on my truck. Somewhere along the way he must have lifted it too high, or just hadn't realised the weight of the rock. It broke my truck in two.

It was soon after that I decided I'd buy a new trailer, put a turntable on the truck and go into container carrying. I had talked to a bloke who told me he could get me some work at Glebe Terminal, an operation which was tied up by Balmain blokes. But when I got there I could tell by the looks on their faces that they weren't too enthusiastic at all about me coming over there to get work. It wasn't about football; it was just about not wanting an outsider muscling in on the available jobs. And they were on strike, anyway.

Then fate dealt me another good card. On a night soon afterwards, I was sitting at home having a cup of tea with my father, lamenting the situation, when the phone rang. On the other end was an uncle I never even knew I had, Sid Moberley. 'Is Stan there?' he asked my dad. 'I was looking for him, I rang your number by mistake.' They got talking and Dad asked him if he was still working down at Vegetable Oils. Yes, he was. 'Sid, young George has just brought a truck, a semi, and he's looking for work – can you help him out?' my father asked him. 'Leave it with me,' said Sid. 'I'll get back to you.'

A couple of weeks later, and with still no work for my

truck, the phone rang with the message that I had to go down and see Phil Fortescue, who ran the transport side of Vegetable Oils. Sid was there to meet me, and they agreed to give me a start. The timing was opportune, in a couple of ways. For starters, my work agreement there more or less coincided with Meadow Lea Margarine coming on the market; it was to prove very quickly to be a boom product. Additionally, I soon realised there was a deficiency and an inefficiency in the way the pallets of Vegetable Oils products were loaded and unloaded. You could take a truckload of margarine up to Davids Holdings at Blacktown or to Coles or Flemings, get there at 7 in the morning – and not get unloaded until 3 in the afternoon. You'd just sit in a line, hour after hour. This was okay if you were on an hourly rate, and getting paid to do that, but I was always on a pallet rate.

I knew that there had to be a better way. And the search to find that way provided me with the great break of my working life.

I've always been a bloke who searched for solutions. I like stepping back from things and viewing the big picture, trying to find answers. Some people might call it 'lateral thinking'. For example, I've spent a good bit of time studying detailed maps of the waterways of Sydney, looking for means by which they could be linked up to provide an efficient all-city transport artery to take some pressure off the roads. And, you know, there *is* a way, and it wouldn't be all that difficult. (If anyone wants to ask, I can show it to them.)

It was that sort of approach that provided me with my big break back in the early '70s, carting margarine and other goods for Vegetable Oils. The products and the business were good, but, as I've said, the system of transportation was slow and inefficient. They were sending out trucks carrying 20 pallets and the turnaround was painfully slow at times. I said to the big boss one day, 'If I could get 40 pallets there in one go, would you be interested in that?' He certainly would be, he told me.

'What are you going to do?' I told him my plan: to build an extra deck on my container trailer, doubling the capacity. So I went ahead and did it, building this deck thing, like an open container. When we first loaded her up and tried it out, the truck swayed around – but it worked. The key to success was to be the first truck in each morning, and to get the quick turn-around so I could get back and pick up another 40 pallets. I was carting 40 pallets a time at $6 a pallet, and once the system was bedded in I was killing them. Some days I would get my 60 or 80 pallets up, and that was good money back then, considering I was paid at a per-pallet rate.

In due course, I took it a further step, buying an aluminium trailer and lining it with fibreglass, so that the trailer would be suitably cool to transport margarine, in line with tightening health regulations. I linked up with an engineer down at Botany, Alec Forrest, who was bloody good, and discussed my ideas about having a system of trolleys on rails in the truck to speed and ease the loading of heavy pallets. He said it could be done. He knew exactly what I wanted and was able to translate the thought into an operating reality. Via a fair amount of trial and error, and the introduction of floating axles to provide some flex-ibility in movement, we came up with something that would work and took out a patent on it. Eventually Alex offered me the chance to buy him out of the patent, and I did that.

The 'invention' essentially consisted of four 'railway lines' on the floor of the truck, and the use of airbags which enabled us to cart two pallets quickly to the back of the van and come back and pick up two more. Once we got it going it was amazing how fast it could operate. Then we put a bar on the walls of the trailer on which we had another floor, operating exactly the same way.

Luck often supports a good idea. And my luck came in the shape of some absolutely terrific blokes at Vegetable Oils, Billy Wocko from the Ukraine and an Italian kid named Frank Bolento. They really wanted me to succeed and they became expert at the intricate task of loading my newfangled truck. The pair of them were just great. If I got back at lunchtime for my second load, they'd put lunch back and load me up first. They were the two best forklift drivers I ever had anything to do with and they played an important part in my success.

It all started to work. I traded in my first truck (the open one) for another aluminium trailer on which we installed the rails-and-trolleys system. Progressively the business grew to the point where I had seven trucks on hire purchase, each of them sporting colourful Meadow Lea advertising on the sides. It grew to be an enormous contract. I was getting more money to go to Pyrmont and back than a bloke who was driving to Melbourne. I was carrying twice the capacity and the company was pumping out so much product that it had to use just about all the cold storage space in Sydney to house it. And the stuff was selling like mad. Everything coincided.

One Saturday morning I did six loads to Pyrmont and back. Nolene said to me, 'You're a hungry bugger,' and I said, 'Listen – I'll work all day if they're going to pay me at this rate.' It became an unbelievable job. The best money I turned over for a week – and this is fact, not skiting – was $36,000. When it was big I could move 240 pallets in six hours, and that was big money. But there were days too, if the oil wasn't in, when you wouldn't earn a penny, days when you would sit idle.

In 1982 we nearly lost the lot. Meadow Lea was the target of a raid by Goodman Fielder that went within a cat's whisker of coming off. Sitting there with six big Kenworths and a White on hire purchase, I was literally sickened. The vans were around $30,000 at that time and a truck $40,000–$50,000. I had a stack of money tied up in the business and was frightened by the prospect of what a takeover would mean to me. After the Goodman Fielder raid failed I asked David Stewart at Meadow Lea if a takeover was likely. He levelled with me: 'Yeah George, it will happen next time.' I asked him the question straightaway: 'Can I sell this business of mine . . . and with the goodwill?' 'Yeah, you can sell it with goodwill,' he said.

I had already had some feelers from TNT, and I let it be known that my business was now officially for sale. I took a call from

TNT boss Ross Cribb and the conversation went something like this:

> *Cribb:* I hear your business is for sale, George.
> *Piggins:* That's right, Ross.
> *Cribb:* What do you want for it?
> *Piggins:* A million dollars.
> [*Ross laughs.*]
> *Piggins:* Ross, I don't really care – it's either a million dollars or I don't sell.
> *Cribb:* Is it *that* good?
> *Piggins:* Have a look at the books and see what you think.

So, they had a look at the books – and paid me $1 million clear for my business. That's $1 million after all expenses were paid – taxes . . . the lot. I was 40 years of age. I always said I was going to retire at 40, and I guess in a way I did, from that part of my life anyway. But of course I pressed on, the work ethic and business sense being woven into my life, with shares in a couple of pubs, a sports store, nurseries and an indulgence in one of my great loves, breeding racehorses. Joining me in various businesses were partners such as Jack Gibson, my brothers Stan and Wally, and Frank Cookson and Henry Morris.

The racing game has provided me with a great deal of pleasure in recent years, my involvement with horses linking me to childhood years in Mascot. I took out a trainer's licence some years ago, and spend a lot of time at the breeding property Nolene and I own in the Southern Highlands. We've had some luck – a couple of horses that topped $100,000 in prize money. Like everyone in the game, the hope is always that the *next* one is going to be the champion. It's what keeps everyone going. Racing has got its lovely side: the horse aspect of the business is that for me. Some of the things I have seen at the stables have been fantastic. And the strong friendships I have made – with the likes of Reg Young, Les Bridge, Jimmy and Grey Lee, and the late

Stewie Bathis and his son Matthew – mean a lot to me. Yet there's a shiftiness about it, blokes who wouldn't tell their mother to put a dollar on a horse in case she might tell the neighbour next door. With some of them, you go to the track and say hello, and they're frightened you are going to ask them for a tip. There are some mean-spirited bastards around. As a trainer and non-punter I'm always happy to share what I know. And I get asked a fair bit, being fairly recognisable through football and the Souths battle. If I think it can win, I'll tell them, and if I think it can't, I'll tell them that too.

It's funny how it worked out. When TNT came calling in '84 it just happened, by chance, that I was 40 years of age. But if I've been 'retired' since that day, I keep thinking there must be an easier way!

I remember an afternoon in the backyard at Mum's some years later when a few of us had gathered, including my younger brother Stan, who had just come back from Queensland. Stan had been through some of the big nurseries up there, and was impressed. 'I'd love to get into that business,' he said. 'Well, I'll tell you where the best site in Sydney is,' I told him. 'The Jockey Club on Gardeners Road would be the best place in Australia for a nursery.' I had worked on the trucks for a nursery in earlier times and had a good idea where most of the outlets were. Flower Power had become big around that time, and bigger, new-style nurseries were just on the move. Here was over a hectare of prime land, on a busy road. The backyard conversation quickly grew into something bigger. Stan said he'd like to have a crack at it and I said I'd go in with him.

The great rugby league coach, Jack Gibson, joined us and so did my other younger brother, Wally. The problem was getting the place. The lease for the Jockey Club was up for sale, but there was a big push for a school to be built on the site. Fortunately the zoning of that area, adjoining both The Lakes Golf Club and the Eastlakes public course, favoured the open-air attraction of a nursery ahead of a school. After a tussle, Botany Council gave us its blessing and we were able to convince the local government head body that a nursery in the district would be a desirable addition.

And that's how I became a nurseryman. I've been pictured since by the media as the grisly old hooker, sniffing the flowers. The place, now Gardens-R-Us, with its beautiful outlook over the golf courses, has become a recreational hub of the district – and a good business. Nursing homes in the district send buses down; the old people can take their time, have a cup of coffee at the Lakeside Cafe and enjoy walking among the flowers and plants.

We branched out further into the nursery business, including into the NSW gaol system, where we put on horticulture classes for the inmates. That proved a productive exercise and good for the blokes involved, I'm sure. The only problem is the turnover! Just when we've got a group well trained and everything going right, that lot is released and we have to get other blokes trained through the classes.

For a million bucks back then in 1984, TNT got a good buy, and I got a fair deal. The thing they were going to find hard to match was the personal service I had provided. I had superintended the whole business in a very 'hands-on' sort of way, making sure the job got done right. If an order came in late when a driver was about to knock off, well, I'd take it myself. In no conceivable way, though, could I claim all the success as my own. I think any successful company owes a large slice of the credit to the workers. There has to be a lot of teamwork in business, as there is in football. I had some great drivers and terrific blokes – fellas like Ray Carriage and Tommy Curran. I remember one time the pair of them asked me to give a mate named Bruce a job, and when the bloke turned up, he had no teeth. When he tried to talk he was like a gummy shark. Realising the importance of dealing with customers I said to him, 'Look, go and get yourself organised with some teeth and I'll pay for them.' So he did, and I employed him.

Anyhow, one Saturday morning the news came through that Bruce had smashed the truck in an accident at Wentworthville. I was concerned about the driver, naturally, but his wife confirmed that he was okay when she rang me. 'What time did it happen?' I asked her. There was a pause on the line, then, '11.30 last night.' I said, 'But he took the truck at 4 yesterday afternoon, and was going straight home!' 'I know,' she replied. 'He went to the club. I'll kill him . . .' Under the circumstances I had no alternative but to sack him.

It happened about a week before this bloke was due to get his new teeth. Bruce wasn't a bad bugger and I wasn't going to be too tough on him. But to gee up the others, I borrowed a set of my mother's old false teeth and stuck them in my pocket. I told them: 'I've had this bloke – he's a smarty. When I pay him out, if he hasn't got the money for the false teeth, then I'm going to take them back off him.' They just looked at me in disbelief.

Anyway, he came around to the sports store at Maroubra Junction on a Saturday morning to collect his money and I took him outside. He was very apologetic, but I said to him, 'I could have done the truck, the load, everything. I can't have you working for me anymore.' We parted good friends. I walked back inside and took the false teeth out of my pocket. 'Here,' I said to John Curran (brother of my driver Tom), who managed the store, 'stick these in the drawer.' I'll never forget the look on his face. When Nolene came in later that morning he asked her, 'Nolene, he took the bloke's *false teeth* off him – is he really *that* hard?'

5. Bloody Battles . . . and a Man Named Churchill

Souths boys are tough. There is a saying about Souths
footballers that they would play footy with a house brick
in the middle of the road if they had to.

Tanya Plibersek, ALP member for Sydney, in a speech to Federal Parliament

THIS WAS NEVER going to be a book of football yarns. It is
instead a book about an Australian life (which happens to be
mine), a book about a belief – that what was done to South
Sydney Football Club by outside forces was a deplorable and
despicable act – and a book, hopefully, that reveals and drives
home to the public that people power can still triumph over the
bully boys' attempts to change society for their own benefit.

Even so, a fair lump of my life – 14 years – was taken up playing rugby league at a senior level with South Sydney. Inevitably
there are stories and characters on that stage which explain and
provide a backdrop for what took place later, and perhaps throw

light on the depth of passion in my fight to save the club. For that reason I will share in this chapter and the next some fragments of a career, of moments and characters I remember.

I played my football in a hard era before the eye of the TV camera closed in on the game. Games were won on a mix of skill and physical superiority, and South Sydney at their best had the blend just right. Like St George before them, Souths were an uncompromisingly hard side, but capable of dazzling skills. Spectacular, free-running football was a club tradition that went all the way back to the beginning when Souths were formed in 1908. My era was one of an eye for an eye, a tooth for a tooth. Referees and touch judges of the time did their utmost to keep the play in check, but there was a wink and a nod to rough justice too. If you got whacked, chances are you'd get the chance to land one back. That sort of approach lasted, probably, until the end of the '70s. I remember Easts' Bunny Reilly belting me one day, squaring off, if memory serves me correctly, for something that had happened a little earlier. One of our blokes, Stevie Little, a policeman, shouted out to the referee, Greg 'Hollywood' Hartley, 'Didn't you *see* that?' 'He deserved it,' said Hartley, on the run, and play went on. I could wear that.

When it came to tough guys, St George's (later Canterbury's) Kevin Ryan might have been the toughest of the lot. He hit me harder one day than anyone else ever hit me on a football field. He really clobbered me, lifted me off the ground. At the Sydney Cricket Ground in 1967 he and our Johnny Sattler came to grips. It felt like the ground was moving. Sattler and Ryan were sort of trading punches on the run, and all of a sudden John O'Neill joined the fray from the side and flattened Ryan, forcing him off the field for a time. These blokes were heavy hitters and I was pleased to be just an onlooker. (Shit! They were really giving it to each other, I remember thinking.) Ryan was a dominant player, a leader. When he went across to Canterbury in 1967 he made a huge difference. Only Bobby McCarthy's intercept beat them in the grand final that year.

Sattler mixed toughness and callousness, and that's a lethal combination. Tough was never in question, considering that he played most of the 1970 grand final with a broken jaw. I'll pick my words carefully, but John probably did things on a football field that a lot of blokes would never do. I mean I could do *most* things once someone tried to do something to me (and I'll tell you my version later of an infamous incident involving me and English forward Malcolm Reilly which might make your hair curl), but there were not many who would instigate the way Satts and one or two others would.

Noel 'Ned' Kelly was like that too. Wests forward Ned hit me on the chin in a match one day and it was reported that he knocked me out. Well, to set the record straight, he didn't. I was fishing for a penalty. In saying that, the punch thrown may not have been Ned's 'best' anyway. Maybe if it had been his best I *would* have been in dreamland. Ned's book (*Hard Man*) records that he was sent off 17 times in his career. My own record stood at 14 send-offs, which is not great, but nowhere near as bad as it seems considering that many of them were for scrum infringements – an occupational hazard for hookers back then when scrums were a fair dinkum contest. Ned Kelly belted me in a Souths–Wests game one day, just after I had landed one on their red-haired forward, Barry Bryant. I went bang and hit Bryant. Ned went bang and hit me. I recall the linesman running on, and Dennis Lee, our prop, rolling me over on the ground.

Geoff Connell, who played for Balmain and Canterbury, was another tough player. He got me in a headlock one day and squeezed so hard I thought my head was going to explode. Rossy Warner from Norths, a butcher by trade, was as hard as anyone I ever came up against. In one game in 1967 he nearly kicked my shins off. I didn't know what else to do – so I kicked him back. We both got sent off.

Ray Higgs (Parramatta), pound for pound, was tough, as was another Eels forward, Bob 'the Bear' O'Reilly. He was an easy-going bloke, Bob, but my theory with him was always: if the Bear is asleep, then let the Bear sleep. Once you woke him or stirred him, he was a bloody handful. I recall the big Irish forward in the

St George pack, Robin Gourley, and a game in which one of our blokes took him on. 'I'll kill you!' Gourley roared and I'll swear the whole scrum shook. He was fearsome, and we were just a bunch of kids at the time. 'Tough' means different things to different people. Just because you can punch someone in the face doesn't mean you are tough. A tough person to me is someone who will take the ball up in a match when his forwards are in trouble, knowing he's going to get belted. At the end of the day, they're the tough guys – the blokes who hit the ball up most.

I don't remember ever being scared on the field, although I suppose anyone who plays a tough body-contact sport like league knows that a serious injury might be part of the deal. But in assessing one-on-one clashes, the referees of my time pretty much adopted the stance that if a bloke was holding his own, then they'd let it go. But no way were they going to just stand there while someone got the living daylights belted out of them. So there was protection to keep it in bounds.

It was a different world from today's game, which is under such a media focus. But you can't tell me that those big, fit kids playing today wouldn't be just as tough as those from other eras if the game was still played that way. Of course they would. There's so much bullshit today in the grading of 'incidents' that take place on the field; they argue endlessly whether it's a 'grade 4' or a 'grade 5' or a 'grade 79'. What a load of shit. A head-high tackle is a head-high tackle, always has been.

I played with and against some great players, and I guess a few opinions are in order. Ron Coote, Bob McCarthy and Paul Sait were the three best players at Souths in my years there. I played against Reg Gasnier in 1967 – a great player. It's funny how little things stick in your mind. In a game against Saints in 1967 I remember him going for a field goal and me catching him in the air with my tackle, right at the exact moment that he kicked.

Of them all, I think Graeme Langlands was the best I saw play the game. I played against 'Chang' a number of times, and toured with him in 1975 when he was Australian coach and I think he was just about the perfect football package, with all the gifts. I went away with him in '75 on the World Cup tour, and we became friends. I like the bloke. I paid the penalty for being in his shadow though, one day in 1973. Chang and I both got sent off on the same afternoon, and when we fronted the judiciary on the Monday night they fined us both $250. The thing was they needed Langlands for a Test match, and so they imposed the fine instead of a suspension. I got caught up in that; they wanted to demonstrate that what was good for the goose was good for the gander. I blew up, I was filthy! I didn't mind playing football for no money, but I sure didn't like giving the bloody stuff away, and especially in a season in which I was on pretty modest payments.

Johnny Raper was another, a great player who stayed late because he loved the game so much. In the SCG match against Saints in 1967, I remember Gasnier saying to him, 'C'mon Chook, we're not going to let these kids beat us!' But the kids did beat them that day. Bob Fulton was another player of my era with plenty of talent, although I never had much to do with Bobby off the paddock.

As far as hookers went, John McMartin (Parramatta), Ron Workman (Penrith) and Max Krilich (Manly) were probably the most skilful I came up against. As a hooker, you lived and died on what you achieved in the scrums, and the No. 12s were a special breed. Back then it would have been unthinkable to shove a halfback or a winger in at hooker as happens in today's no-contest/non-event scrums. In the scrum you did what you had to do. I remember playing St George one day and they had a couple of young second-rowers in who belted me in an early scrum. Next time we packed I just went 'whoof!' and roofed them both in the scone (the head). They left me alone after that. The way I looked at it, if someone belted me, well, I belted them back.

The scrums were a battleground. Probably my luckiest escape came one day at the old Sydney Sports Ground in 1965, when I was playing third grade against Parramatta. The Parra hooker was a bloke named Val Shoudra and as a scrum broke up, he head-butted me hard. I felt my teeth to make sure everything was intact. Then I snapped; it must have been the look in my eyes or something but he took off. I chased him and hit him on the back of the head and knocked him down. I don't know what it was, I just saw red and I kicked the shit out of him, really 'roofed' him. A touch judge came steaming on, flag upraised, to report me to the referee, Brian Barry, who was having his first grade game. 'He chased him, then he hit him, then he kicked him,' the touchie reported. But the rookie ref had been told not to send anyone off so he left me on the field. There was no citing in those days, so I was safe. The *Telegraph* the next day carried a story on the incident under a headline along the lines of: 'What is rugby league coming to when they leave this madman on the field?'

The incident, of which I am not proud, had its repercussions. Second-grade coach, selector and former international Les 'Chicka' Cowie was particularly crook on me because of it. One of my team-mates said to me back then: 'The only way you're ever going to make first grade is to leapfrog right over second grade.' Anyhow, in '66 I *did* get called up to seconds, much to the coach's displeasure. Chicka was mad on fitness and at the first training session we were doing an exercise I disliked intensely, where you jumped up in the air and clapped your hands over your head. It used to tighten up my calf muscles. 'I hate this bloody thing,' I said to no-one in particular. 'What did you say?' snapped Chicka. 'Nothing,' I said. He repeated his question. 'Well, I said I hate this exercise,' I told him. 'Why don't you piss off then,' said the coach. The atmosphere was very heated now. 'No, why don't you and I go behind the shithouse and settle this!' I snapped. He didn't come – and I don't blame him for that. I was a good few years younger than Chicka. But it was something I never forgot.

It probably worked against my career at Souths as I'm sure I never got any favours from Chicka Cowie. He used to take us on road runs, which I ran in bare feet. I always trained barefoot – road runs and all – until Jack Gibson made me wear boots or trainers when he was Souths' coach. It was just a continuation of earlier years. I had hardly ever worn shoes as a kid. I recall a newspaper photo of me once in old-fashioned ankle-high boots. 'The poor people of rugby league,' said the caption. In fact I had paid $300 to have the boots tailor-made!

One night Chicka took us on a particularly long circuit out from Redfern Oval to St Peters, and wending a long way home. Heading back, the pressure was on and past the Mount Lachlan Hotel in Elizabeth Street, Waterloo, Chicka, who kept himself very fit, lobbed alongside me. I wasn't going to let him beat me and I upped the pace. Suddenly Chicka was gone; he had hit the gutter and come down hard. I kept going and beat him back. When he arrived he was covered in blood. 'You didn't stop,' he said to me. 'Yeah, I knew I had you beat when you fell,' I replied. For all our differences early on, Chicka was a great and loyal Souths man, and I'm pleased to say that our relationship mellowed to the extent that we became firm friends and training mates in later years. Rugby league can be like that.

The scrums were a war zone at times. Heads would slam into each other – and if you look at my eyebrows today, they tell a story in their own right. There must be the leftovers of a couple of hundred stitches in them. Against Easts in a second-grade match in 1968, Bill Schultz, the New Zealand hooker, kicked me in the face and broke my jaw. I thought he had just knocked some teeth out, but my jaw kept slipping sideways while I tried to hold it, and my teeth, in place. My jaw had been snapped in two places.

Probably the fiercest battering I ever took was on a day I wore the green-and-gold Australian jumper in a match against Wales in the 1975 World Cup. They had a big pack, and a pretty tough one. There was their hooker, the ex–boxing champion Tony Fisher, big Jim Mills, Colin Dixon, the coloured second-rower, and Eddie Cunningham. They seemed to be bent on getting me off the paddock that day and they really gave it to me. In the dressing room at halftime our coach, Graeme Langlands, said to me: 'You should see your head, it's up like a balloon!' That was a fierce game. I finished up booting Cunningham in the head and the crowd came over the fence, and Wales coach Les Pearce got involved too. They didn't miss me that day, the Welsh, but blokes like our back-rowers Terry Randall and Ray Higgs stuck solid. They stood their ground. And we won.

When I reflect on tough games in a tough sport that went over the top now and then, there is one match that comes to mind, one which attracted little attention. But it was pretty sensational all the same. In early 1968, Souths firsts played the reserves at L'Estrange Park, Mascot. From the first scrum when there was a big collision as we packed, it was obviously going to be 'on'. The first-grade front row was Sattler, Walters, O'Neill. The reserve-grade front row was Dennis Lee, Piggins, Rodney Gorman. I can remember Rod saying to me very early on: 'Mate, if this is going to explode, I'm with you.' And I can recall Ronny Coote running over the sideline at one stage and calling out to Denis Donoghue, Souths' president, 'Call the frigging thing off – this is going to blow up!' It was a hard, heated game, contested about as fiercely as a football match can be. And the seconds won, 6–3, two tries to one. I'll tell you just how hard it was: during the game there were challenges to meet behind the sheds at the end and settle things one-on-one; none came to anything.

Coach of Souths firsts then was Clive Churchill, voted as the greatest footballer to have ever played rugby league in Australia. It is with pride and appreciation that I look back and reflect that I knew the man, and played under his coaching. It would be remiss of me not to talk of him, to share a thought or two.

Clive Bernard Churchill was rugby league's Bradman. He died prematurely and 16 years earlier than the great Sir Donald. But his name lives on in rugby league legend, and always will, despite the disgraceful slash-and-burn approach which has seen much of the game's past shunned, torn down and discredited. In two polls, conducted by the respected *Rugby League Week* magazine and by the *Daily Telegraph*, Churchill was named Australia's greatest rugby league player of the century. It is a source of pride in my own career that I played under his coaching, and especially so in 1967 when I played 16 first-grade games as hooker in a South Sydney side that won the premiership. It was my first year in first grade, and Clive's first year as coach. I had never met him or seen him before that year, although I felt I knew him. In any muck-around game of football I ever played as a kid involving my mate Ronnie Coleman, Ronnie was always 'Clive Churchill'. He was a fullback, you see.

In the years since the Churchill coaching era at Souths, I have occasionally heard disparaging remarks about Clive along the lines that he was 'no coach', and that a side which was both a team of champions and a champion team just went out and did it. In fact, Churchill was the shrewdest of league men with a wonderful football brain. He coached with a light touch because he knew he had the troops and didn't need to interfere too much. I have often thought that his own words summed up perfectly a brilliant five-year period in which Souths won four premierships and lost the other (1969) under questionable circumstances. Clive said, 'I had a team of champions, and my main task was to keep harmony in the place. They weren't dumb, they were smart young blokes who could play football and my job was just to make sure we didn't ever let it get off course.' Yes, Clive Churchill could coach alright. He won four premierships in five years, and should have had a fifth. Sure he had a championship team, but he handled that side just right, expertly and without fuss.

His manner and style were light years away from those of some of today's ego-driven, overpaid coaches, whose interfering, heavy-handed approach (based no doubt on the firm belief that they are God's gift to coaching) threatens to take away all initiative from the players. Frank Hyde has written of coaches delivering their post-game match summaries to the media as if sharing the Sermon on the Mount, so wise and all-knowing are they. Churchill was never like that.

So, give me modest Clive Churchill any day, with his careful guidance, an ever-present twinkle in the eye and his determination to let a champion football team play the sort of football it was capable of playing without being shackled. When I went into coaching myself in the '80s I took a leaf out of Clive's book. I think it's fair to say that I coached 'lightly', determined that the good players I had could play to the limits of their ability and enjoy themselves along the way.

At about the time he was diagnosed with cancer in the 1980s I ran into him one morning down at Coogee Beach, when I was out early walking my dogs. He had received his bad news and was out having a walk on his own, no doubt thinking about it. We walked and talked for a while and along near the surf club I asked him, 'How are you going financially?' Things weren't great. So, I said, 'How about if we put a testimonial dinner on for you?' 'That'd be great, mate,' he said. So we all got working – the likes of my (then) tennis partners Ron Coote, John O'Neill and Gary Stevens and our wives – and the outcome was a fantastic night at the function centre at Randwick Racecourse, highlighted by Clive's entrance, and by a speech in which he showed he had lost none of his sense of humour. Clive was completely bald then and related the story of how he had told a taxi driver that it was the result of a visit to an Irish barber named 'Kim O'Therapy'. That night was our first meeting with Alan Jones, a man destined to be so closely linked to Souths in years ahead. The *Telegraph*'s Mike Gibson recommended Jones to us as compere–special speaker – and Alan did a mighty job. I don't think there was a dry eye in the house after his tribute to the great Churchill. We raised a lot of money, no less than the game owed to such a man and player. Clive's death in mid '85 was a huge blow, although expected, and the funeral was enormous, certainly one of the biggest in Sydney until the death of another great Souths man, John O'Neill, on August 9, 1999.

After Clive's death, O'Neill and his wife Clare and Nolene and I included Joyce Churchill, Clive's widow, in our regular Wednesday night dinners at Souths' Chinese restaurant. It's something we do every week. But it's a bad club to be in. John's gone now too, so I'm the only male left in the Wednesday night get-together!

I suppose you could say that the sort of spirit and emotion shown publicly on the deaths of blokes like Clive Churchill and John O'Neill was evident to some extent in the fight to save the South Sydney club these recent seasons. And I know that people rallied round – and I don't want to sound ungrateful – but gee whiz, if we had *all* dug in a little bit harder, stuck a bit more solid, you know, News Limited would never have got its way with rugby league. Some of the things that happened as ARL men and clubs crumbled meekly (and much more of this later!) simply couldn't have happened in the days of the tough, loyal old breed of league officials for whom the game was always the thing. It would be unthinkable to consider even just a few years back that fellow clubs could have turned against Souths the way they did – signing affidavits that put the knife right into the Rabbitohs. Of all the things that happened, that action was one of the most unbelievable.

But there *were* good things that came out of it too. I think of quality blokes like Mick Cronin, Peter Wynn and Bob O'Reilly who came along to our rallies because they believed in the principle involved. And I think of someone like Cliffy Lyons, a player from the old school, putting his hand up to play for Souths as we battled around the countryside in early 2001, trying to raise funds for yet another struggle in court.

Those personal gestures were a reminder of what rugby league used to be about, the things I mentioned in the Introduction of this book – mateship, loyalty, camaraderie, about doing the right thing . . . or trying to. Since 1995 it has not been about any one of those things and the game is diminished because of it. I doubt it will ever be what it was, but that is the challenge that all of us in the league now face.

6. Blood 'n' Thunder Days: Playing the Game

Piggins wasn't the sort of man to back down in any challenge. He took on board what I had to offer that day, then came right back at me, giving me just as good as I gave him. A hard man, George Piggins – but a very straight one. Rugby league could do with more of his kind.

Malcolm Reilly

I PLAYED 251 GAMES for Souths, 118 in firsts, 100 in reserve grade and 33 in thirds. Out of all those matches I am remembered for three things perhaps: my fight with Englishman Mal Reilly in the middle of the Sydney Cricket Ground in 1973; a try I scored against Western Suburbs at Lidcombe Oval in 1976; and my game for Souths when we won the grand final over St George in 1971. In the course of a career all players have stories to tell, of days that went very right or days that went very wrong. Most people would put the Reilly fight into the second category.

My brawl with Reilly took place at what was then football's 'home', the SCG, on an afternoon in 1973 when Souths were playing their keenest rivals, Manly.

Malcolm was a very tough player, and a bloody good one. Manly paid a fortune to bring him from England, and he gave them value, despite hobbling on a crook knee for much of the time. Anyone who tries to tell you that Englishmen aren't tough . . . forget it. Reilly pretty much introduced the lethal elbow into football and, boy, he did some damage in the seasons he played. Anyhow, we were playing Manly at the SCG in a second-round game. These matches always had plenty of sting. Manly were our main challengers in that era and the defending champions that year, having won their first title in 1972. But there was no existing feud or anything like that between me and Reilly. What happened, just happened.

At a certain moment in the game, I tackled him head-on, across on the Ladies' Stand side of the ground. Reilly had kicked me in the mouth in an earlier tackle, damaging my jaw, and I had put a shot on him then. When they separated us, we had both been cautioned. This second time he came down on me and as he got up he virtually played the ball on top of me, and his boot crashed down onto my jaw, the sprigs raking my mouth, ripping and tearing flesh from around my teeth. When that happened I thought, 'You bludger, you did that on purpose' and I whacked him. We grabbed each other and there were a couple of headbutts and punches thrown. Meanwhile the game went on. Laurie Bruyeres, a sergeant-major style ref who officiated with his collar stiffly starched, ran past. 'Cut it out!' he yelled. 'If you keep going, I'll send you off.' We had hold of each other at that point and I said to Reilly, 'If we carry it on, we'll be off the paddock.' 'Yeah,' he said.

I relaxed my hold and next thing he let me have it – a big Liverpool Kiss. Then it was really on. I grabbed him and came up hard with my head in close. I had a bit of strength and I was able to fling him to the ground and lob on top of him. I'm try-ing to give it to him, and he's trying to get me off and get back to his feet. In that sort of situation, I am a street fighter. It's win at *all* costs. Anyhow, it got a lot worse when he shoved a finger in my eye – I don't know whether it was deliberate or not, it could have been accidental. But I saw red. 'Oh, you want to gouge, you bastard!' I yelled at him. I went straight for one of *his* eyes, and I'll swear I had it out in my hand. Ray Branighan, an ex–team-mate with Souths who had joined Manly, ran in at exactly that moment and pushed me, and Reilly's right eye popped back in. Then referee Bruyeres, who had followed the play, was back on the scene and sent us both off. It was Laurie Bruyeres, incidentally, who sent me off in the first grade game I ever played, at Redfern Oval on Anzac Day, 1967, with the old Newtown warhorse Clarrie Jeffries. Clarrie and I were pinched that day for 'repeated scrum infringements', a regular event then and generally caused by referees who overreacted.

Anyhow, a couple of nights later when Reilly and I fronted the judiciary, his eye was badly inflamed. And my jaw was swollen to buggery. At the NSW Leagues Club in Phillip Street before the hearing, he said to me: 'Who did *that* to you?' And I said, 'You did, you bludger.' Anyway, Reilly asked me if I was going to have a drink. I said fine, and he bought me a schooner of lemonade. Then we went upstairs and faced the judiciary and were each suspended for three weeks. The charge was 'head-butting'. 'What went on wasn't good for the game,' said judiciary chairman Dick Dunn. I could only agree with him. 'It was good for nobody,' I told the media blokes. After that incident I never had any problems with Malcolm.

What happened was a silly thing. As a footballer I didn't go looking for fights, but if I did get into one, the only thing I wanted was to win. I never went looking for stinks, although a few found me over the years.

Much more positive from a pure football sense was the try I scored against Wests in 1976, on a ground which has long since disappeared from the list of major rugby league venues. I didn't score too many tries and this one was probably my best. I remember a few things about that day. For starters it was blowing an absolute bloody gale and the tin roof on the big old shed they had at the back of Lidcombe was lifting ominously. I was thinking, 'We'll get our heads cut off here.' It was one of those games that went my way. I am a short bloke, but I had a fair turn of pace for a short spurt, and I played my football at 92 kilograms, or just above. The try was just one of those moments that can happen in football. It came in a hard, tight match against a Western Suburbs side which included the likes of Les Boyd, John Elford, John 'Dallas' Donnelly and Tom Raudonikis. The game was played before a crowd of more than 17,000. I'm not quite sure how it happened, I just saw the line from 20 metres out . . . and kept going. The photos show me apparently well held by Wests forwards Peter Young and Graham O'Grady but I just kept driving towards the tryline, bumping past some other defenders. We lost the game 17–13, but the try gained some attention. In fact Channel 7's Rex Mossop was so impressed he incorporated the footage into the opening sequence of his Sunday sports show for some seasons to come.

The match got away from us right at the death, and I remember that just as clearly. On the bell, close to the line, one of their big blokes, Geoff Foster, hit the line hard. I had him covered, I thought. I was underneath him and stopped his progress and lifted him. Next thing he had come down over the top of me and plonked the ball over the line. Two of our blokes had come charging in and, instead of dragging Foster backwards, they had added to his momentum when they tackled him, virtually pushing him over the line. Wests beat us, but at least the try is there for posterity and I got quite a kick when I saw it again on video some time ago.

When it comes to all the games I appeared in over 15 seasons, I'd say I am remembered most for my contribution to the 1971 grand final, when we played – and beat – the Jack Gibson–coached

St George. And if the game sticks in other people's minds, as it seems to, I can tell you that no-one in the world got more satisfaction out of that '71 grand final than me. It provided one of the biggest thrills of my life. We won a real good hard game 16–10, and it was an afternoon I'll never forget. As much as anything else the victory provided me with a deeply satisfying feeling because it made a certain bloke eat his words – the leading referee Col Pearce. Pearce shafted me back in 1967, and he shafted me again in 1971 with something he wrote in the papers. I have absolutely no doubt that Pearce had a big influence on what happened to me in '67, my missing out on the grand final after I had played virtually the whole year in first grade. And I could never forgive him for that. In fact, he gave me a terrible time throughout my career.

What happened between Pearce and me was this: in a match in '67 we clashed, and I abused him, using crude words. Yes, I'm sure I offended him, but he must have been *very* offended, considering the way he carried that grudge. For some reason Pearce was down on me hard in that game in '67 and at a certain point I just blew up and abused him. It was a strong spray, admittedly, and he took it very badly – badly enough to subsequently tell a certain selector at Souths that I could cost the club the premiership that year. I have been told that the message was something along the lines of: 'If you want to win this year, you're going to have to get rid of Piggins. He gives away too many penalties.'

Souths took the tip. Now that you know of my ongoing differences with Chicka Cowie, you don't have to be a Rhodes scholar to guess who the selector was. In a way, I couldn't blame Souths. Clubs are always looking for 'the edge' and when the leading ref hands out a tip, they're inclined to listen. Oh yes, Col Pearce shafted me about as badly as was possible for a player to get shafted. I have no doubt that his opinion, as the game's top referee, was a strong factor in me losing my first-grade spot to Elwyn Walters, something that virtually destined me to play reserve grade for seasons to come. I will just say this: I am clear in my mind and conscience that I never did anything near bad enough to Col Pearce or the game to warrant his vindictiveness towards me. I can tell you now that the events of '67 left a bad taste in my mouth. I thought I had acquitted myself well as a first season first-grader and to be shafted by an outsider was a bitter pill to swallow.

And he was still at it in 1971, writing in the press that I could be the downfall of Souths in the grand final. I was filthy with that. He was *still* into me. To his credit, I suppose, he backed off after the grand final and admitted he was wrong, writing that the 'leopard' (me) had changed its spots. As far as I'm concerned, Col Pearce never changed his spots. What he did to me in '67 was a bastard act, and he was still that way four years later. I will never forgive him.

But to say that I didn't enjoy my football after '67 would be wrong. I did. It was after 1967 that business started to pick up for me and by the time '71 came around, I was pretty well entrenched. Maybe if I had been playing first grade, I wouldn't have been able to pay the extra attention to my business that I did. My life might have been very different.

When 1971's chance came around, it had been such a bloody long wait for me. After the lost opportunity of '67 I only ever got a run in first grade when Elwyn was injured or away on Test duties. In 1971, it was an injury to Walters in the major semi final against Manly that opened the door for me. I was very nervous before the game, but then I always got nervous before playing football. Right through my career I would dry retch before a game. This particular game was an especially big challenge. I knew I was undertrained, coming out of the seconds, where there was less emphasis on training and you played 10 minutes less football per match. And towards the end of the grand final, with the pressure on, I was battling against leg cramps. I remember Johnny Sattler saying to me at one stage: 'Get up . . . You've got to keep going!'

It was a great day for me. I pipped St George's Col Rasmussen in the scrums, giving our blokes the share of possession we needed; I had a hand in a couple of our tries; I did my share of tackling; and by being alert I managed to pinch back possession from dummy half at the play-the-ball a number of times, importantly so in the last 12 minutes when we were under real pressure at 11–10. I used to study the way blokes played the ball. And at that time in the game the play-the-ball was what the rules had always intended it to be – a mini-scrum, where the defender could strike for the ball, if he did it legitimately, when the ball hit the ground. The rule has now been thrown out, in the dubious interest of television, or on the whim of some genius official or other. It's crazy. The ruck rule as it was back then added uncertainty to the game, a healthy factor. One of the great tragedies of the game now is that the legislators have killed the contest for the ball. The play-the-balls are no longer contested and the scrums are a namby-pamby joke. Blokes put their head into them already knowing the outcome.

When I was playing, I would watch on television how particular footballers played the ball. The ones you could 'get' were the ones who would plonk the ball on the ground as they got to their feet. When I ran out for the grand final I knew the ones in the St George team I could get, and with referee Keith 'Yappy' Holman applying the play-the-ball rule fairly I managed to win the ball enough times to make a difference in the match. I remember pinching one back off the great Graeme Langlands and one from centre Ken Maddison.

We led 11–0 with only 15 minutes to go but they came back at us and we finally won 16–10 against Saints. It was a relief when Bobby McCarthy scored the clinching try after a forward drive up-field in which I had played my part. Afterwards the mob gave me a huge cheer at the leagues club. I think the fans appreciated how long I had battled away in reserves, waiting for the big chance. Now it had come and I had grabbed hold of it, providing me with perhaps the greatest football day of my life.

Viewed from down the track there was great irony in that night of celebration. Souths now stood at the very pinnacle (four premierships in five years). Unbeknown to us all, it was downhill from here.

Souths in '71 were in football's classic position: about to become victims of their own success. Football is bad business. The more successful you are, the more it costs you. And it is certainly not like other kinds of business, where the more successful you are, the more you make. At the club there was a collision of various forces at that time: a decision to spend up and renovate the leagues club; the fact that the club's first- and lower-grade sides were successful, with players on good money; the reality that the club was run by old footballers, who admittedly gave us wonderfully good times between 1964–71 (for which I am forever grateful), but who lacked sharp-edged business 'nous'; and the appearance of predators from other clubs, cheque books poised to throw big money at Souths' best players.

The sound of that grand final night was the sound of the club song: 'Glory, glory to South Sydney'. In the background, however, there was also the sound of alarm bells ringing . . .

Progressively after that, our stars drifted away: Coote, Branighan, O'Neill, Walters and later, McCarthy and Stevens. At different stages I could have gone too. Balmain made an offer in 1969; I went out and spoke to Wests at one stage; and Easts expressed an interest in the year that Elwyn Walters joined them (1974). But Souths suited me just fine. And the longer you stay with a club, the more tightly bound to it you are. Everything about Souths was fine. It was near where I lived, and I worked long days; I'd be gone by 5.30 in the morning, and I'd stay on the job as late as I could. I just didn't feel like logging off and having to jump in the car and drive to bloody Manly or Parramatta or anywhere. Rosebery to Redfern – that was easy.

I was never a mad-keen footballer type of bloke. Don't get me wrong, I loved the recognition, and I loved the game itself, loved the sporting contest of it. I suppose if I was around these days and someone said, 'George, if you come up to Parramatta you are going to get $600,000, or you can stay at Souths and get $100,000' I suppose I'd see the benefit of getting a cab out west every afternoon. But it's all about balance. For me, to move would have been to lose out in my business. Sure, I could have made some more on the football, but the bottom line was the same. And I was a Souths bloke. So I stayed until my body told me it had had much more than enough.

At Souths I got a real sense of the wider, deeper things that a much-loved football club can be about, and why the 1999 decision to cut Souths was so terribly wrong. Back then I remember Roger, the blind boy, whose mum took him to every Rabbitohs game. And Bobby Reilly, a gentle bloke who suffered from Down's syndrome, and who trained at Redfern when we did. When he died he was buried in a Souths jumper I had given him years before. The club was his life.

Give me the choice of playing overseas for Australia or playing for Souths and I'd take Souths every time. In saying that I'll add that to have played for Australia, at home, at the Sydney Cricket Ground, would have been enormous. That chance never came my way. For me, playing at home always had more appeal than playing overseas. At home you had the ultimate, you were playing your game, for your club, before your fans. Playing for Souths in big years like 1967 and 1971 provided the chance to play before 30,000–40,000 people. I used to love it. The crowd was so important. They were part of the whole pageant, part of what you were doing. Yeah, I loved that more than anything: playing at 'home' at the SCG in the atmosphere of a big crowd. All the above, perhaps, explains my dilemma in season 1975.

In '75, having been an 'early bloomer' in life to an extent (leaving school at 14, married at 17), I scaled the greatest heights of my career and played for Australia as a 'veteran' footballer of 31. I had played for New South Wales in 1974, and was to play with them again in 1976, but in 1975 I went to New Zealand to play a World Cup match against the Kiwis, and on return was named in the Australian squad for the northern hemisphere 'leg' of the World Cup.

I can reveal here that for the first and only time in my career I feigned an injury in a bid to try to get out of it. And in the end it was only the persuasion of my father and my wife Nolene that convinced me to go on the tour. When I got back from New Zealand on the plane after playing in the match, in which we beat the Kiwis 24–8, I was reported to have an abdominal injury. Fullback Graham Eadie was also on the 'doubtful' list. He had a crook shoulder, a fair dinkum injury. At the airport we underwent a medical and the talk among the officials was: 'Taking two injured players is sticking our necks out . . . cutting the squad down.' And I said to Kevin Humphreys, who was then ARL and NSWRL chairman, 'Look, Graham would be more important to the side than me.' I was pretty much saying to him: 'Take him . . . don't take me.'

Kevin thought it was such a lovely gesture that he got them to take me down to the Domain and put me through a fitness test to give me every chance. I knew I wasn't injured, but I had to go through the whole bloody charade. I just didn't want to go.

Anyhow, I went, and today I'm glad I did. To have won an Australian jumper in the game I played means a lot to me. I saw sides of football on that tour that I thought were fantastic and I saw things I thought were pretty bloody disgraceful. Being a non-drinker puts you into a different category on a tour like that. Early on, a few of the blokes, John Quayle and John Peard among them, organised a pub crawl. I went with them and, look, it was interesting. You would go into some old pub with a plaque on the wall reading 'Oliver Cromwell slept here' or some such thing, and in which they had a tradition whereby they changed the sawdust on the floor at the same hour every night and had been doing it for 400 years or more. England just reeked of history, and I enjoyed that. But a pub crawl is of limited interest when you don't drink, and when those around you are getting drunker.

When Quayle dislocated a shoulder in the match against Wales, and they were going to send him home, there was some agitation for someone to go with him, a bit of a gee-up actually.

I put up my hand and volunteered. I was ready to come home, but they made other arrangements.

I roomed with Arthur Beetson and laid down the ground rules very early. 'Arthur, this is the deal: anything that is on the floor goes into the laundry basket.' I'm a tidy sort of bloke and Arthur is a bit the other way. On that campaign, Arthur spent plenty of time looking for his clothes. If they were on the floor, which they often were, I automatically put them in the basket and sent them down to be laundered. Arthur reflected on the experience in a column he wrote a few years later:

> This was the understanding we had: that George would handle the catering and make up the room if I kept Tommy Raudonikis and 'Igor' Randall out of the way. Tommy and Igor loved to annoy George who would get out to the shops and come back whistling and carrying his gear, only to find our room all messed up. But there was only one George Piggins. When he used to train, and I stress the when, George wouldn't wear any boots, even when it started snowing, it was bare feet all the way. He and I had our fair share of meetings on the field too and there were times I expected to turn around in the shower after a game and see him standing there waiting to borrow the soap. He used to follow me around on the field like his long-lost brother.

Food over there was comparatively expensive and after a night out in a restaurant during which I was served lamb chops about the size of 20-cent coins (when I told them I wasn't paying, they found some chops of a more sensible size), I made a decision to 'eat in'. I told Beetson: 'It's too costly to eat out; I'll go to the markets and buy the food and cook it here.' Arthur and I proceeded to eat pretty well – to the stage where one woman we met one day was convinced we were sumo wrestlers. Steve Rogers came up to the room one night and when he saw the way Arthur and I were eating, he said: 'I'll shot the money in and eat with you!' 'Steve,' I replied, 'I'm not your mother . . . I'm not looking after you.'

Managed by Bob Abbott with Graeme Langlands as team coach, the tour was an eye-opener for a boy from Mascot, and a success on the playing field. I played against England, and Wales – in the wild match in which I took a hammering and during which TV viewers saw the unusual sight of the Welsh team coach, Les Pearce, and some spectators in the middle of a punch-up. And I played in a couple of club games including a wild one against St Helens during which we copped plenty from the crowd at Knowsley Road. It was tough football. Canterbury's Peter Moore was on tour too and I admired him back then. He was all Canterbury, albeit undoubtedly ruthless and cunning in his bid to do the best for his club. To see what he did later, sell out the game and jump to Super League – despite his protestations of innocence – shocked me. Maybe Peter Moore was disappointed in rugby league back then, but not anywhere near as much as the game of rugby league is entitled to be disappointed in him for what he did to it. If Canterbury hadn't taken the bait, there would have been no Super League. But more of that later.

One night on the '75 tour, Langlands stooged Tommy Raudonikis, Allan McMahon and me. It was in Toulouse, and Chang talked us into going to this place downtown. 'It's a terrific feed and a terrific night out,' he said. The minute we walked in I could tell it was a clipjoint. The girls were pretty, the champagne corks were popping, and the warning bells were sounding in me. 'What have we walked into here?' I thought. Anyhow, the champers had been opened and the bill was $300. I wasn't paying that, as a non-drinker, and neither were the others. The bloke eventually let us out.

One of our blokes, dirty on the way things had turned out, produced his party trick of running up the backs of parked cars and over the top. I thought to myself, if it was the front of my place and there was a silly Frenchman or Englishman running up and down on my car, I'd bounce his head off the pavement. But he did it to half-a-dozen cars or so, then tried it on a little Citroen with a canvas top – and finished up inside! I could hear the gendarmes coming and I took off, along the canal and over the bridge, back to the hotel. I passed Langlands in the foyer. 'You can laugh if you like,' I said, 'but they'll get pinched.' I kept going straight up the stairs and to my room. I could have done without that night. And there were other things that happened on the tour which soured the experience for me.

Out of the World Cup campaign, I finished up with just one Australian jumper as a memento since someone pinched the others out of my bag at the airport. I was happy to get home at the end of it. I missed Australia a lot. We are blessed to live in this place; the climate, the food, the sea, the mountains behind. What we have here is just unbelievable.

I played three more seasons with Souths after the World Cup experience of 1975, dragging it out an extra year when Jack Gibson came to coach the club, providing me with the inspiration to keep going. I was captain that year and enjoyed the experience of working with Jack, even though the combination of Father Time and injuries was wearing me down. At the end of '78, Jack said to me: 'You've got one more season left in you.' 'Jack,' I told him, 'I couldn't play again if Jesus Christ asked me to.' I was 34 and that year I just couldn't get out of bed in the morning after a match.

I remember that last year when Jack put the tackling tyres on at training and I refused to do it. I said to him: 'I'll wheel the tyres to the other boys, but I am not tackling them.' That didn't suit Jack and we had an argument. I finally said: 'Jack, I can tackle tyres on Tuesday and again on Thursday nights if you want me to, but what I can't do is play football on Saturdays if you make me do it.' Every game was taking me a week to get over. I was 34 and I was gone. There was no enjoyment anymore. The pain was just too bad. Jack relented in the end, and I didn't tackle the tyres.

These days, the game offers me many painful reminders that I played it for 15 seasons. Injuries were, and are, travelling companions. The old Sydney *Sun* newspaper made a fuss one day in 1976 when I headed into a match carrying (according to its list): a broken nose, two badly corked thighs, a groin strain and a severe hamstring strain. 'I don't believe in missing matches,' I told them. I've always had a neck problem because of all the scrummaging, and my legs give me plenty of trouble too. I've had operations on my knees, and snapped an Achilles tendon. These days, my ankles give me hell and my hips, my neck and my shoulders are all playing up.

I had all the trouble spots x-rayed a while back, thinking about some repair work. 'Where do we start?' asked the doc. 'You've given yourself some awful wear and tear over the years. I suggest you shed a few kilos and when the first body part gives up on you, then we'll do some work on it.' And that's where it stands.

So, these days I work at it, keep myself active. I'm often at the track at Randwick. Three days or so a week I'll be down at the farm, at Burrawang in the Southern Highlands, and when I'm there I work 12-hour days.

My dogs help keep me fit and moving, the two boxers, Sam and Sophie. And they're true mates of mine. If you had five friends in your life as loyal as them you'd be doing alright. I've always had boxers, always from the same people, Warren and Robyn Knox, and they have beautiful and undemanding natures. I'm happy I can still walk with them. I figure that if I'd gone along with Jack Gibson's wish and played the 1979 season, I might have been sitting on a bench throwing a ball for them, and that would have been about it.

7. The Coaching Caper: Simple Truths

A good coach needs a patient wife, a loyal dog and a great captain – but not necessarily in that order.

Bud Grant, US football coach

IN 1979, SOUTH SYDNEY dumped coach Jack Gibson. Sacked him cold. I thought that what Souths did, and the way they did, it, was very ordinary. As a fairly direct result of what happened to Jack, I was estranged from the dressing-room area for the next six years or so – a bizarre situation when I reflect now on the passion and effort I put into the last half-dozen years in trying to save the place. Nolene and I didn't miss a game in that time though. We supported the team as spectators.

Jack, who became a friend and a business associate, came to the club in 1978, the year my body gave up on me and forced me into the role of ex-footballer. Getting Gibson was a tremendous coup for Souths; by then he had the first two of his five premiership scalps dangling from his belt and was on the way to becoming arguably the most influential, innovative, maybe *the* best coach ever.

In a single season, Jack took Souths from a 3-win, 19-loss record in 1977 to a 12–1–9 (one game being a draw) and seventh placing in 1978, and to victory in the pre-season Craven Mild Cup. Season 1979 was patchier (a 9–13 record) although the club was on the move, with the lower grades both making the semi finals and a $500,000 sponsorship deal bringing the club out of struggling seasons and into the light. There is no doubt that the Gibson influence and presence was a major factor in the good things that were happening. Jack and I became good mates. As he might have put it: he liked my head, and I liked his.

But the club brushed him, bringing up Bill Anderson to coach the side in 1980, and throwing Anderson supporter and current high-paid Parramatta coach Brian Smith a coaching job with the under-23s. Smith had been skipper of reserve grade in '79. Anderson went on to have solid success in 1980, a Tooth Cup victory and a fifth placing on the premiership ladder – and good luck to him. But Gibson had guided the club through a significant building phase, and should never have been dumped the way he was.

Into the second half of the '79 season, I knew what was going on, that promises were being made to Anderson and Smith that involved the sacking of Gibson. I was privy to what was going on because at that stage I hadn't declared myself as a Gibson follower. When the club announced its decision on Jack, I made my feelings known: 'I can't work it out. You have the best coach in the game and you're going to sack him. The Lord himself couldn't have achieved any more than Jack did this year.'

Anyhow, they did it, and on the day it happened, Jack came around to my place. 'They just sacked me,' he said. 'Yeah, I know,' I told him. 'What d'you mean you know?' he asked. 'Who's got the job?' I told him. Ron Massey, Jack's offsider, refused to believe me, and even had a go at me. 'You shouldn't go around saying things like that,' he said. Well, Jack and Massey were at my place again the next day and by now they knew. 'You were bloody right . . . those bastards!' they said. Their original disbelief was easy to understand. Jack, Massey and Billy Anderson were very close – a real team, with Jack having full faith in Anderson as his reserve grade coach. I'm sure Jack felt he had been stabbed in the back by what took place.

I didn't appreciate what had been done either. We were a club without funds and we didn't have the best football side going around, but we had the best coach. Having a coach of his status would always be an attraction in bringing promising young players to the club, and it was pretty disrespectful to replace him with lower-grade blokes who had benefited from the Gibson years and learned many things from him. To me, if they had wanted to sack Jack, it would have been preferable to bring someone in from outside.

Because I disagreed so strongly, when the chance came later in the year, I decided to try to do something within the football club: I challenged for the presidency. I almost got in too. Norm Nilson just beat me. From that time, I was on the outer – way offside with the blokes running the club. I still never missed a game. I'd sit with John O'Neill, who was a selector in 1980, and he'd say: 'C'mon, come down to the [dressing] room.' But I couldn't do it. My belief is that the coach has got to be seen as boss of the dressing room, and to have people like me coming in there who were virtually not talking to him and didn't hold that much respect for him wouldn't have been right.

I kept the lines of communication open with Terry Parker, the club secretary, and with some of the players. Anderson coached until the end of 1982, and then Ron Willey took the reins for seasons 1983 to '85. My situation, being an outcast at a club where I had played 245 games, lasted virtually up to 1986 when, against the odds, I became coach.

People have often asked me what it was like playing under Jack Gibson. It was good. Jack has got a winning aura about him and he brought enthusiasm and motivational ideas to Souths at a time when the club was really struggling. In his autobiography,

Peter Sterling suggested that during his career he wanted to win more for Jack than anything else – that's how much he thought of him. I don't quite agree with that; I think you have got to want to win more for yourself than anything else. Football to me was like fighting. Once I started, I wanted to win. And if I got beaten I didn't want to get beaten by 12, I wanted to get beaten by one. I could never imagine anything less than giving full effort. In '78, my last playing year, the great quality that coach Gibson introduced at Souths was enthusiasm. He had the knack of lighting a fire in you, whatever your age (and I was 34 then!).

Towards the end of the 1985 season, Rod Gorman (ex–Mascot and South Sydney first-grader, and an old and close mate) and Frank Curry (ex–Zetland and Souths lower-grade player) came to see me and asked if I would put in for the first-grade coaching job the next year. They were interested in coaching the lower grades, and wanted us to apply as a sort of package. I had probably drifted away from football a bit, but I decided I'd give it a go. I wasn't high on the club's priority list, I knew that. Souths offered the job around to various high-profile people, including Bob McCarthy, but when they couldn't get a taker, the rumour was that they finally decided they'd throw it to me, with the thought that there was no money to buy players and I would probably fail – and they could get rid of me altogether if we didn't do any good.

It was offered to me in unusual circumstances, at an unlikely venue. At the wake which followed the huge funeral tribute to Clive Churchill in 1985, Souths secretary Terry Parker asked me the straightforward question: 'Will you do the job and coach the firsts next year?' I said I would, stipulating that I wanted Rod Gorman and Frank Curry as my lower-grade coaches. I had no official coach's certificate and the rules of the time deemed that you had to have one, but they rustled one up for me, no questions asked, and all of a sudden I was an accredited coach.

I took the job because I believed I could make a success of it. Among my aims was something fundamental, but important:

to re-introduce the old South Sydney spirit into my teams. I wanted to get back to a situation where kids around the streets of our district were busting to wear the red and green. And I told them at the club that at the end of the season my performance must be assessed only on what had been achieved, not on friendship.

Life was by then a yearly struggle at Souths. The going was tough for the leagues club in comparison with the big wealthy clubs and we did not have the access to funds of some of the others. And I had been pretty outspoken at some of the things that had gone on. But it's easy to be critical, and to be fair, it wasn't officials such as Norm Nilson or John O'Riordan – men who had been at the helm in recent times – who had plunged Souths into their financial black hole. It was the generation of officials before them who did that. Even in saying that, however, the generation at fault were largely blokes who had been part of a wonderful Souths era in the '50s. And when they came in as selectors and coaches and administrators, Souths went through another purple period (1965–71).

Unfortunately Souths were plunged into such a hole financially that the doors of the leagues club were closed in 1973, and the struggle to keep our heads above water has pretty much gone on ever since. Success in football is an expensive business, kicking up players' wages. That inflation, added to renovations undertaken at the club and a general determination to provide a good time during what was a golden era, finally brought a financial crash.

I'll say this about what happened: yes, no doubt there was some rorting at Souths. But I don't think the rorting at Souths Leagues Club got into the same ballpark as what went on at some other licensed clubs. At some places I could name, the increase in people's living standards has been nothing less than miraculous. At Souths, there was a lot more sharing and generosity – the trips, the holidays they put on for players, the spending money they dished out on those trips. You can call it rorting if you like, and if it was that, I suppose you could say we were all part of it in different ways. But whatever anyone might have got out of Souths then wouldn't be anywhere *near* what some of the smarter ones ripped out of other places in more recent times. Don't think rorting was limited to licensed clubs either; in my experience it is right through business.

At the end of the 1985 season, I was coming to terms with the fact that I was about to be a first-grade football coach at a club where expectations for my success were probably not sky high. I had never coached before but I had played under blokes like Churchill, Gibson and Clem Kennedy, and learned some things. Interestingly, the more I thought about it, the smarter I realised Clive was at the coaching caper, despite him never getting a mention when 'great coaches' are under discussion. He won four premierships in five years, and on the day his team was beaten (by Balmain in a highly controversial grand final in 1969), the referee, Keith Page, had plenty to answer for in my view, tolerating Balmain's questionable 'go slow' tactics and hammering Souths in the penalty count (16–7). Clive was very, very smart in the way he handled the top-quality players he had. A rookie coach like me could take good things from the lessons taught by Churchill, Gibson and others, and also from soaking up 15 years' experience playing the game. And that's exactly what I planned to do.

I put faith in some fundamental truths too: that you have to go forward to score tries. It doesn't matter how scientific and complicated some of the 'genius' coaches of today try to make the game, things like that don't change. Today's players are much fitter than when I played – and they should be. They're highly paid, full-time professionals. The demands of television have made it a fast, razzle-dazzle game – although, strangely, the quickest players today wouldn't be as quick as the speedsters of my era. Today it's all quick, quick, quick (the late John O'Neill described football today as being like a very hard game of touch), with the replacement rule (which was thankfully modified in 2001, at least) undermining one of the game's great, traditional qualities – the 'wear-down' factor, when one side gradually wins the ascendancy over 80 minutes.

I'll tell you something else that has changed too: the noise content. Football was a rowdier, more exciting experience when the game was tribal, and when factors like attrition and courage over 80 minutes were its foundation. In 1986, as I got ready to take over as coach of Souths, the game of rugby league was somewhere in the middle, positioned between what it had been and what it would become in the television age.

I coached Souths for almost five seasons. The experience bound me tighter to the club and its struggles, and readied me for the fight that lay ahead a decade later to try and save what we had.

By the time I parted company with the first-grade side – as coach – in early August 1990, I was club chairman, thoroughly aware by then that we would have to battle strong and smart as a club if we were to survive. The alarm bells were already ringing. Until a troubled 1990 season, my coaching years were like a roller-coaster ride, producing much excitement, a good deal of success, and plenty of personal enjoyment. Up until I actually took over the side I had never thought of myself as a coach. I was always sort of outside the right guidelines. One thing I knew was that I didn't agree with 'over-coaching'. In potted form the story that followed was this:

1986 We ran fourth, beaten only by a point for the minor premiership, then lost two straight semi finals, the second in a highly controversial match against Balmain (more on that later). Frank Curry's under-23s won the premiership.

1987 We finished fourth again, qualifying in that position in the semi finals, then beating Balmain (15–12), in the preliminary semi. The next week Canberra gave us a real shellacking (46–12), snapping the door shut on a season of great promise.

1988 We finished eighth, just short of the top group after being derailed by the NSWRL's decision to penalise us two premiership points for inadvertently using 17-year-old President's Cup player Scott Wilson as a replacement in a match at Brookvale (in which we beat Manly 28–14). My sending-on of Wilson was a technical breach of the league rules.

1989 A sensational year in which we won 12 matches straight, an all-time South Sydney record, but petered out disappointingly in the semi finals. We finished third. We won the President's Cup, the club championship, the minor premiership and gave the League a glittering season with our front-running contribution. People were reminded of the old saying: 'When Souths are going well . . . rugby league is going well.'

1990 We hit the wall. Serious injuries to key men such as Michael Andrews, Wayne Chisholm and David Boyle, plus the departure of Ian Roberts to Manly, cut a deep hole in the side. A drug raid mid-season, instigated by the NSWRL, was a shattering event. (More of that later.) We lost 13 games straight and in early August the club and the coach – me – parted company. Frank Curry took over the next year.

As mentioned earlier, there had been people at the club who had only gone along with the idea of me getting the coaching job because they thought I would fail and quickly be out of their hair. With the disappointments of the 1990 season, there was the possibility at last for some people on the board to wield the big stick on me. The relationship between the board and me had soured anyway. It was time to move on. As a coach, I used the things that had helped me build a successful working life: commonsense; a simple, straightforward approach; hard work; and the ability to bring out substantial contributions from good people around me. And I drew on the experience of all those seasons I had as a South Sydney player. To me, rugby league was always a simple game. Things that worked in life have always worked on the playing field too: solid preparation, determination, teamwork, strong focus on the job at hand which in football is basically about going forward to get the ball over your opponent's line and stopping them by being dogged in defence.

I took up coaching not long after I sold my trucking business and around the time I bought my farm in the Southern Highlands. Part of the training routine at one early session was for the players to gather up all the old seats from Redfern and pack them on my truck. I was taking them down to the farm to use as fences. I tried to schedule training at times when it best suited the working blokes. And I set out to make it more of a pleasure to come to training than a slog. With someone like Mario Fenech, if you gave him 25 laps and 50 sprints, and training with the ball for two hours, he would say: 'Good session.' But not everyone is like Mario, and I tried to find a happy medium. There was a good atmosphere at our training in those years. I wanted both training and playing to be enjoyable for the blokes involved.

I suppose people who know me would say that I have an ability to 'think outside the square' too. An innovation I introduced in my first year proved a winner for the club. Traditionally, rugby league clubs held their 'trials' in February, just as the season was kicking off. The drawback of that was one of players coming 'new' into a season, probably well below peak fitness, and unlikely to show their best. Why, I suggested, didn't we hold our trials at the *end* of the season, when the players are match-hardened and fit after what they have been through? The club agreed, and in October 1985 we held our trial day. It was a big success; I think in that first year we unearthed five players who went on to play first grade, including Paul Roberts and Rod Maybon. We used that trial system for a while, and then everyone was doing it. Eventually trials were superseded by what happened in league, with club scouts videoing promising kids all over the state, and clubs signing schoolboys on the evidence gathered. There were no more secrets.

The budget for the entire Souths coaching staff was $10,000.

That was for everyone. I had to pay the two lower-grade coaches, my conditioners, selectors, rubbers, and then take what was left. If anything. Today, 15 seasons later, there are coaches 'earning' $600,000 a season – a clear example of what inflation and reckless spending has done to the game. But even back then, the $10,000 budget was at the bottom of the scale. I know of one bloke Souths approached who was offered $50,000 to coach the team. I got $10,000 and it didn't get any better in the seasons ahead. But I didn't worry.

I didn't have a lot of cash to spend on players either that first year, but I targeted one I knew could add value to the club: Phil Gould. Gould, then 28, was with Canterbury in 1985, had played under some good coaches, and had talent above the ordinary. I always felt with him that if he had applied himself more to fitness and training he would have gone all the way in the game. His lifestyle had tended to get in the way. Phil liked a good time and a punt – and was not over-rapt in training. But he was an exceptionally skilful player with football 'nous' above the ordinary, and I suspected he could be a big help in what we hoped to achieve. That is why I went after him. I'm happy to say my judgment was spot-on.

At an early training night at Booralee Park, Botany, in 1986, I pulled Gould aside. 'Gus, I've been out of the game for six or seven years,' I said to him. 'I've still got a good idea about how this game is played, but I know things have changed to an extent. I'd like you to run the side tonight.' So he did, and in the course of the session he was talking to the players about colours, about red zones and green zones and all sorts of other jargon that was new to me. Shit! I *have* been out of this game a long time, I thought to myself. After training, Gould and I stayed back to talk. I think we pretty much agreed that when it came to winning football, things hadn't changed that much, and that the game was still about running and tackling hard. But the language of the game had changed, and the approach to matches had become more detailed.

Gould's knowledge of the 'new way' injected enthusiasm into

the team and stimulated the players. Virtually from that day, Gould became my on-field adviser and he was a very great help to me in my first year as a coach. I remember one of the players coming to me to express his dissatisfaction with Gould's workrate on the paddock. I said to him: 'Look, we're in a learning process here. I'm doing everything I can off-field as coach, and when Gus goes onto the field, he carries it on. Yeah, you might have to do one or two extra tackles for him in a match. But we are learning a lot, all of us, and we are in a process of rebuilding.'

Around that time Gould was under some pressure. One of the selectors, Colin Berwick, voted him out of the team and Gould got wind of it and fronted him. To his credit, Colin stood his ground and said: 'Well, that's my opinion.' Gould was upset at what had taken place, which was a human enough reaction, and I said to him: 'Phil, not everyone likes you, and that's just the way life works . . . so why worry about what someone thinks? You're here, you're in the side and the side is going well, let's just get on with it.'

It turned out to be a bloody good year for us. We got beaten by a point, unluckily, by Parramatta. Otherwise we could have been minor premiers. But it was a great turnaround from ninth the previous year, and I felt I had taken a giant step ahead as a coach, aided by the arrangement that worked so well with 'Gus' Gould. The blend was good, and for him too. I'm sure that as the season went on, the realisation hit him: 'Hey, the legs are getting old . . . and I'm getting on as a player, but I'm handling this sub-coaching side of it well.' I was happy to share the credit with Gould for anything we achieved. In August I told *Rugby League Week*: 'He's been an integral part of our success this year, you can't give him enough credit. He has an incredible football brain, he's got control and he's got coolness. He virtually guides the kids.'

We signed Gould for two years, but at the end of '86 he came to me. 'I know it's a two-year contract,' he said, 'but I can get the second-grade coaching job at Canterbury. Would you release me?'

'Not a problem,' I said. I was greatly appreciative of the

contribution Gus had made, and I knew he would be a success elsewhere. I knew, too, that he felt a lot for Souths, and it was no surprise at all how resolutely Gould, as a highly respected league commentator and columnist these days, backed Souths' fight for life from 1997 onwards. That was greatly appreciated.

I was 'hands-on' as a coach and the media made a good deal of something I did now and then at training to emphasise the importance of defence in underpinning the other skills we had in our sides over those seasons. In tackling sessions near the end of training, I would take the ball and try to batter my way through the forwards. My watch became a casualty of that and one journalist wrote: 'The South Sydney coach smashes his watch as regularly as time itself.' We were a tough, hard, physical side and any team which lined up against us knew it was never going to be easy.

We bowed out of the premiership race in great controversy in 1986. It was 8-all in the semi final when referee Kevin Roberts, an ex–Souths player, sent off our hooker Mario Fenech, for 'gouging' Balmain's Benny Elias. In my opinion, Elias was the best hooker-forward to play the game, and in the first half at the Sydney Cricket Ground he was giving us the run-around – and I said so in my halftime talk. I thought we were right in the game if we could put a bit of extra work on Benny. Close him down. 'I'll take care of Benny,' Mario offered. There was no love lost between the pair. 'No you won't,' I said. 'Just keep playing your game and forget all about that.' I asked Les Davidson to make it his job to put some pressure on Benny, but Mario, such a whole-hearted player, was about as subtle as a brick when play resumed. He grabbed Elias in a scrum just after halftime, and Roberts sent him off for it. It was a big call. You don't hurt people by grabbing them on the face, although you might annoy them. Twelve against 13 was too much for us against a talented Balmain side, and they finished up running over us 36–11. And so the season was over.

Mario Fenech, who these days is trotted out as some sort of

resident funnyman on *The Footy Show*, was unlucky to have
never played for Australia. He had all the attributes, but I'm sure
that whoever put him in as a hooker in the first place did him a
disservice. I shifted him out of there to second row, then prop in
the latter part of his stay with us, and I don't think he ever went
back. Mario would have been an ideal second-rower in his
younger days. If Mario Fenech had been schooled as a prop or
second-rower early, I have no doubt that his career would have
reached greater heights. His send-off at the SCG that day cost us
dearly but it doesn't change my opinion of Mario in any way. He
was a very good footballer and a bloke with high values in life.
A very decent human being. With no disrespect to his parents,
who are really fine people, he was probably always more interested in what they thought about him than anyone else, and that
approach probably didn't help his career.

There is a bloke I have never forgotten from that first year of
coaching, 1986. We recruited him from Illawarra, a young player
with Paul Newman good looks named Rick Posetti. Rick was a
second rower who drove a sports car and looked like he had
everything it took to succeed in football. He moved to Sydney
and boarded with his auntie as he began his career with us. Long
before the season started, we had buried Rick Posetti. Struggling
with his breathing at training he went to a doctor, and was diagnosed with cancer. Within eight weeks or so Rick was dead,
crash-tackled by that most savage of opponents. It was a tragedy
that made all of us at the club think about our lives; about just
how uncertain life can be, and how the trick has *gotta* be making
the most of the time here, and the possibilities and abilities you
have. I still remember Rick so clearly – how he arrived at the
club with such hope and anticipation. And then he was gone.

I won two coach-of-the year awards during my tenure at Souths
and enjoyed much of the experience. I was never a 'professional'
coach by any means. I demanded the simple things from my
players: that they were punctual for training, that they were fit,
and that they worked hard at their game to be as good as they

could be. But I also believed the game was about some fun and enjoyment, and I made that part of the mix too.

Controversy seemed to follow us through the years I was coach. Sometimes it was good, other times not so good – maybe there's always been something about a team like Souths that attracts extra attention. As the old league journalist, Claude Corbett, wrote so many years ago: 'There is a glamour about South Sydney football which has always held the public.' I know one thing for sure now: the game missed that quality badly in 2000–2001 when Souths were out of the game.

In 1987, another season of considerable success, the biggest controversy again came on our last day, and centred around winger Steve Mavin, who will probably never forget the nightmare 16 minutes he played, as Canberra scored three tries from his fumbles on the right wing. What happened that day was a crying shame. Mavin was a terrifically talented young player and to see him today – to see the assistance he has been to Souths at rallies and in our fight against the NRL – is to see the real picture. I suspect that for a time back then in '87, Steve was leading a life that brought him undone. It became very apparent early in that semi final against Canberra that something was horribly wrong, that he was not focusing on the ball or what he should have been doing and that his co-ordination was dreadfully out.

The first time they kicked the ball to him I don't think he would have caught it with a fisherman's net. The real Steve Mavin, the one we knew, would have fielded the ball and taken it back 30 or 40 metres down-field. But on this day it was not the same Steve Mavin, and I will not speculate any further about the reasons. Laurie Daley and the Raiders twigged that there was a problem and set out to play to it. They put a couple more to him, and Steve stuffed them up too. Three tries resulted, and we were virtually out of the semi final. As coach, I had to make the hard decision. And I did – I took him out of the game.

Steve was gone from the ground by the time we gathered in

the room after being beaten 46–12. I rang him at home later and asked him to come to the club. 'Steve, we lost a game of football . . . life goes on,' I told him. Later, he came and joined us at the leagues club. I held no grudge, then or ever, against Steve Mavin.

In 1988, our standout controversy came early – April 26 – cost us two premiership points and probably stopped us making a third successive finals appearance. That day, with six minutes to play, we led Manly 28–14 at Brookvale Oval and had the match safely won. In the heat of battle and looking to briefly 'blood' a greatly talented young player, I sent 17-year-old Scott Wilson into the fray to get a taste of first grade.

Scott had played President's Cup for us earlier in the afternoon. At that time the NSWRL rules were that a player who played President's Cup was not permitted to play in a senior grade on the same day. Journalist Peter Frilingos from Murdoch's *Mirror* or *Telegraph Mirror*, or whatever it was in those days, rang me with the news: 'They're going to take two points off you.' A couple of days later, the NSWRL board docked us our two winning premiership points.

Yeah, I fouled up, and they hammered us, even though Scott's presence on the field had no impact on the result. The event knocked the guts out of us. I believe to this day that it cost us a semi-final spot (we finished eighth, just behind the top group). I was furious that night and I told the media:

> I made the mistake but the 15 players are copping the flak. I feel like a bloody idiot, but I find it hard to believe that the League could take two points off the team. What would have happened had we lost? Obviously we would have been fined – which means there are two different penalties for the same offence. We didn't try to ring in a Wally Lewis or a Gene Miles . . . This was a 17-year-old kid out of the President's Cup who had played well and who we had decided to reward. The punishment for a nothing crime is far too severe.

Sydney Morning Herald journalist Alan Clarkson supported us with a strong editorial. I wondered what would have happened if the boot had been on the other foot. Would Manly, with their friends in high places, have been hit as hard as we were if they had erred?

Scott was a wonderfully talented young player, as good a natural talent as ever came out of the district. I remember Nolene and I going to watch him play for NSW Schoolboys one day and coming away thinking that he could have been 'anything'. But Scott instead became a victim of what was happening in society, and in football, and never really fulfilled the talent he had. My replacement blunder at Brookvale in 1988 gained him instant notoriety that he could have done without, and in 1990, my last year at the club, things got much worse for him after the NSWRL-backed drug raid at Redfern Oval. The Australian Drug Agency arrived unannounced at the ground during a training session on June 18, and 12 days later it was announced that 10 players had tested positive to drugs. Nine were never named. The tenth was Scott Wilson and, as a result of the storm that broke, the club sacked him. I disagreed vehemently with the decision. I think they decided to make an example of one player – and it was Scott.

At that time, just like now, you'd have to believe in the bloody tooth fairy if you thought there weren't players in the game dabbling in drugs. I am told that the ecstasy culture among the young generally is enormous. So why not in football? These days a footballer given large amounts of money, courtesy of his free-spending football club, has two choices: treat it with care, invest it and begin building his future, or say, 'You beauty! What a great period of my life, I'm going to have a ball!' And if you set out with a pocketful of money these days with the idea of having a ball, well, chances are you'll soon enough run into drugs. With the exception of marijuana, today's drugs weren't around when I was playing football. I can say truthfully that I never puffed pot, but I'd like to put a lie detector on some of the blokes making the rules these days and pose the question: 'Did you ever smoke pot?'

The NSWRL's targeting of Souths back in 1990 was disgraceful and disgusting. It picked us, an inner-city club down on our luck at that time, and hit us with what was virtually the first major drug test done in football. The League didn't go anywhere near the upmarket sides. And it caught a 19-year-old boy. I remember we were called downtown to Phillip Street – club president Norm Nilson and myself – and confronted a media frenzy of TV and print blokes wanting the kid's name. And someone gave it out – the League gave it out – and handed Scott a suspension.

What was done to him was shameful. The NSWRL took Scott and exposed him to the world. I told League CEO John Quayle what I thought: 'Would you do it to your own child, John? Somewhere along the line there has to be responsibility. We took this kid on when he was 15, put money in his pocket and brought him along, then he got hooked up with older kids, went into areas he shouldn't have gone, and all of a sudden when he stubs his toe you want to shot him to the wolves.' Norm Nilson intervened, 'You can't speak to [Quayle] like that,' he said. 'Pig's arse, I can't,' I replied. I was furious.

Scott, after all, was no different from many other young blokes of the time. How fair was it, to catch 10 and make an example of one? This was a greenhorn kid from my club being treated like they had just caught him coming through Sydney Heads with a container load of hard drugs. It was an example of shocking overkill, and in early 2001, the NRL, feeding the media frenzy when the two Wests Tigers players Craig Field and Craig McGuinness tested positive to drugs, showed that in no way had it learned the lesson. It's too easy for the people running the game to look on from some lofty height at a kid and say, 'He's a bad image for the game . . . we'll get rid of him . . . we'll drug-test him.'

I remain highly suspicious today about the whole thing. There was increasing talk then about drugs in sport, and that the game of rugby league had to be pulled into line, which was fair enough. But my question is: why just single out Souths – why not attack everybody? We were not the only club with a problem. I believe it was no coincidence at all that the raid at Redfern came at the time when our financial plight had been laid openly and publicly on the table. We were struggling, and we had informed the League of our decision to pull back for a time on our financial support of the football area, and to concentrate in the medium term on trying to get the leagues club to work, because of our belief that the financial future of the football club lay in the strong growth of the leagues club.

I suspect very strongly that the NSWRL wanted us out of the competition, just as it had kicked Newtown out in the early 1980s. Anyone who thinks that the Super League geniuses were the first to think about culling sides is kidding themselves. Without a doubt there was an earlier agenda. I remember back in 1994 – Alan Jones's first year with us – and John Singleton wanting to bet me $5000 that we wouldn't be around the next year. There were people who *knew* something was cooking. Later, when Kerry Packer got Nick Politis and me together it was no accident. His son, Jamie, was tied up with Easts, and I think Kerry thought he'd give it a go, to help out. He realised soon enough that we were miles apart and no merger was possible.

I think now that it was all the beginning of what was to happen to Souths publicly a few years later. I believe that somewhere a great big blueprint existed of which clubs the powers-that-be wanted in, and which clubs they wanted out, and I believe that Souths was on the second list. In other words, the ARL had already targeted Souths for the scrapheap, long before Super League did. The drug raid of 1990, and the tipping-off of the media was all part of that.

The drug problem in rugby league can be solved, I believe, and without too much trouble. And let me say that I agree that the game should take a hardline stance on drugs, educate players and spell it out to them that the taking of illegal drugs is not going to be tolerated, and that if they want to take drugs, fine, but they won't be playing rugby league. If the blokes running the game want to be purists, a straightforward and effective solution would be this: to introduce a system whereby six players from each club are randomly tested, via blood or urine tests, each Monday morning.

The apparent trend in the game now is that whatever drug-taking is going on – and unquestionably there is some – takes place *after* matches. So the time to hit, and hit regularly and randomly, would be on the Monday, when the drug traces would still be in the system after the weekend round. It would be no difficult thing and the problem would disappear overnight. I'd make it three strikes and you're out, too, and no debate entered into. But does the NRL have the will to do it . . . or would it much prefer to just catch someone occasionally and sensationalise that to buggery, to show everyone what a terrific and responsible job it's doing? And if that means sacrificing a player or two along the way, well, no worries. Think of the headlines. Sometimes I think that's what the NRL's more interested in, rather than trying to rehabilitate some kid who has run off the rails.

The brilliance of our 1989 season, the highlight of my time as a coach, faded fast in the struggle of 1990. But I can still look back with pride on the achievements of '89, the honours won (although, regrettably, not a premiership) and the way a near-great South Sydney year set the pace for the entire game of rugby league as it had done so many times in the years past. We were probably light on a couple of centres that year, and losing prop Ian Roberts through injury was a critical blow. At that stage of his career, Roberts was just awesome on the field. The achievements of winning the minor premiership and the club championship were outstanding ones. I remember one bloke saying to me that 'we'd had the side to win the premiership for the past three years' but that our blokes virtually never got a look in when the rep sides were being picked, except for Les Davidson. When I look back, I know we did a very good job, achieving what we did. We were probably a couple of internationals short of winning a competition.

For me, the coaching caper was an enjoyment – like playing

again. I loved to win. And when we got beaten I would analyse it in depth, trying to figure out why it happened and how to prevent it next time.

There were special individuals in the team. If we'd all been as dedicated as Mario Fenech we'd have won a comp for sure. But we probably would have gone mad too . . . Mario was so intense. Craig Coleman, who enjoyed the good life, was probably unaware of the great opportunity that was his. He was a halfback with the ability to control a match, but if he had matured earlier, into the person he has become as a coach, he would have been a much more lethal player. Phil Blake was outstanding for us, and he should have played for Australia. And Ian Roberts? On what he did in the '89 season he would have to go down in my book as one of the best footballers I have seen play the game. We had very tough working forwards in Michael Andrews, Wayne Chisholm, Les Davidson, David Boyle and Mark Ellison. Neil Baker, who scored heaps of points for us, didn't realise deep down how talented he was. Jim Serdaris was outstanding that season and won 'Rookie of the Year'. Then we had a talented player in fullback Bronco Djura, who just wanted to laugh and enjoy his life. It was quite a mix.

A coach can take a player to the door, but he can't take that next step. The player has to do that himself. There is only so much you can do and I wasn't earning enough money out of Souths to concentrate on them 24 hours a day. Similarly, the players weren't earning enough to be full-time professionals. So we found a balance in between, gained some success, and enjoyed ourselves.

By 1990, with injuries, the departure of players, the crushing blow of the 'drugs' publicity and the increasing financial fight to stay afloat, it was all falling apart. It occurred to me that if the League had applied the same enthusiasm and planning to the out-of-control player payments problem as it did to 'nailing' Souths via the drug raid of June 18, then the game could have secured its future and been sound and strong enough to thwart any Super League raid. The one cure the game needed was to solve the problem of outrageous payments to players. There were, and are, ways of doing it. But the League never seemed to have the resolve.

Funnily enough, I am firmly of the view that the 1990 season, although our worst by a fair space as far as my coaching years went, was also my *best* year in holding the club together. By that time we were in serious financial difficulties, our best player, Ian Roberts, had been pinched by Manly, and the effect of having top-line forwards Andrews, Boyle and Chisholm on the sidelines had a devastating effect on the side. Morale crumbled for a time, yet we were able to hold it together so strongly that by the end of the season not a player wanted to leave the club. We just couldn't give some of them the money they wanted. But the fact that in terribly hard times we still had a club, and were still able to keep a nucleus of our players, was a significant achievement. I probably couldn't have done it in '86, but the rapport I had built up with the players enabled us to stay strong deep down, despite the disappointing results we returned and the problems we faced.

So, 1990 was a bad year for us results-wise, and sometime in its wake – the exact date escapes me but probably early the following season – I had a conversation with a well-connected league man, Bill 'Break Even' Mordey, that convinced me finally that Souths were pencilled in on some secret blueprint, in which merger or extinction were the only choices for the club. Bill was then the NSWRL's media manager and at Redfern he said to me: 'Souths and Easts are going to have to merge . . . That's all there is to it.'

I could only presume there was fire somewhere behind the smoke, as I had suspected for a while.

8. Tea at Kerry's Place

It is the *gift* rather than what is given that matters.

William Edward Stanner

THE MEMORY OF my conversation with Bill Mordey came
back to me a few seasons later when a message arrived via Jack
Gibson: Kerry Packer wanted to talk to me, the chairman of
Souths Football Club. It was pre–Super League, sometime in
1994, at the time Alan Jones had arrived at Souths as general
manager of football operations. Alan put in place arrangements
for us to go see Packer and Easts chairman Nick Politis at the
Packer family home in Bellevue Hill, and joined me for what
was to be a night I'll never forget.

Before the meeting, I was aware that the subject for discussion
was a possible 'merger' between Easts and Souths. After struggling
in the early '90s we came to such a meeting from a position of
some strength. In the 1994 season, with Jones coming in, we won
the Tooheys Challenge Final (over Brisbane) and a run of seven
successive victories mid-season gave signs of better days ahead.

Alan Jones's arrival brought financial support too, although the battle, as always, was never easy. To tell you the truth, I was a bit overawed at the thought of bowling up at Packer's house. There's not much difference between us in age but Kerry Packer is Kerry Packer.

We had some oysters as an entree to dinner and the talk turned to the possibility of a merger. Nick outlined the Sydney City (Easts) point of view, which was pro-merger, and then it was my turn. I said I could see where he was coming from and that I understood that there were some aspects of it that could have benefits for the game. At the end of my few words, I said to Politis: 'I have a question for you, Nick: What say would Souths have in the running of a combined club?' Politis looked straight at me. 'None,' he replied. 'Well, I know I'd be tarred and feathered by the members of the football club under that arrangement. The answer is no,' I told him. There goes the main course, I thought.

In fact we continued on to finish our meal and at the end of it Kerry Packer said goodnight to Nick Politis and Nick headed off. Subsequently, Packer told me he was a Souths' supporter. I nearly fell over and I said to him: 'How come you haven't helped us?' 'You've never asked,' he replied. 'Well, consider yourself asked,' I said. Packer invited Alan and me to jump in the car and head down with him to the Cosmopolitan Hotel at Double Bay. There, he asked me the question, 'How much do you need?' I thought, nothing ventured, nothing gained, so I looked him in the eye and said, 'Two million!' He looked straight back at me, 'I'll give you seven fifty [$750,000].' After we left Kerry Packer, Alan Jones and I headed back to his place and there Jones said, 'We'll keep this under our hat . . . it'll get us going.'

It was a great and generous gesture by Packer. And the fact was that he always *had* been a Souths supporter, tracking back to the high-flying days of the 1960s. I had been dead honest with him. At that time we did need $2 million to get us buoyant again in the premiership, to make us a force. If he *had* given us $2 million at that time, maybe we would never have run into the stormy seas of these recent years. His contribution of $750,000 came at a time when it was really tough for Souths, with no grant from our leagues club, and no specific support package from the Juniors outside its traditional and strong input in running the extensive junior league competitions. At the time it helped us stay on course, but it was not enough to take us to the next step. A sizeable grant from the Juniors at that time, added to the Packer money and the money we generated ourselves, could perhaps have kick-started a new era.

Later, I think Kerry had the impression we wasted his money. I know he made some comments along those lines. But we didn't. We used it carefully and with appreciation in the struggle to consolidate and begin a rebuilding process at South Sydney RLFC. Now, $750,000 is a lot of cash but in reality he had given me a popgun to fight some bloke wielding a machine-gun. It helped keep us alive, no more. What Souths needed was a steady $5 million a year from a leagues club, i.e. the Juniors. The two clubs – Souths and Souths Juniors – were completely separate organisations, albeit on a similar mission: to develop and produce talented and successful rugby league teams and players for the district. The relationship had been a slightly wary one over the years, with the Juniors hanging back whenever it was suggested that it should be a full-scale financial backer of the senior club.

In our later time of strife I did a survey of pubs in our area, and wrote letters to them all, asking if they would assist us in the Souths' fight. I didn't get a single answer of support back. They'd been quite happy to have people in their pubs over the years watching Souths on TV but not one of them said, 'We'll give you something, George.' Not one. At least Kerry Packer did that.

In my dealings with Packer, I found him a down-to-earth bloke. I remember him saying how much he would have liked to have been a top sportsman. Blokes who have the sort of wealth that he has can fulfil many dreams. Maybe that was his, although just out of reach, even though he was a top polo player, a darned good golfer and apparently a crack rifle shot. Maybe he would have liked nothing better in his life than to have played for Souths.

Nick Politis never saw a merger between Easts and Souths as anything less than a takeover, slanted the Roosters' way. But I'll say this: had it eventuated that Souths could *not* get back into the rugby league competition, it would've been better for Easts to take over the whole district, and at least retain some local identity. Having said that, I would never have stuck around to watch it happen. You can present a case that Easts (Sydney City) stepping in would've been in the best interests of the game, but not with me at the helm. Souths are my side; Easts (I always think of them as 'Easts' despite fancy name changes) would never be my side. I'll say this for Politis: he was dead straight. An Easts man through and through, he wasn't going to shot anything away. He was fair dinkum about that. The team was going to be known as the Eastern Suburbs Roosters, was going to play in red, white and blue, and be based at the Sydney Football Stadium. And he was going to have 51 per cent of the say in running the joint. His opinions on Easts were just the same as mine on Souths.

The only two 'mergers' that were ever seriously discussed at Souths through all the turmoil were the one with Easts (which was a straight takeover, of course) and one with Cronulla, something I wasn't involved in, but was aware of. There were various red herrings doing the rounds on the supposed approach from Cronulla, a proposal that met with acceptance from certain forces within Souths in 1999. Some of the talk was very promising, indicating that Souths would come out of any such deal in a strong position, virtually in control. I was talking to *Sydney Morning Herald* sportswriter Roy Masters one day at that time and I said to him, 'Roy, if you can get that sort of a deal for us [i.e. a takeover of Cronulla by Souths], we'll take it.' The supposed arrangement was for a team running around in the red and green and carrying our name. Roy took the question directly to Cronulla chairman Barry Pierce. 'Is he mad?' responded Pierce.

In fact, it was all bullshit, and yet there were agendas afoot within Souths, people fuelling the fire of this Cronulla 'deal'. I think they thought: 'Yeah, we'll get this bloke Piggins to the discussion table and we'll break him down.' When I learned the truth of it, I didn't give them a chance. I went straight to Barry Pierce, a decent bloke, and asked him if there was any truth in the stories doing the rounds at Souths that we would be the dominant partner in any deal. He denied it straight out. Cronulla coveted our juniors and wanted the deal their way. As far as I was concerned, that was the end of it.

I'll repeat what I said above: if South Sydney RLFC stayed out of the equation because the law had backed up the NRL's determination to kill us, the only possible deal that would've made sense in allying the club with another would've been with Eastern Suburbs. For Souths to have linked with Cronulla, 17 kilometres away, a club with which we have nothing in common and, more than that, a club struggling financially, would've been crazy. It was on someone's agenda to push this. It sure wasn't on mine.

The problem for Souths back at the time of the Packer meeting – and virtually ever since 1973 – was that we were always struggling to match it financially with the big clubs, with their unlimited leagues club backing, season after season. Particularly in these later seasons of the '90s when the fight was really on to save the club, we were always on the bite. We had great and continuing support from high-profile people in the media, busy people like Alan Jones, Andrew Denton and Ray Martin who gave all the help and time they could manage. But if it was tough in the years before, it was a hell of a grind from 1997 onwards. We had to keep chasing the cash to keep the fight going and we were always on the edge of wearing out our welcome. In 1999 and 2000 it was tremendously difficult, considering that the biggest sporting event in Australia's history, the Olympic Games, was soaking up just about all the available money.

I think that the various boards of South Sydney RLFC since

the day the leagues club hit the wall in '73 should be commended. Not a single one of those years since has been easy. While other clubs rested on a cushion of leagues club money, Souths did it the hard way, with no grant and each season being an endless scramble to raise the money that was needed. I think the fact that Souths were able to do that, and keep doing it, says a tremendous amount about the spirit of the club. For a club to survive in big-time modern football for almost 30 years without a single substantial grant from its leagues club is near enough a miracle. That Souths did survive was a tribute to the various boards who had been in charge of the annual struggle. The board before the one I chaired was not overly fond of me, but I've got to say they did a good job to keep the club going. The club survived because people wanted it to survive. They still do. I'd love to see what a club like Parramatta have received from its leagues club by comparison since 1971. It would be over $100 million, I'll bet.

In 1990, when I became chairman of Souths Leagues Club, we had made a far-reaching decision that I firmly believed was in the best interests of what we stood for. It was a decision to put our focus on refurbishing and regrowing the leagues club, in the belief that a strong and successful leagues club could be a permanent foundation for a strong football club. I supported that approach 100 per cent, even though I knew it almost certainly meant some sort of sacrifice of the football club's playing strength in the short term.

The football club was in serious trouble then, to the extent that the previous board had been poised to sell a portion of our property at Redfern – the carpark. I remember the chairman, John Riordan, saying at a meeting that if we didn't take that step, the football club wouldn't last another two years. I was strongly opposed to any property sale and eventually the old board stood down, and a new board went in, with me as chairman.

I went down to Phillip Street to see John Quayle, the League's CEO, and I told him we wouldn't be able to assist the football club, which was carrying a $1 million–plus debt. I told Quayle I would not be prepared to sell the assets of the leagues club to finance the football club.

I then went looking for another solution and found it in the one-twelfth share of the NSWRL Narellan Golf Club property that Souths Leagues Club owned. It was the only asset we had, apart from the leagues club property itself. The theory was that we wouldn't be able to sell our share because the other clubs wouldn't agree to it, but I set about trying to prove that wrong, by talking to the other clubs, and got their agreement. I also went to the people at Souths Juniors and asked them straight if they would buy out our share. They agreed, and paid us $1 million – enough to wipe out the football club debt. Henry Morris, chairman of Souths Juniors, said at the time that if we ever ran into some money, we could buy the Narellan share back. I'd love to get it for $1 million today!

In my talk with Quayle, I'd said this: 'John, we both know that the biggest source of income for a successful football club is its leagues club. [Even at that stage there were clubs putting in $5–$6 million a year, where we were putting in next to nothing.] What I am proposing is that we forget about the football side for three or four years. I want to put our leagues club in a position where we are creating profit, to the point where we will be able to strongly underwrite the football club.'

With the help and guidance of Alan Jones, we borrowed $6 million from AMP to back the strategy that had been decided on. When we took over the leagues club in 1990 it was in debt for around $2.5 million, with assets of $3–$4 million. When I stepped down as chairman in 2000, we had a debt of $6 million and assets of $13 or $14 million, and by then 150 poker machine licences, worth around $10 million. We borrowed money, focused on the leagues club and refurbished and modernised it to the extent of the last dollar available – and put faith in the strategy we had taken. A move from Redfern to the Sydney Football Stadium, generating some more revenue, helped keep the football club afloat during difficult times. The value of the club-plus-licence now shows that we were probably on the right track.

Running a football club like Souths for the past 20 or 30 years with little financial support from the leagues club has been an amazing and challenging juggling act. Souths had been in survival mode since 1973, when the doors of the club were shut. But we got through, and paid our players and our bills. The great tragedy is that just when we were getting on top of it, Bob Carr's NSW Government changed the law to allow hotels to have poker machines. A government's job surely is to look after the best interests of the community, and licensed clubs support hospitals, charities, the disadvantaged, sports and social clubs. Yet Carr gave poker machines to fat-cat hoteliers and let them put the money in their pockets, inevitably taking money away from clubs, and so from the many community organisations and sports that they support. And they have the front to say they are 'Labor people'. It bloody amazes me.

With Henry Morris (then Souths Juniors chairman), I went to see Carr before the decision was made – to lobby against what the government was contemplating doing. Henry and I and some others had taken on the government earlier – in 1997–98 on its plans for increased poker machine taxes – and had had some success. (At one point during that battle I had threatened to stand against Bob Carr in the seat of Maroubra.) At the time this second issue blew up, Henry and I had shares in a pub, the Charing Cross at Waverley, but we disagreed strongly with what the government was considering. 'God, why didn't someone tell me earlier?' the premier said when we told him the damage the decision would do to clubs as community-support organisations. What a cop-out! When you are in charge of something, you can't plead ignorance. And when the Government gave the pokies to the hotels, it was a disgraceful decision. Carr and his government have changed sport forever in New South Wales, because licensed clubs will no longer have the money to pour into sport as they once did.

When it was obvious what was going to happen, I went to Henry Morris with a proposal: that the Juniors buy up every hotel in the district. 'Do that, and we'll become the greatest

Left: Just a kid from Mascot squinting into the sun in the family backyard. I'm about three or four here, I reckon.

Centre: Class 1M at Gardeners Road Primary in 1951. That's me fifth from the right in the second top row. Nolene Jones, who was to become my wife in 1973, is in the picture too: fourth from the right, second front row.

Below: The Mascot Juniors F Grade, premiers in the Souths Juniors competition of 1957. I'm third from the left in the front row.

Above: A photo I will always cherish – the Souths team of 1971, winners of the premiership. Back row (left to right): Bob Grant, Gary Stevens, Keith Edwards, John O'Neill, Ray Branighan, George Piggins. Front row (l to r): Denis Pittard, Bob Honan, Eric Simms, John Sattler (capt.), Ron Coote, Paul Sait, Bob McCarthy. Ball boy: Denis Donoghue Jnr.

Right: Grand Final Day, 1971. Souths president Denis Donoghue (left) and trainer Fred West (right), brandishing a giant-sized rabbit, celebrate the win over St George. Clutching a soft drink and sporting a Saints jersey, I'm soaking it all up.

Far right: Late in my football career, running with the ball at Redfern – the best little ground in town for watching football.

Left: Nolene Jones and me on our wedding day, August 30, 1973, at the Wayside Chapel at Kings Cross.

Below: Behind the wheel. Trucks became my working life, and helped make my life what it is today.

Left: The immortal 'Little Master' Clive Churchill, pictured in his coaching days in the late 1960s. Clive had a great Souths side at his command and, in my view, he coached them perfectly – with a light touch. (Rugby League Week)

Below: I didn't score too many tries in my career, but here's one on the way: against Norths on July 16, 1972, at Redfern Oval.

Right: On March 19, 1978, we won the Craven A pre-season final over Canterbury (10–3) on a Henson Park mudheap. It was so wet, even the cup was wrapped in plastic. Here, as captain, I'm enjoying the moment, flanked by Gary Wright (left) and Rocky Laurie (right).

Above: I won my first NSW jumper in 1974, but for some reason wore a Manly one to training at the Sydney Cricket Ground No. 2. Here, I'm with Bob McCarthy (left) and Cronulla's Ron Turner.

Below: When Souths Leagues Club re-opened its doors after the troubles of 1973, I was behind the bar, pulling beers. The line-up of happy customers is headed by Rabbitohs stalwart and ex-international Bernie Purcell (right).

Left: It's Saturday, July 21, 1973, the day Manly and Great Britain lock Malcolm Reilly and I came to grips famously at the SCG. This photo shows the threats and angry words as the fight begins.

Below: Reilly and I pick ourselves up from the ground, both of us significantly the worse for wear. Referee Laurie Bruyeres (out of picture) has sent us off. The touch judge with the flag is Gordon Hedger.

Left: With a couple of old mates, Bob McCarthy (left) and Paul Sait, after playing my last game at Redfern Oval, August 13, 1978. We copped a hiding from Parramatta that day, 50–10.

Right: Coaching is a tough and stressful business; it's not easy to sit passively on the sidelines while others do the work. Here Souths chief executive Terry Parker (left) and I rise to a tense moment in a match in 1988. (Rugby League Week)

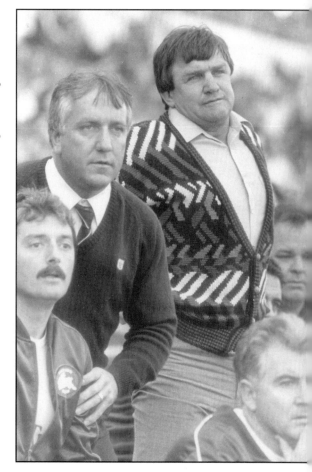

Above: Mario Fenech (right) was a passionate and intense player, and an outstanding one. I suspect that Mario would have fulfilled his dream of playing for Australia if he had been selected and schooled early on as a back-rower rather than a hooker.

Left: Flanked by two of the key Rabbitohs in 1986, my first year coaching Souths. Phil Gould (left) was my trusty lieutenant and a huge help in guiding me into modern coaching. Ian Roberts (right), a fine bloke and a champion footballer, had emerged as one of Souths' most outstanding juniors in many years.

Above left: Nolene and I have had boxer dogs for 30 years, and we have loved them all. I can't imagine life without them. Here I am in the 1980s with Jenna (left) and Jay. They were regulars at Souths training when I coached the side. (Rugby League Week)

Above right: Messing about with horses has been an interest of mine since my growing-up days at Mascot. I'm pictured here with a couple of thoroughbreds at Les Bridge's Randwick stables. The footballers looking on weren't bad 'uns either – Craig 'Tugger' Coleman (right) and Mario Fenech. (Rugby League Week)

Right: I love getting out into the countryside and I love plants and flowers. The nursery at Eastlakes (Gardens-R-Us) has been a real commercial success and is a place where I enjoy spending time. I'm pictured here in the glasshouse. (Rugby League Week)

Above: Up the steps of the Town Hall, with John Sattler just behind … and behind him a crowd (estimated at 40,000) which added up to the biggest sporting protest ever made in Australia. It's October 10, 1999, the day of the great Reclaim the Game rally, five days before the NRL kicked us out of the competition. (Action Photographics)

Below: Ringed by a huge media contingent on October 3, 2000, I try to find the words to express Souths' disappointment, after the long case in the Federal Court, at Justice Paul Finn's finding against us. (Action Photographics)

Our two remarkable mid-city rallies galvanised Sydney as rarely before. Football fans and people with absolutely no interest in the game alike came along because they believed in the larger principle of what we were fighting for. The banners sent hard-hitting messages to News Limited and the NRL. (Action Photographics)

Right: Former Souths captain and current football manager Sean Garlick's passion for the cause shines through in this photo as, with son Jackson on his shoulders, he addresses the huge crowd of 80,000 at the second rally in November 2000. (Action Photographics)

Left: I couldn't have fought the fight I did without my wife Nolene whose belief in the cause and determination to take it right to the wire was as strong as my own throughout. Nolene became the 'hub' of Souths' struggle.

Left: A great bloke and a great mate: with John 'Lurch' O'Neill, late in John's life. The photo was taken at an awards night held at the AJC Centre, Randwick, in 1998. (Rugby League Week)

Below: The relationship between Henry Morris (right) and myself ebbed and flowed a bit during the long fight as we pressured Souths Juniors to commit heavily to the Rabbitoh cause. On the day of this photograph, July 5, 1996, we were in full agreement, ready to tackle a NSW Government proposal to increase poker machine tax. (Fairfax Photo Library)

Above: As he headed for fame and fortune in Hollywood, Russell Crowe, Rabbitoh fan, found time to support us. Here, he's 'at the game', flanked by Craig Coleman (right) and the club's runner, David Lyons (left). (Action Photographics)

Below: The ruling against us in the Federal Court in October 2000 brought real distress to many people to whom Souths meant so much. Surely photos like this one, taken outside the court, must have registered deeply within News Limited and the NRL. (Action Photographics)

How sweet it is! It's the afternoon of July 6, 2001, and back at the leagues club even the chairman can manage a smile after the full bench of the Federal Court decides in our favour. (Action Photographics)

football club in the world,' I told him. 'We can buy every good pub and every bad pub. We'll close the bad ones down and we won't lose a customer. They'll either go to the next pub, or to one of our clubs. We'll own the lot.' It was obvious the pubs were going to become cash cows from the moment the poker machine decision was announced. The Juniors had $24 million at its disposal, and could have done it. Henry's people said no. I think the idea was too big for them.

The poker machine glut is a tragedy that the government imposed on the state. The spread of the machines into pubs has harmed society, but you can only go so far protecting people against themselves. Within the leagues club framework when I was involved there, it used to worry me greatly to see pensioners coming in and losing their money. It was immoral, I believed, for us to be continually taking it from them. They weren't there out of the sheer enjoyment of playing the machines; they were there daily with the dream of winning. And the machines are set up so that you *can't* win, not in the long term anyway. At least within the club framework I thought there was a chance of doing something about it – and I tried to set up a points system under which people who came in and, by choice, played the machines and lost their money could get to eat in the club for nothing. Under the scheme, people who played the machines would be graded as 'A' members – after all, they were the ones supporting the club by playing the machines. It didn't happen. But such a system *can* at least be applied in leagues clubs. It will never happen in pubs. And people can have a shot at me, claiming hypocrisy. Yeah, I had a pub for a while, and in the end it had poker machines in it. But I always thought the principle of the pubs getting the machines was immoral and I was happy to get out of the hotel business.

The poker machine decision effectively killed our hopes for the leagues club, and for a long-term football future based largely on its success. But by then the league world had been turned upside down, anyway, by the events of 1995. Nothing was as it had been.

Late in the year that I had talked with Kerry Packer sitting in his car in downtown Double Bay, after he'd agreed to give Souths three-quarters of a million dollars, the rumours began that rugby league was to be bulldozed with a takeover bid. For Souths, as the rumours came true, it was the beginning of an ending. Some people would have preferred that it was 'the end', but I was never going to allow that to happen.

PART TWO

Take the strong icons that once held us together, like
football – now adjuncts of capitalism. The very things
that hold Australia together are being threatened. I think
football is being threatened.

B.A. Santamaria

9. Super League: The Monster that Ate Rugby League

Is the globalisation of the sport worth the price that has to be paid if that price is the death of clubs with years of history, tradition and cultural involvement in their communities?

Simon Kelner, To Jerusalem and Back

THE SUPER LEAGUE WAR that tore apart rugby league in the years 1995–97, leaving behind scars that may never heal, had its beginning in the boardroom of the League's only privately owned club, the Brisbane Broncos. Sponsored in 1994 by News Limited–owned companies Traveland and Queensland Newspapers, the Broncos seemed constantly at loggerheads with the NSW and Australian Rugby League, and sometimes in bitter dispute with the Phillip Street strong men, chief executive John Quayle and chairman Ken Arthurson. In that discontent, the idea of a breakaway 'Super League' was born, driven by Broncos executives such as John Ribot, Paul 'Porky' Morgan and Barry Maranta.

Up to that time, rugby league in Australia had been under the control of the NSWRL and the ARL, right from when the game began in 1908. During 1994, when the battle lines for pay TV dominance in the Australian market were being drawn, the Broncos 'sold' the idea in principle to Rupert Murdoch and his giant News Limited conglomerate. Sport was seen as the perfect market leader in the chase for subscribers, and rugby league was a brilliant TV sport, at the height of its powers after record-breaking achievements in season 1994. The fight that ensued was a lot more about TV rights than it was about football. The old 13-a-side code was no more than a pawn in a much larger game.

So it began. Ribot, the former Test winger, held a vision of a 12-team 'super' competition, backed by American-style razza-matazz and with worldwide appeal. News Limited considered, and said 'Let's do it.' Rumours about the pending revolution reaching back almost 12 months became fact in February 1995, when News executives Ken Cowley and David Smith went through the 'front door' to present the Ribot–Broncos vision, now the News vision, to representatives of the 20 clubs at a meeting at the NSW Leagues Club. Kerry Packer's booming appearance at that meeting, with his threats that he would 'sue the arses' off clubs if they rose to the Murdoch bait, is now part of rugby league folklore. From there the movement gained unstoppable momentum, culminating in the 'April Fools' Day' raids when News Limited agents signed battalions of players to Super League contracts. The war was on, leading to a destructive, vicious, nightmarish period unprecedented in rugby league's history.

Through it all in the seasons that followed – split competitions, falling crowds, widespread public disgust – there were only three winners: the lucky players who signed hugely inflated contracts with one side (Super League) or the other (the ARL), the player agents, some of whom became overnight millionaires, and the legal eagles, armies of them, who lined up as the two sides slugged it out through the courts. To paraphrase an overworked cliche: rugby league was the big loser. Today the game is still contending with the alarming fallout, the negative effect of the Super League war having diminished league at every measurable level.

As mentioned, there had been plenty of whispers and some media speculation that there was movement afoot in the game in late 1994 and early '95 (if not before), but my first direct involvement in the changes came when John Quayle rang me at home one Sunday morning. From memory, it was December 1994. 'Have you heard?' he asked. 'Heard what?' I said. 'There's talk of a raid on the game,' said Quayle. 'News Limited is trying to take us over and set up a Super League. Can I count on your loyalty?' I told Quayle: 'John, my loyalty to you will be as strong as yours is to me. That is what you can count on.' 'Fair enough,' said Quayle. In the course of that conversation with the NSWRL chief executive, I mentioned the idea of a loyalty agreement; that clubs sign a five-year agreement in return for which they would get a five-year licence to play in the competition.

Things had changed by then at Souths, the arrival of Alan Jones in 1994 as general manager of football operations guaranteed that. Jones's arrival had brought with it enough financial support through his powerful business contacts to enable completion of the multi-million-dollar renovation project at the leagues club. The season had started with a bang – a wonderful win in the Tooheys Challenge final in Albury, 27–26 over Brisbane – and ended in drama and controversy with allegations of match fixing in a game in which Wests beat us 34–26. A police investigation subsequently cleared our players and the club.

My thoughts are that allegations that aren't proved aren't worth talking about. But, in saying that, I'm not naive enough to think there mightn't be the possibility of funny business in matches, especially considering the cricket experience, and the way that gambling has been encouraged to get into bed with rugby league in recent years. John Quayle and Ken Arthurson attempted to keep gambling at arm's length, but by the 2001 season it had reached plague proportions, with the bookies and the TAB between them betting on just about anything you could bet on in a football match. The arrangement was so cosy that the TAB was involved in a sponsorship deal with the NRL. It was unhealthy. As if the people of New South Wales didn't have enough to bet on, what with the poker machines, the gallopers, the trots, the dogs, Keno, Lotto . . . and who knows what else. Now football is in the mix. The climate of the game is such now that the possibility exists of deals being done to 'fix' matches, although in a game like league it would be hard to pull a side up.

Allegations emerged in a *Sun-Herald* story of September 11, 1994, that players in a Sydney first-grade team had bet against themselves in at least one match during the year. Two days later, at a sponsorship launch at the club, Alan Jones revealed that he had asked police to investigate 'monstrous and heinous' allegations that several Souths players had 'run dead' after backing Western Suburbs to win the match on August 14. Wests had won the game 34–26. Later came allegations that a former international had placed bets of $20,000 on Wests to beat Souths. On October 18 the shadow lifted when a six-week police investigation cleared the club of any involvement in match fixing.

In my own career I was never aware of any matches which might have been 'hot'. If I played in any, I know nothing of it. But league's past is dotted with rumours and innuendo about crooked matches, with the finger invariably pointed at the referee. And if I was going to tie anybody up in a football match, that's who I'd be talking to: the ref. He's the man who wields the power. Historians will quote you various matches that remain clouded in doubt, the 1952 Souths–Wests grand final and the 1963 Wests–St George grand final being at the top of the list. And ask any of the Souths guys that played in 1969 (against Balmain) and they will tell you that that grand final was one of 'those' games also. Or maybe it was just great tactics by the Tigers. That match has been much discussed down the years; how Balmain slowed it down in the second half by feigning injuries, causing frequent stoppages in play. Frustrated and rarely able to build any momentum, Souths never really got into the groove in a game for which they were 3–1 on favourites. A hefty penalty count of 16–7 awarded against them by referee Keith Page did not help the cause.

The supposed 'scandal' of the Souths–Wests game in late '94 quickly faded from memory with the events that overtook rugby league in early '95. Quayle's concerns, of course, were spot on. News Limited, cashed up, fed by malcontents within the game, was circling.

I remember very well the February 6, 1995, meeting downtown at League headquarters, where News Limited's architect of the plan, David Smith, and chief executive Ken Cowley presented their blueprint to representatives of the 20 premiership clubs. There were all sorts of questions flying around. I asked Smith if he could tell me which of the ARL clubs he had spoken to. 'No,' he said, 'but I can assure you I won't be speaking to you.' 'Yes, you can count on that,' I assured him in return, 'you've got no chance of talking to me.' They made it very clear: News didn't want to talk to the 'brokes' like us and Wests.

Canberra chief executive Kevin Neil spoke in favour of the News Limited plan. This was the way to go, he said, a great chance for the game to be put in a positive light around the world. He was adamant. 'How have you the right to sell the game?' I asked him. 'You agreed to play in this competition . . . it is *our* game, it is not your game to sell.' And Neil got this kind of sheepish look on his dial. It's now well known that he was in the thick of it from the start. Club director Barry Maranta spoke for the Broncos and said that he had a lot of money invested in the club, and didn't we people from the League realise that the way to go was into franchises? There was all this lovely money to be made out of the game, he reckoned.

The proposal presented – one that was not new to many in the room owing to secret talks already held – was for 12 licensed, privately owned Super League teams. The 20 existing teams would remain in state-based competitions and would be shareholders in the Super League teams. Smith showed a slide that outlined 12 teams in Australasia, a Euroleague, world TV coverage and sponsorship, financial stability and high salaries. Players would receive such benefits as superannuation and medical insurance, would share in merchandising sales, and would be trained for careers after football. Well, they got the bit about the high salaries right!

John Quayle's ploy to get Kerry Packer along to the meeting was a great tactical move. Packer was typically blunt and direct. He had contracts with us, he said, contracts with the ARL which, in his opinion, bound every club to Channel 9, and this was a warning to anyone who tried to break those contracts.

The demand that day for clubs to sign the ARL loyalty agreements really showed how badly organised this coup to hijack the game was. It just panicked the other mob, and every single club signed because it didn't have the guts to stand up and say, 'No, we're going with News Limited.' I have no doubt that they signed because of the lack of trust among themselves. They were all lured by the bullshit talk of what was being proposed for this 'Super League', but they couldn't trust each other to stay solid. I would have respected them more if any one of them had put up a hand and said: 'Hang on a sec, we're not going to sign this, we really believe there's something good for the game in what is being proposed, and we want to look deeper into it.' But none of 'em did. They signed the ARL document, then snuck away in the dead of night and signed with News – players and clubs.

The five-year loyalty agreements on which the ARL v. Super League court cases would be fought, supplementing and supporting the original agreements signed in late 1994, were sent out the day after the meeting, with a demand that they be signed and returned by 9 am the following day. All came back signed, albeit with expressions of protest from Canberra and Brisbane, the Broncos dragging their feet longer than any other club.

Rugby league is a great game, a tough game, a hard game. But you wouldn't have thought so if you'd seen the piss-weak effort of some of the club officials back then. Not one official from Canberra or Brisbane or any other of those who would defect had the ticker to dig his heels in. Instead all clubs signed the ARL loyalty agreements. Every single one of them! I wonder what Murdoch thought about that? Here he was about to bankroll the greatest breakaway movement ever seen in Australian sport, and not one of his connections at the various soon-to-be Super League clubs would put up a hand on Rupert's behalf. Talk about staying solid and being loyal!

It seemed that, from the start, News Limited listened to and put its faith in rugby league men who didn't deserve it. Another truly shameful performance from officialdom came later, at a meeting held at Souths Leagues Club, and involving all the clubs. I can still remember the moment when Roger Cowan from Penrith got up and said, 'We'd like John Quayle to leave the room' – and everyone just sat there in silence. Can you imagine that? And they put it to the vote and it got through unopposed, except for me. They all tried to justify it later by saying: 'Well, making it "clubs only" gave everyone the chance to speak out freely.' What a load of shit! When Quayle walked, I walked with him. And I said to them, 'I wouldn't have allowed this meeting in my club if I knew you were going to do that to him.' It was a bloody disgraceful thing they put on us as host club. Our top man, CEO of the game, deserved to be treated with more respect.

To me, the whole thing was unbelievable. Here were Murdoch and co. walking in off the street and taking over football. It would be like someone declaring martial law and saying no-one goes to work today, you've all got to stay at home. I'm sure Australians would say, 'Pig's arse, we're going to work and we're going to keep this country going.' That was the way I felt. I was filthy. I thought, who are *you* to come and take away this game which I have played for most of my life, and which my family played and on which my life is based? Who are you, sitting there telling me there's going to be some new competition, that you'll be taking away what the ARL built over all those years?

Rupert Murdoch and his cronies never wanted to plough the field. They just wanted to pick the crop. From the word go, News Limited wanted the league community – all the way from the leagues clubs down to the bloke who sells the raffle tickets – to grow the crop for them, and to do all the work. Murdoch would then reap the harvest and sell the produce to reap huge dividends via pay TV, etc. That he got burned badly, with News Limited so far having lost something like $750 million or whatever it is, represents no more than just desserts. And if News could somehow turn the clock back to 1995, they'd do exactly that, and never again go within a bull's roar of rugby league. Somehow a company that you've gotta think is one of the smartest in the world got itself smashed financially by listening to untalented malcontents within the game and to the odd lightweight entrepreneur. How News Limited execs fell for the thimble and pea will always amaze me. Any mug in the pub could have told them back then that you don't make money out of football clubs, and that their 'vision' of rugby league as some glittering game that would sweep the world was just bullshit.

The way Murdoch's allies collapsed at the meeting that day in February 1995, and in the immediate aftermath, should have sounded the loudest of warnings to him. Broncos CEO John Ribot, Canberra CEO Kevin Neil, Cronulla chairman Peter Gow and Canterbury Bulldogs CEO Peter Moore and others had run secretly with the idea, something they would never have had the backbone to do without the Murdoch empire behind them. And here was their very first trial of being loyal to their new master . . .

I am still amazed that News Limited didn't slam the door shut straightaway. Instead, for some misguided reason, it carried on with it, still did business with these people, still peddled this propaganda about the game being in a shocking state and News having to rescue it. The game in fact was in excellent shape.

Canterbury in particular handled Murdoch beautifully. They eventually took $32 million off him in payouts and settlements associated with Super League. I suspect that after that first meeting, which must have been a huge shock to the News Limited mob, Canterbury's 'Bullfrog' Moore, being the operator he was, was able to regroup his people, straighten them up – put a broom up their arse – and get control again. Canterbury's jump to the Super League side clinched the deal for News Limited. Without Canterbury, a traditional Sydney-based club, there would have been no Super League, and that's a truth that must still create great disquiet within the Bulldogs, and should forever. The ARL's chairman at the time, Ken Arthurson, has gone on the record with his belief that the Canterbury signing was the whole key to Super League. Until they signed, the breakaway League had only virtual newcomers and blow-ins to the game, clubs which had not built the tradition that made rugby league the game it was. But in Canterbury they had the double-whammy, a powerful Sydney-based club, and a club with more than 60 years of tradition, and success. That first day, Peter Moore – like the others – chose not to, or couldn't bring himself to, stand up and declare himself pro-Murdoch. Both Nick Politis and I challenged him at the meeting because by then rumours were circulating that the Bulldogs were locked in negotiations with Super League forces.

A few days later I told the *Sunday Telegraph*'s Mike Coleman that I believed Moore was 'duty-bound' to turn his back on any Super League approach. Accused at the February 6 meeting of 'double-dealing', Moore defended himself in Coleman's article. I told the journalist: 'Last November we all entered into an agreement to stick together and we expected that agreement to be honoured. I can understand the pressure that someone like Peter (Moore) is under but when you stick your hand out and shake on something, that's it as far as I am concerned. Peter entered into an agreement and if he was put under pressure by News Limited he should have made the League aware of it.'

A few weeks later, March 20, 1995, I received a letter from Bullfrog Moore. It read:

Dear George,
I was never about to cancel out the great association that
I have had with your Club, and your family.

Public criticism does not bother me when it comes to the like of Nick Politis – he doesn't rate as a friend or administrator.

However, you are a friend and a very respected administrator who would influence a lot of people.

The article says that you said I reneged on a handshake deal. I never have and I never will.

The article also says that you said that I should have made the League aware of the pressure that had been put on me by News Limited. To this very day, no-one from News Limited has ever spoken a word to me about Canterbury-Bankstown joining a Super League.

George, I was only upset because I have the highest regard for you as a friend and a man.

Anyway, George, I don't carry grudges and I don't think any less of you for what was in the paper. I know how they can put comments out of context.

However, I do think that you owe me a lunch.

The real story about the Bulldogs' position came out in a letter sent to all members in May that year – and signed by the Bullfrog and club president Barry Nelson.

In part, this is what it said:

Despite the obvious need for a drastic reduction in the number of Sydney teams, we strongly believe that our Club has fully earned the entitlement to continue in its own right – to stand alone and retain our tradition, heritage and history.

Super League has recognised our Club's right to maintain our destiny in Rugby League and has given our Club this unfettered right.

Under an ARL rationalisation of 11 Sydney Clubs, our Club was faced with the certainty of compulsory amalgamation – an ultimatum that we must forsake our tradition, heritage and history. In place of the Sydney

136

Bulldogs, we would have certainly been, say, 'Western Bulldogs', amalgamated with, say, Wests and Balmain and never again to wear our beloved 'Blue and White': I don't think that any of us would ever have gone to watch this amalgamated team. It would not be even reasonably close to our hearts.

There have unfortunately been many emotions exposed over the last three months but we have reduced our emotions to only one – survival of our Club within its own right.

Loyalty to the ARL was certainly a factor.

However, loyalty to our own Club is a deeper loyalty.

Once I had the utmost respect for Bullfrog Moore. But I lost that totally because of what he did in 1995. And it was a bloody shame, for them to turn me against a bloke who I had thought once was so good for rugby league. I didn't even go to his funeral when he died in 2000. In my view he was a Judas, even though he always protested he was dragged into the Super League takeover bid by circumstances, by his players and the coach, his son-in-law Chris Anderson, making decisions to sign with Super League. For God's sake! He *ran* Canterbury, knew every bloody thing that was going on there, and had done for 25 years, and he was a delegate to the ARL. He was one of the men in charge of the entire game! I have no doubt he looked at the News Limited proposal and decided it was in his own best interest to go and in the best interest of his club.

Moore's stance created an awkward situation for ARL chairman Ken Arthurson; the pair had been best mates for many years. To Arthurson's credit he dragged together a strong ARL defence in the battle against the Super League mob. He fought hard. I have no doubt he could have jumped ship early and taken his beloved Manly to a safe and secure stand-alone position in Super League forever more. But he stuck – and fought. And the irony came only later, when Norths and Manly, desperate to prove they should be stand-alone clubs, both fell on their swords as they threw money about foolishly, trying to seal their positions. Eventually they were pushed into a merger, which ranks as one of the dumbest and most uncomfortable decisions that any football hierarchy ever made. The two clubs hated each other, yet you had the geniuses at the NRL shoving them into a joint venture, so desperate were they to get their 14 teams. The Northern Eagles promptly spent the millions of dollars allocated on player salaries. Again. By the end of 2000 they were a million in the red. Topped up by News, they were $1 million–plus in debt again in 2001 and looking certain that they would be heading right out the back door, with reports of a $1.3 million debt in late June, and News declaring 'No more!'. Before too long, the partnership collapsed.

Peter Moore was just one of many who jumped ship. In early 1995, Mal Meninga, as Australia's captain, got up and took the oath at the ARL's huge season launch in downtown Sydney. In quick time, Meninga was gone from the ARL game, leaping to the truck full of money that Super League was offering him.

And along the way he managed to say one night, famously, that the game of rugby league had done nothing for him. When you look at rugby league there are not so many doctors, pilots or company directors within its ranks. In his working life, Meninga had been a policeman in the Queensland Police Force. Chances are that rugby league opened that door for him, as it has opened many doors for the men who play it over the years. I know that it opened plenty of doors for me, and fortunately I had the commonsense to go on and make something of that. I think the countless players who have been provided with wider opportunities because they played league at a high level, even if they didn't take those opportunities, should be appreciative of what the game has given them.

Look at the blokes who were offered cartloads of money and took it, and put yourself in their place. What they didn't have to do was kick the game, as the likes of Meninga and Laurie Daley did. I had more time for the blokes who probably thought deep down they were doing the wrong thing by the game in joining Super League, but who at least joined quietly and without fuss, and without feeling the need to justify themselves by lashing out at a game which had been good to them. Rugby league was fighting for its life at that time, and if blokes were going to sell out to Murdoch's money they should at least have attempted to be a little bit humble and understand how people like me felt, seeing the things that we had followed all our lives going by the wayside. A bloke like Laurie Daley probably later regretted what he said – about players being treated like 'dogs' and so on – and maybe he was fired up by someone in the background. Still, he shouldn't have said what he said and should have had the character to show more respect for the game. Daley knows better than anyone that the game of rugby league has provided him with his great opportunity in life.

For all that, I can in the main forgive the players, but never the officials who sold out rugby league. Their duty was to put the game above everything else, instead they saw Murdoch's raid as a chance for themselves, and grabbed it. It will suit me just fine if I am never again in the same room as the blokes who turned traitor back in 1995, and beyond.

Some of them got their comeuppance in the stinging Federal Court judgment of Justice James Burchett, delivered on February 23, 1996. In his finding in favour of the ARL against Super League's challenge, on the validity of the loyalty clauses, Justice Burchett didn't mince words. He told the truth. His 220-page judgment is a scathing document, but only selected items got into the papers because of the media's handling of it. It was powerful stuff, but it got swept under the carpet to an extent because some of it was going to embarrass and humiliate people on the Super League side. The things that Burchett said have never been denied, by other courts, or by anyone. They couldn't be, they were true.

Justice Burchett's words on the secret assault on the game and the likes of John Ribot, Peter Moore, Ken Cowley and Barry Maranta must have cut like knives. The words and phrases are powerful: 'completely corrupted', 'clandestine', 'connivance', 'complicity', 'deceit'. Of Peter Moore, Justice Burchett said: 'He was revealed as a man who was overwhelmed by the magnitude of his temptation. He was completely corrupted, and shut his eyes to his obligations to the club and the League.' Of Barry Maranta: 'Mr Maranta was engaged in a deliberate exercise in deception.' Of John Ribot: 'Mr Ribot does not emerge from cross-examination as a reliable witness and I accept his versions of events only where it accords with my view of the probabilities.'

Justice Burchett wrote also of the Super League methods: 'The secrecy, deceit and suddenness that were intended to be the hallmarks of this assault upon the League are apparent at every turn in the evidence . . . The evidence makes it plain that News Limited and the Super League companies acted in the relevant sense, with dishonesty.' He found that News Limited and its Super League companies had acted with 'dishonesty' in trying to induce rebel clubs to breach their contracts. He called their tactics 'infiltration by the back door', an assault on the league establishment 'well outside the norms of proper and acceptable commercial conduct'.

But as early as that afternoon in February '96, it was certain the fight still had a long way to go. Ken Cowley told the media: 'Our resolve is undiminished. We will respect the law but we will not walk away. In the future this will be viewed as a temporary, if painful, reversal.' As expected, News Limited appealed the decision.

Six years later, history has delivered its own judgment on the likes of John Ribot, Peter Moore, Peter Gow, Paul 'Porky' Morgan, Kevin Neil and their other fellow travellers. They stuffed a bloody great game. In a few short years, because of what they did, a game that had survived strongly for 90 years or so has had its roots torn up and its traditions destroyed. It has gone from being what it had always been – the number-one game on the eastern seaboard – to a trailing number three.

The game has lost ground everywhere. And the AFL really

rubbed rugby league noses in it when, on the basis of a competition in which traditions have been retained, it signed a huge TV deal in 2001. It's a deal incidentally that spells trouble for rugby league. Yet, the blokes who conspired to steal away rugby league, such as John Ribot and Kevin Neil, are still in the game, still spitting out their opinions. Morgan and Ribot headed the charge, having links to News Limited via company-linked sponsorship of the Broncos. When 'Porky' Morgan died, he was afforded tributes that suggested he was somewhere up in the territory of Jesus Christ. I didn't know the bloke, and that suited me. I only met him once. On his death they all wanted to say what a great job he'd done for Queensland. I didn't give a shit what Morgan had done for Queensland – what I do care about is that he stuffed up football for most of the people in Sydney.

In 2001, John Ribot made a minor admission of regret at the way things had turned out. In a television interview in March, Ribot stated he was not proud of helping start the war that ripped rugby league apart: 'Where we were heading probably wasn't the right way and we had a fight that probably would have been nicer behind closed doors.' Adding some typical bullshit, Ribot said there was no use dwelling on the 'skirmish', but he hoped all parties had used it as a learning experience and moved on to better the game. He couldn't bring himself to say sorry. We have all done wrong things in life and when we've been caught, we're sorry. But that was Ribot.

I wrote him an 'open letter', but by then there was effectively a blackout on Souths in the media, the latest tactic, and it barely rated a mention. This is what I said:

March 10, 2001

Dear John,
I read with interest last week in the *Sydney Morning Herald* that you had admitted to having some regrets over the rugby league civil war.

Let me start by saying that I think it is a good thing

that someone can come out publicly and show regret for things that may have happened. However, to be quite frank and honest it is not enough. You have to go further.

At Souths we have no regrets in regards to our actions during the Super League–ARL war. We can look back and say we acted in good faith at all times. We did not sacrifice our integrity. We refused to give up our heritage and tradition at any cost.

Our only regrets are that so many people suffered so much pain and anguish as a result of this civil war over sport.

I regret that women and children have cried openly in public because their football team was taken away from them.

I regret that Souths, the club that had done more than any other to promote and foster the game of rugby league in Australia over more than 90 years, has been treated with such disdain and disrespect by so many people in the game.

I regret that ordinary everyday Australians have had to contribute more than one-and-a-half million dollars to fight in courtrooms for their right to be entertained by the only football team they care to follow.

I regret that the opinions of people such as Ian Heads, Frank Hyde, Jack Gibson, Roy Masters and Phil Gould no longer seem to matter in rugby league.

I regret that players stood by, doing so little to ensure that so many of their fellow workmates were not deprived of the game in the future.

Such a letter obviously was never going to appear anywhere in the Murdoch media, Ribot having had a sweetheart relationship with them since it all began in 1994 (amazing when you consider the amount of money he has cost Murdoch). I don't buy the Murdoch papers and haven't since 1995. In fact, like a lot of people, Nolene and I made conscious decisions a long while ago not to support any Murdoch products. As of recently, however, we do have Optus on the TV, although the rugby league channel was not part of the package. As long as Souths remained on the outer, I did not watch the game.

I'm sure I was an embarrassment to the people who were trying to justify what has been done to rugby league. They knew deep down that I was defending something that was true and right, and they knew that they had nothing they could defend. Until that pretty pale statement from Ribot in early 2001, there hadn't been a word of regret from the blokes who brought it all about, although people like Wayne Bennett, a Super League supporter at the beginning, have gone on the public record with their serious misgivings about the whole thing. Bennett, one of the most respected coaches in the game, has said he would have never got involved in the Super League thing if he had had the slightest inkling as to the way it was going to turn out. He had suggested 'better ways' (i.e. a promotion and relegation system) to preserve club identities . . . and maintain hope. I'm sure many of the people who jumped originally must think like that now. Rupert Murdoch especially. And if it hadn't been for pay TV, the whole bloody thing would never have happened.

Right from the start I think John Ribot was only interested in one thing: he wanted to become a rugby league powerbroker. When you look at all the things that have gone on, the certainty now is that if you had any part in creating Super League or the NRL, then you didn't have the best interests of rugby league at heart. Rugby league sold Rupert Murdoch and his son a pup. Sometimes the best of us get conned. And that's what happened. The people who sold the idea to Murdoch must have done a mighty slick job. And once he was in there offering all that loot, clubs fell over themselves. Clubs that didn't have leagues clubs had everything to gain, and clubs that *did* have leagues clubs had even more to gain because they were going to get rid of the burden of the bloody football side. This became even more important when hotels were granted poker machine licences. Inevitably, as discussed, this gesture would affect licensed clubs, lead to reduced patronage and reduced profits, and limit the amount of money that could be given to football clubs.

The vision presented by Ribot and co. was always false. There is a saying in church communities: give us a child until he or she is seven, and we'll have them for the rest of their lives. It's the same thing in sport. Once a kid starts off young in a sport, chances are he'll stick with it. And children inherit their sporting loves from their parents. All this is why John Ribot and his Super League supporters with their phony 'vision' were so far off the mark: this bullshit picture of rugby league sweeping the world, of the game springing up like mushrooms in brand new lands where the sporting heritage had long been represented by other sports. And News Limited fell for it.

During all that took place in rugby league in 1995, I thought now and then of the brotherhood that had once existed in the game – when clubs stood together, and bailed each other out if there was trouble. But from '95 that was gone forever. It was every man, and club, for himself.

Not that the ARL was blameless. It had let player payments get out of hand and the long-term TV deal it had done with Packer had hobbled the game. The introduction of the four new teams for 1995 (Perth, North Queensland, Auckland and South Queensland Crushers), in the interests of expanding the competition to a genu-inely national status, was always fraught with danger because of the cost factor. The ARL's eventual goal was that the 20-team competition would gradually reduce by 'natural' means. 'If they're smart enough and active enough, they'll survive. If not, they won't,' said John Quayle, setting the agenda for the clubs. I doubted right at the start that we could sustain the costs that were automatically introduced into the game in '95. Perth and South Queensland fell before long, and only huge subsidies provided by News Limited propped up North Queensland and Auckland. Further clubs were quickly sacrificed once the going got tough (Adelaide, the second Newcastle team, the Hunter Mariners, and the Gold Coast).

The now-famous February meeting was followed by the April

raids at which clubs and players jumped like salmon swimming upstream. The thing was never going to lie down, even after the 'loyalty' signings that followed the February meeting. The rumbles were still there. Souths were right out of the loop by then anyway, so it all sort of washed over us. We stuck fast with the ARL, but there was no emphasis on saving us, even though we had been the highest-rating club on TV in 1994, and there was no interest whatsoever from the other mob (Super League). The ARL didn't prop us up or promise us revenue, it just counted us among the numbers, and cut us adrift. Everyone thought we were in financial trouble. Well, we weren't *in trouble*; we were poor but we weren't living beyond our means as others were. The decisions by then were no longer being made by rugby league people anyway: the game was in the hands of Packer and Murdoch.

One of the many top-line players who took Super League's hugely inflated money in 1995 was Ian Roberts, a great product of the Souths junior system. I have plenty of respect for Ian Roberts. He is a decent person who cares about others. As a footballer he could have become one of the best players ever if he hadn't suffered a serious groin injury which blunted his career. One of the first times I saw him play he broke quickly from a scrum, raked in a pass and sprinted down the wing.

There were rumours about Ian's 'lifestyle' from early on. As coach, I talked to him about it one day, to let him know that there were rumours doing the rounds that he was a homosexual. He denied the stories, which was natural, I suppose. Later some of the players came to me and said, 'You are going to have to say something because he's hanging around [a gay haunt].' And I told them, 'If you've got a problem, *you* tell him.'

Ian's decision to finally 'come out' in the book written about him in the late '90s was no doubt a brave one, although I've got to say I'm from another era and I have mixed feelings about broadcasting your sexuality. I prefer some discretion about that side of one's life. And that discretion, I reckon, should apply to anyone: homosexual, heterosexual, or whatever.

Ian Roberts, footballer, was a strong, tough man. I remember a game he played against Canterbury in which the other mob were sledging him, but they weren't too keen to take him on that day when he cut loose on the field. He could fight, and he could play football. I wasn't too surprised to learn later that his father had been a good middleweight amateur boxer in England.

He was, and is, a heck of a nice young person, and it was no doubt because of that that some people took advantage of him in his business dealings. He came to me one day with this deal he had been approached about, to do, of all things, with buying prawn trawlers in Dubai. A couple of the South Sydney Juniors guys were on the verge of going into it at that stage, too. It was at a time when I had just sold my business and was cashed up. Ian told me that he was caught for $40,000 and if he didn't find the amount he'd lose the investment opportunity. When I told Nolene that I had decided to lend Ian the $40,000, she rolled her eyes. I made it very clear to him, however: 'Ian, I am not in the deal. I am lending you forty thousand, and in six weeks I want it back.'

The full story may never be told, but the outcome was that Ian Roberts lost virtually everything he had, and it was a couple of years before my $40,000 came back. I want to stress here I was never in the deal, and was filthy with what happened. I told the two blokes involved in the scam what I thought of them. They had taken advantage of a young high-profile player. I even went up to Windsor one day and waited for one of the blokes behind the whole thing. I told his wife I was going to hang him off the Windsor Bridge when I caught up with him. (He didn't turn up.) Ian was probably lucky that Super League came along. He benefited from that and was able to make up the financial ground he had lost in that bastard of a scheme.

Roberts also got big money out of Manly (1990–94) before Super League arrived. His pirating by Manly was a pretty disgraceful event, and one which added weight to my theory that Souths had already been marked down as lame ducks at some high-up level in the game, bound for extinction. How else could you read it? Roberts was our gun player at Souths, more or less holding the side together, and the game's hierarchy allowed a situation where Manly, the club with whom League president Ken Arthurson was associated, were permitted to steal him cold. The ARL had no device in place to stop it and it needed a hard decision at the top, a stiff direction to Manly along the lines of: 'For the greater good of the game . . . don't touch him.' At the top of any sport, I reckon, you need people who have balls enough to make unpopular decisions, but those decisions should be made on only one foundation: that they are for the good of the game.

I didn't blame Roberts for his career decisions in football. When we talked at the time of the Manly signing that there was no blame as far as I was concerned, that I understood he was bettering himself, working towards setting himself up for life.

The Super League war magnified a problem that was already in the game by 1995: that of players being paid much more than clubs could afford. As I've mentioned already, the trend had needed checking well before Murdoch came along. Back then it had to be the ARL. Admittedly, it had tried, but couldn't bring it off.

As far back as 1990 the NSW Rugby League introduced a salary cap system to try and apply a brake on reckless club spending. The cap, aligned with a player draft giving lower placed clubs the first pick of available talent each season, was at the heart of the League's search for balance and responsible management in its competition. Both have never been bedded down in the game, although other codes (such as AFL), and other countries, manage it. The draft was buried by a decision of the full bench of the Federal Court in 1991 and the salary cap, although hanging on in the game, has never had the full faith of anyone due to weak policing and the many twists and turns that clubs can use to get around it.

Of course there should be a salary cap in place, and at least the current mob are trying to do that. It should be maintained by a points system, and heavily policed by the NRL and ARL with the agreement that a club can't buy a player without releasing another. That way we could spread the talent around.

But the player payments genie was out of the bottle back in the early '90s and there wasn't the will to try and find a solution – even though the game became an outrageous bidding war in which the rich robbed the poor, and even though the entire future of rugby league was put at risk. League went on to virtually bankrupt itself through the hyperinflation caused by one company's colossal overestimation of the game's potential value.

Maybe it needed the members of the leagues clubs to revolt at that time, to go to the directors and say: 'Whoa! Enough! We're not going to let you keep ruining football by pouring all this money in.' In fact, the inflation was easy enough to stop. It just required the leagues clubs to get together in a sensible, businesslike way and put a cap on what they were going to pay to football clubs each year. It would be a completely justifiable stance. By doing it in the current tough climate, the licensed clubs would be preserving the foundation of what they have.

Such a decision is probably the big hope for the game, restoring balance and commonsense. But do you know why it didn't happen? Because the blokes running the football clubs, who in many cases also ran the leagues clubs, didn't want to kill the goose that was laying the golden egg, that's why. Around this time, club secretaries (dressed up in their new titles as 'chief executives'), often blokes with little business acumen or expertise, were drawing salaries of $250,000 a year! No way were they going to vote to change that.

Many years ago there were perceptive league men who reckoned that the arrival of the leagues clubs would be the ruination of the game because they created a false market, and one that was ultimately unsustainable. With the pubs now having poker machines, those predictions are closer to being proved correct. The days of leagues clubs handing over 70–90 per cent of their profits to prop up poorly run football clubs are surely at an end.

And today, football clubs are still falling into the same trap, spending money they don't have for players, then somewhere along the track asking, 'How the hell are we going to pay for all this?' Then the end of the season comes and there's red ink everywhere and they haven't won the pennant. But the real irony is that for the poor silly bastard who wins the trophy, he's got a surefire blowout in player payments for the next year if he wants his club to hold together. And so the merry-go-round goes.

I remember a seminar at Wollongong a few years back at which Kerry Packer was the guest speaker. He made the simple point that there was no money in football, not for the clubs, anyway, who have always been more about 'survival'. It was not a business, never would be, and that was that, he said. It was so true and yet it was a warning that was never heeded. Clubs these days kid themselves that they are running businesses, but they're not. They're running a heavily subsidised sport, propped up artificially by poker machine revenues from licensed clubs. The game has been overpaying its players for too many years and the game's leaders have never been able to apply the brakes.

The game can't afford to pay players $600,000 or $800,000 a season. If this madness hadn't taken place, I'm sure footballers would think themselves well paid, compared with the average bloke, if they were on $150,000 a year with the best of them getting a bit more. But it's going to take a hell of an effort to wind back from current levels. The emergence of professional rugby union with lashings of cash has further muddied the waters, creating a new market for high-profile league players and nudging rugby league clubs into paying more than they should to keep them.

At Souths, we tried to be responsible in what we paid players. We accepted that as a football club we were going to be a non-profit organisation. We always had been. But we had to make sure that we were a non-loss organisation too, because in the difficult '90s we had no way to make up losses (unlike Parramatta, pelting in $8 million or so from the leagues club) – other than by cutting back paying staff. And we got kicked out. Our approach was that the bottom line of a season should never, ever be compromised. You pay players the amount you can afford. And the division can be on a percentage basis, with the best players getting the most money. Brad Fittler deserves to be the top-paid player at Easts, but not at $800,000 or whatever, per season. There can never be justification for a player getting that sort of money.

But because clubs are their own worst enemies, in many cases run by people lacking business skills, the head body (NRL) must have powerful checks and balances to prevent the financially self-destructive behaviour that takes place. A strong salary cap which couldn't be rorted would be one part of the equation. The need would be for a no-nonsense committee putting a value on players, dictating the maximum that a club could give to a certain calibre of player. There would also need to be rules and regulations that would protect the game itself. If it had been protection of the game that was paramount, I most probably wouldn't be writing this book today.

Souths, with two potentially wealthy leagues clubs in the district, with the best junior league in the business, with a history and tradition unmatched by any other club, and with a proven ability to produce more top-flight players than any other club, would have been a prominent and permanent member of the competition. Instead the League allowed a situation to develop where other clubs were allowed to pirate good players from us . . . once the word was out that our book had been marked.

I have a document which is a reminder of the appeal of South Sydney back at the time when the Super League snatch-and-grab raid was cooking. By then, Souths had been marked down by some as having no future in the game. But a letter to the club from Channel 9's network director of sport, Gary Burns, tells of Souths' wider appeal, even when our team was struggling to match it on the field with the big spenders. Burns wrote to tell us that Souths' game against Penrith at the Sydney Football Stadium in mid 1994 had achieved the highest TV rating so far that year, peaking at 30.6, a figure that translated to 750,000 viewers across Sydney. Yet, there was already an agenda to kick us out.

One quality that went out of the game because of what happened in 1995 was respect. Within the game to that point, certain clubs might have been arch enemies, but they *respected* each other. After '95, Judases appeared within the clubs, supporting the News Limited corporate raid. It was shocking. And it killed something very fundamental in rugby league.

I blame just about everyone involved at a high level. The ARL appeared to be sitting on top of the world at the end of 1994, yet it was taking the game to a (financial) situation where it couldn't support itself. I certainly level initial blame at the ARL for its inability to keep in check the unsustainable payments to players. Then, the dead-of-night News Limited/Super League hijack was brutal and immoral. I don't believe the damage done can ever be rectified. The public saw the other codes – AFL, rugby union, soccer – sticking far closer to the old values of camaraderie and loyalty, and turned their backs on league.

League, after all, had been just a game, another sport, but a good one. But from 1995 it became a business, and a bloody bad one. Suddenly all these people were running around, the likes of 'Porky' Morgan and Graham 'Richo' Richardson. And blokes like Bob Fulton and Frank Stanton were going to England, on what was virtually a 'spoiler' operation on behalf of the ARL, to spend vast amounts on UK players who were never seen in the Australian premiership. Money was being thrust at anyone who moved . . . except Souths.

The agenda to get rid of South Sydney was around for quite a while, I'm sure. A good example of that was the way the annual Optus money, pledged to ARL clubs during the period of the war, was distributed in 1996 to the 'loyal' ARL clubs. It was no level playing field; it was paid out unfairly on a scale of success. We were at the bottom of the scale and it was very hard for us to be competitive. We didn't get the chance to get a single one of the 'Canterbury Four' (Jarrod McCracken, Dean Pay, Jim Dymock, Jason Smith), who were paid huge loyalty incentives to hop back over the fence. Instead, Parramatta got all four.

The disgraceful thing is that with some reasonableness and some care for the game, the whole bloody thing could have been worked out back in '95. They could have sat us all down in a room and we could have come up with something so much better. An option: a 12-team city/NSW competition based on all the traditional local derbies and feuds and old values of the premiership could have quite comfortably been kept going. And if there was this great push for the 'national' competition, that too could have been done. For example, Easts-Souths-Balmain could have owned the 'City' side and the national competition could have been played on a Wednesday night, or even a Friday night, so as not to interfere with the nuts-and-bolts premiership competition. The big difference between this and the Super League 'vision' would have been that the main focus in Sydney, the game's heartland, would have remained in the traditional premiership competition. Oh yes, there were solutions for sure, and all of them better than the mess we ended up with, but sadly too many people were pushing their own self-interest and their own agendas. Not enough respect for the game itself.

One of the greatest ironies of the whole Super League she-mozzle was that the bloody thing virtually saved Souths, in the short term anyway. The arrival of the Optus money, $1.8 million in 1995, got us out of a huge hole. That year things went on at the club that disappointed me, and prompted me to call in an outside audit team, KPMG. We spent more on players than we should have and it had been hard to get the complete picture of our finances. To my bitter disappointment the auditors found that we had gone into the red by $1.1 million and that we were being let down in some areas by over-optimistic estimates on incoming money.

When Optus, via the determination of its top man, Geoff Cousins, vigorously joined the fray against the Super League invaders, it saved Souths. The grant got us out of trouble. And today I feel desperately sorry for Optus, who was such a loyal and staunch supporter of the ARL side of the game (albeit in the interests of underpinning its pay TV rights). Optus didn't flinch and in the end it finished with the crumbs, Murdoch and his Foxtel having won the day.

As I write this book, I see that Optus is taking action against some of the clubs it supported because of recent deals done with rivals Telstra to display Tesltra signage. Good luck to them, I reckon. I believe that Optus showed itself to be a company possessing principles and the old quality of loyalty in the way it supported the traditional game so resolutely, although I recognise that its business rights came first.

The 1995 financial blowout at Souths was a big disappointment to me. When I'd come in as leagues club chairman in 1990, with the football club more than $1 million in the red, and we managed to settle the debt by selling the leagues club's share in the Narellan Golf Club, I told Terry Parker, CEO of the football club: 'This will never happen again here.' But it did happen again – in 1995. I was increasingly concerned with what seemed to be developing in the football club, having trouble getting answers, and it was then I called for an independent audit. Things had been done that shouldn't have been done. The move to the Sydney Football Stadium had been a success; what had been negotiated for us there had been unbelievable, with hundreds of Origin tickets and grand final tickets going along with the deal. It shouldn't have gone wrong, somehow it had, and the club was in debt. We had a budget and hadn't stuck to it. The firm brief was that the football club had to run within its means, the plain instruction from the board back in 1990. Terry Parker had been at the helm when that instruction had been breached and he should have followed what he knew had to be done. He resigned in December '95 in the wake of the audit by KPMG.

Parker knew the deal; he knew that if the club ever got back into debt, he was gone. I was bitterly disappointed. 'I could fight this,' he said to me when it came to a head and it became apparent that he had to go. 'Well, whatever happens you won't be here, Terry,' I replied. We let him go quietly and gracefully. I think he should appreciate that.

The years 1995–96 were bloody awful ones for rugby league, with the game on the paddock almost totally submerged by what was happening off it. Fans stayed away in droves and TV and radio ratings plummeted. Rugby league was changed forever and many dilemmas for the game's future emerged.

One of them was whether selfless unpaid officials would continue to align themselves with a game in which first-graders were paid obscene amounts of money, traditional clubs were cut or merged, and a media company, concerned overwhelmingly with the bottom line, ran the game for its own end (to flog pay TV subscriptions). Hardworking people – in the juniors, in the bush, and linked to the great clubs – were once the lifeblood of the game and have provided its support base since 1908. For them the reward of involvement had nothing to do with money. It was to do with enjoyment in seeing young kids come through the grades, and perhaps go all the way in the game. It was in the love they had for a club made up of like minds. Winter lives of countless thousands over the seasons had revolved around that. In 1995 there was a change, and suddenly everyone wanted a dollar out of the game, or, preferably, bucketloads of them. A respected league historian, Dr Andrew Moore, wrote that he believed the lifeline that had always linked the players and the working-class people who supported and loved the game had been severed forever once the players were suddenly elevated to the huge payments levels that came post-1994. The $30,000 worker with a mortgage could no longer relate to the now $500,000-a-year footballer who had once lived down the road.

For Souths, they were unsuccessful years. We fielded teams that were under-funded, in a period in which the focus was on developing the leagues club, and during which we operated with the aim of keeping football club spending to what we could afford. At the time the war broke out, the refurbished leagues club had just re-opened its doors. Alan Jones was on board at the club, bringing many positives. A bloke who tends to polarise people, Jones had his critics too, and increasingly so as the losing performances mounted. But it was a period of regrowth, and a difficult one. Clubs go through different eras, and this was one of ours.

Alan Jones has been a terrific fighter for the principle of Souths' right to survive, never taking a backwards step on that issue. Whenever I have gone to him and asked for help, he's been only too happy to do it. Between him and me there is friendship and respect. Plenty of Souths players have benefited from the help that Alan has provided. But we have had our differences. I remember at the time the big wharfies' dispute was on, he had taken the government's side, and given the wharfies a big pay, on TV and radio. He was in the club the following night and I said to him: 'Alan, do you realise where you are? You're in Redfern. If you keep going on the way you've been going on about the wharf labourers, Big Tosser will finish up grabbing you by the scruff of the neck.'

'Who's Big Tosser?' he asked. I told him that Big Tosser was the *real* big bloke who sat on the stool just inside the door of the downstairs bar. 'I'll have a go, y'know,' said Alan defiantly.

It was in late '95 that we started the long process of talks with Souths Juniors, seeking a merger arrangement and a financial commitment from them that would see the Rabbitohs through. The Juniors at that time had $19 million in reserves, and spent around $1.3 million a year running the junior league. Our board, me included, was prepared to step down and hand them control if the deal came off. The concept virtually was for 'one club', with two successful leagues clubs.

In August '95, we went to them seeking a $5 million rescue package to get us through the next five years. The Juniors had earlier sparred briefly with Super League, endeavouring to get a general overview of what the possibilities for the game might be via the blueprint. Juniors chairman Henry Morris told how three separate calls had been made to Super League headquarters. Requests to 'ring back' were never answered. 'We were prepared to listen to them,' Morris said. 'But after the third call we told our people, "Don't bother, don't ring again." ' The Juniors supported us and yet they baulked at taking the financial step of regular substantial sponsorship that would have guaranteed the future of the South Sydney Rabbitohs forever. In the months ahead, the situation led to some bitter exchanges between Henry Morris and myself.

The thing between us and the Juniors was like bloody *Blue Hills*. It went on and on over a lengthy period, fuelled by the media, and ebbing and flowing in what was some sort of a tactical battle as we kept the heat on them to support and save Souths, and they moved around trying to figure out what sort of commitment to make. I can say now it was never my intention to 'take over' the Juniors and shot all the money into the Redfern club and the football club. I was much more intent on them saving us! I'll tell you right now, I don't really like being a club director. At my stage of life there are other things that provide me with far more enjoyment. I just wanted to see Souths survive. I put the pressure on Henry and his board, and we tried to show the Juniors people that if they didn't stick with us in the strongest possible way then we'd be out the door. Which, sadly, came to pass.

South Sydney Juniors had it in their hands to come up early with a strategy that would have saved the Rabbitohs into the future. I did my best to ram this truth home to them. What I was talking about was saving football in the district, securing it at both senior and junior level. I never said that I was the person who had to run it, or even be part of it. And I always said that I'd be happy to walk away if people wanted someone else to do the job.

The annual turnover the Juniors had was higher than any other leagues club in Sydney, probably with the exception of Penrith. But their ratio of profit to turnover wasn't what it could have been. They were making around $2 million a year, a bloody poor return when I compared that with the (lesser) turnover and (considerably higher) profits being made by other clubs.

They were a club in the comfort zone. I went to Henry Morris and said: 'Henry, I think it is time we went and had a look at some of the other leagues clubs. To look at how they are sprucing themselves up. If we are to maintain our status as a football club in this area we have to move with the times.' But nothing happened. Souths Juniors are in an area where they have very good membership. The club started with a bang, with the energy and innovation of George Wintle, the driving force behind the foundation of the Juniors, and a man who became known as 'the King of Clubland' and 'the Pokie King' in Sydney life. To a fair extent the club has stood still since, however. And when you look at clubs like Canterbury, Eastern Suburbs and Revesby Workers, it's hard to get any other impression than that the Juniors – once the front-runners in the club world in Sydney – have stayed asleep these last 15 years.

The Juniors were offered a 100 per cent takeover of the football club and the South Sydney Leagues Club at Redfern and the chance to build something strong and lasting. They declined. If they had done it, the Rabbitohs would never have been so vulnerable as to lose its position in the NRL.

Based on revenue figures from 1996/97, I showed them that a combined operation would turn over $84 million annually, and that profits would be in the vicinity of $15–$17 million per year. Take $3 million out of that to run the Juniors (football) and, say, $5 million per annum to support the Rabbitohs, giving us a hell of a base for success, and that would still leave $9 million a year to spend on members' facilities and grants to inner-city sporting clubs! And we were offering them an asset in the leagues club now worth around $24 million; that's a licence worth $10 million, a building worth $20 million, minus the money owed on borrowings, $6 million.

In one way I could understand the Juniors' reluctance to get on the financial merry-go-round that had been created in the game by the ARL and made worse by the Super League war. Other leagues clubs had been pouring huge amounts of money annually into the black hole of football. But the Juniors didn't have to go that far.

Without a doubt, $2.5 million a year from them would have made Souths secure in the NRL with the hope that common-sense would have prevailed in the long run, and player payments brought back to acceptable levels. We would have survived that way. And the resultant security (and hopefully success) may have acted as 'bait' to attract support from someone like Kerry Packer. All Henry Morris and his board had to do back in May 1996 was nod, but they couldn't bring themselves to do it. If they had, Penrith and Cronulla, or two others, would have merged and that would have been that – we would have been in.

Rather than making the full commitment, which would have guaranteed the Rabbitohs' future – and would have got us safely through the criteria used in 1999 to judge the future make-up of the competition, notwithstanding the disinclination of News Limited to have us on board – the Juniors eventually pledged a lesser amount. Morris and co. granted us $1.5 million per year for three years, and later for an extra two years, on the condition that there were changes made to our board. I put their reluctance to go the whole way down to a lack of vision and a collective lack of confidence in their ability to run the combined enterprise we were proposing. And when they gave the $1.5 million to us they knew they weren't handing over anything that was going to save our necks. We needed them to stand taller than that. It was never my intention to up the prices on everything at the club, or to have members lose entertainment or facilities. I just suggested that they meet with a high-profile accountancy firm and work at putting a better business plan in place, one that would generate more profit on their turnover so that there was more for everybody – including the bonus of the people of the district still having the football team they had enjoyed and followed for more than 90 years.

Despite the publicity Henry Morris and I attracted at that time, we didn't have a major blow-up over it. I created embarrassment for the board at the Juniors, I know, by publicly exposing the club's annual figures. I did it to build pressure on them to implement a better business plan that would bring in a bigger profit, simply to save Souths.

The pressures on Souths grew in 1996, and especially after an awful day on which the team was beaten 62–0 by Easts (Sydney

City). One of our greats from the past, Jack Rayner, provided some balance to the criticism we were copping when he recalled his first two years at the club, 1946–47. In those two seasons Souths won one game in 28. In sport, success comes in waves.

In May '96 the Juniors knocked back our request that the two clubs merge, and that they virtually take us over. The newspapers called it a 'fatal blow'. 'Souths sink: Juniors bolt, Jones jumps', declared the *Sydney Morning Herald*, with a reference to the fact that Alan Jones was to leave the club at the end of the year. I was bitterly disappointed at the Juniors' decision, made by seven directors without any consultation with rank-and-file membership. I told the media I thought it was up to the 50,000 members whether they wanted their district to have a first-grade side. We were up the creek without a paddle, but I wasn't going to give up just yet.

In the weeks ahead, the newspapers speculated widely and wildly on our possible future. We were linked to the idea of an inner-city 'super club' when SFS Trust chairman Sir Nicholas Shehadie called a meeting, involving us, the Juniors, the Tigers and Easts. It came to nothing. Then there were proposals that we would unite with the Sydney Kings basketball franchise and soccer's Sydney Cosmos in some sort of across-sport deal. The following year there was speculation about us doing a deal with our district brother-club, Randwick rugby union. None of them got off the ground.

The deal that would keep us going was done closer to home, and closer to the heart, in July '96: a $4.5 million commitment from the Juniors to support the Rabbitohs ($1.5 million a year for three years, 1997, 1998 and 1999). It was a lifeline; not enough to guarantee our long-term future, but appreciated all the same. With it there came conditions – the setting up of dual-club retention committees and the appointment of Juniors board member Frank Cookson to replace Alan Jones as football operations manager.

At the press conference to announce the deal I paid tribute to Alan Jones: 'If it wasn't for him we wouldn't be here to make this announcement.' It was true; Jones had worked flat out to help keep the club alive. In the *Daily Telegraph* Ray Chesterton wrote: 'It [the $4.5 million] is a sizeable amount that ensures Souths' survival until 2000 . . . what happens from 2000 is still uncertain.' They were prophetic words.

10. The Day the ARL Threw in the Towel

> Every Kingdom divided against itself is brought to desolation; and every city or house divided against itself shall not stand.
>
> *Matthew 12.25*

IN EARLY OCTOBER 1996, the full bench of the Federal Court stiff-armed Justice James Burchett and the decisions he had made in favour of the Australian Rugby League. Justices Lockhart, Sackville and von Doussa overturned every decision that Burchett had delivered, although leaving completely untouched his scathing written judgments on the shameful way people on the Super League side had behaved during 1995.

The finding was based on section 45 of the *Trade Practices Act*, which essentially says that if two competitors get together and make a deal, they can't exclude other competitors, or exclude receivers of their supply, or a portion of the market. Super

League won the case because it established that to injunct it permanently from setting up its own competition was an unfair denial of services – unfair exclusion. (There was a later irony in this decision, when we used that very argument in going to the full bench of the Federal Court with our appeal in 2001.)

Even if the legal world collectively nodded its head in technical agreement, for the traditional side of rugby league it was a shocking and bewildering turnaround. As Ken Arthurson later wrote, it was like winning a match 100–0 one week, then losing 100–0 the next to the same team, the only difference having been the appointment of a new referee. The full bench decided, as it had to, on strict legal grounds; the unchallenged fact that deceit, dishonesty and immoral business behaviour had backed the Super League raids counted for nothing. The decision, backed by the later High Court rejection of the ARL's application for leave to appeal, meant there would be two different competitions in 1997 for the first time in the history of the game. It also convinced me that the law, very often, is an ass.

The Super League victory left many people with decisions to make. 2UE's Ray Hadley was one. Hadley had seemed to be in there fighting pretty strongly for us and the ARL in the early days. But Ray, seemingly, had an instant change of heart on rugby league in the wake of the Federal Court decision, and switched in the blink of an eye.

I remember where I was when I heard Ray's announcement – down at our property at Lake Conjola. I heard the news of the court decision on 2UE and then Hadley making his declaration, which was along the lines of: 'The full bench of the Federal Court says the future is Super League, and I'm afraid we have to like it or lump it. In my case I'm going to like it. It was an unarguably comprehensive win for Super League and News Limited and we have to accept that. It does not matter whether your sympathies are with Super League or the ARL – the battle is over. After Friday's decision, I'm afraid the slow lingering death will be that of the Australian Rugby League.' In a single bound, he had jumped straight back over the fence. Gee whiz, Ray, I thought to myself, I'm glad I'm not fighting alongside you in the trenches!

The *Telegraph Mirror*'s Peter Frilingos, who worked with Hadley on 2UE then, had aligned himself with Super League from April, 1995. Until then he was seen as a journalist very closely linked to ARL heavies John Quayle and Ken Arthurson (some at the paper thought *too* closely) and in 1994 he had written a strong anti–Super League piece under the headline 'Super-league: It won't work'.

In addressing the rumours filtering through the game of a Super League breakaway, Frilingos had written:'Which brings me to the latest and most stupendous game of chance ever promoted since league kicked off in Australia in 1908 . . . instead of a game of chance involving the rank and file punters, it will feature those standby backers, media tycoons Rupert Murdoch and Kerry Packer.' Frilingos continued: 'The only vocal supporter at this stage is Bronco boss "Porky" Morgan who believes his club will continue to be ravaged by those running the game until his version of how the game should be run is in vogue. There is also said to be limp-wristed support from Canberra and the Auckland Warriors, but nobody wants to put their hand up in public. If the Warriors' involvement is a fact, they should do the decent thing and pull out of next year's premiership to prepare for their own Mickey Mouse competition, wherever that may be.'

Frilingos posed the question: why would News Limited, a front-runner to replace Winfield as the game's major sponsor, plot to dismantle one of the world's most successful premierships? Why indeed! Concluding his article, he called on the people behind the 'breakaway league' to 'at least have the gumption to spit out their agenda and admit their motivation is the dollar, not their version of what's allegedly good for the game'.

Despite the undoubtedly honest sentiments of what he wrote in '94, Frilingos quickly 'saw the light' – a very different light – in the wake of the Super League April Fools' Day raids of 1995. News Limited is a large and powerful organisation and he had worked there for a long time. On a single day, he became the frontman for the new movement via his newspaper, and a true believer to boot. I've known Frilingos for a long time, and I'd have no problem talking to him if he rang tomorrow and wanted to talk about football or anything else. There is nothing personal. He probably did what he believed best within the organisation that he works for.

There was a lot of fence-jumping, soul-searching and soul-selling, and the game and its culture are so much weaker for all that. A lot of people benefited from what happened in 1995. Some blokes that you would expect to be solid just crumbled.

In early 1997, stories appeared in the papers suggesting that I could be in line for the presidency of the NSWRL/ARL, with Ken Arthurson's days numbered. I thought little of it at the time, but on reflection now, I wish they had given it to me, despite the fact that by the end of '97 the ARL was no more than a Claytons organisation because the game belonged to Murdoch.

I'll tell you something, we would have had a solid business plan in place now (one that made sure that player payments were kept within reason, for instance). I would have loved to have taken over the job, to pick solid blokes who weren't afraid to have a go and didn't have vested interests and agendas – blokes who only cared about the best interests of the game. With the right people along-side me I could do it right now, turn the bloody thing around, hopefully rescue something solid and good from the mess. But I'm a realist too. I accept that at my age I've got a use-by date. I'm not going to be in league for any sort of long haul. You can't be some silly old fuddy-duddy wanting to run the game for the rest of your life. The quest should be to find smart young blokes of principle and work with them to lay down the right platform, away into the future. It's pie in the sky, of course – you'd need a nuclear weapon to get the incumbents out.

In the split competitions of 1997 that followed 1996's Federal Court decision, the ARL had far the better of things, particularly thanks to a great Newcastle v. Manly grand final, a wonderful game, snatched by Newcastle in the last minute through a Darren Albert try. And the other mob knew that; they knew they were running a very poor second and embarrassed by a pathetic 'World Club Challenge', which was supposed to have been a highlight of their season.

It didn't worry me one bit when the Murdoch mob went their own way in '97. I knew where the true and real things lay, and that was within the ARL comp. Souths' season was a struggle – a good start under Ken Shine's coaching and then a decline to a 4–1–17 record for 11th placing.

By the end of the year, the game belonged to the boardrooms of News Limited and Kerry Packer's outfit. Packer had to put in to keep clubs like Souths going, and he just didn't want to keep doing that. In the end he probably had what he wanted, the good sporting 'product' for his TV network, and the other bloke (Murdoch) got to run the game. The game's new administration talked the rationalisation bullshit, clubs crumbled, and if Souths hadn't bucked so hard they probably would have got away with it. The general theory back then was that Souths would automatically go into a merger with Easts. There was only one big stumbling block with that: Politis and Easts were only interested in a takeover.

In January '97 had come final proof that rugby league had lost control of its own destiny. Kerry Packer jumped the fence and got into bed with the 'enemy': Channel 9 announced that it would be televising Super League matches. Packer had been very good to Souths, with his gift of $750,000 back in 1994. I hoped he admired the tenacity of our fight. I remember a day when young James Packer came up to me and extended a hand and thanked me, and said how appreciative he was that Souths had stuck so strongly behind his father's organisation. Now, Packer and his TV channel were with Super League. Business and the bottom line had won – and it was a huge disappointment. Kerry Packer had seemingly been rock solid with the ARL since that February meeting in 1995. Then suddenly – bang! – and he's over the fence.

At the time it happened, I recalled something that had taken place some time back. On a handshake deal I had agreed to sell a house to a bloke I knew vaguely. He was heading into a real estate agent's office at the same time that I was going in to put my house on the market. 'Are you in the market to buy a place?' I asked him. 'Yeah, George,' he said. 'Well, I've got one for sale . . . if you like it, how about we do a deal, and cut out the agent's fees?' So he had a look, and he liked it, and we shook hands on the deal. Previously, I had offered the house to my brother Wal, who'd turned it down. Close to settlement day Wal came to me and said: 'Listen, I've changed my mind . . . I'll take that house.' At almost the same time, the bloke I'd shaken hands with contacted me: he'd hit a hurdle and couldn't settle on the agreed day. Technically I could foreclose on his deposit of whatever it was (two or three thousand dollars perhaps) but I said to him: 'Mate, no worries. If you're telling me you're going to buy it I'll keep it for you until you have the money.' It was a deal and it had to be done. If I had done the wrong thing to that bloke it would have worried me for the rest of my life.

Channel 9's directors had walked in and done a rock-solid deal with the ARL. Now, in the twinkling of an eye, they had changed their minds. I hope it worries *them* for the rest of their lives. There are things in life that come under the heading 'principle'. When you've done a deal with people and you fight a battle, you don't just dump them and join the other side. What Channel 9 did certainly wasn't the South Sydney way. Did Kerry Packer forget the 1965 grand final? Did he forget '68 and '71 and all the pleasure he'd got out of the bloody joint over the seasons? He knew that sport was sport, not business – he'd said that in a speech he had given at Wollongong. And yet he'd jumped. As someone said to me afterwards, when it comes to big guns of business, if it's a matter of insulting each other or insulting the masses, they'll insult the masses every time. Kerry Packer had threatened us with his 'I'll sue the arses off you' declaration in 1995. Back then he had told the meeting at Phillip Street that, as far as he was concerned, the contract he had with the game was with every single one of us. Well, I believed I had a contract with him too, and that he should have stuck with that. But he didn't. He just shoved us to the wolves.

The other side of the coin was the Optus people. Geez, they were solid. They did a deal with us early and they stuck. I haven't got a clue how many millions they poured into the game. They were old style in their approach. To them, a deal was a deal.

Only in the cold, hard business sense could I understand Channel 9's decision. Packer well understood that there was no money in football, but he knew too that his TV station, and pay TV outlet Optus (in which he held 5 per cent, with an option for another 20 per cent), were in danger back then of being cut off from the product, rugby league. But I still believe if he had stuck with the ARL in the 12-team competition he would have got what he wanted.

I honestly believe, too, that if the ARL clubs had stuck together and toughed out one more season, in 1998, that Super League would have fallen on its face, and News Limited would have packed its bags and departed, poorer, but wiser. That belief held by Souths was the reason we voted against the 'amalgamation' plan trotted out at the meetings – the blueprint to bring the two competitions together and eventually reduce the number of teams to 14 – held at the Sydney Football Stadium in December 1997. Despite all the hype, Super League had had a poor and unconvincing season and vast amounts of money had been poured into that black hole. At one stage the *Sun-Herald* ran the headline 'Let's face it – Piggins has rolled Rupert' above a story recording how badly things were going for Super League. I doubt Murdoch would have been impressed.

The World Club Challenge – touted as being a highlight of the season – turned out instead to be one of the greatest farces ever perpetrated on the Australian sporting public, with ludicrously one-sided results as the Australian teams dominated, and with no crowd interest. We had the other mob on their knees by the end of the '97 season but we let them get up because of the incessant PR spin that called for the end of the war – a war that we hadn't started. By eventually going over to the new merged competition – a competition owned and funded by Murdoch – we allowed the ARL 'fleas' to triumph.

I did my best to convince the ARL clubs that we were in front and should keep going. There was plenty of wheeling and dealing going on in the background, and I doubt that we were being told the full story at any stage, as Neil Whittaker (ARL) and Ian Frykberg (Super League) worked in secret to try to find the solution that News Limited and Super League desperately needed. There were a lot of lies told at that time about the inflated financial standings of ARL clubs. It's now very apparent that there were many things not disclosed, or fibs, told about the likes of Manly, Norths, Wests, Balmain, Illawarra, Cronulla and Penrith. Because of the way the game had been administered (or not been administered) clubs were in deep trouble financially, thanks to the willy-nilly spending on players and a joke salary cap. Clubs had become expert over the years at disguising their financial standings. I have no doubt many of the ARL clubs saw the prospect of News Limited money in a united competition as a godsend, as something that could rescue them from the deep shit they were in. It was an easy option for them to forget tradition, ignore the shameful things that had been done to the game, and vote to get into bed with the enemy.

The amount of double-dealing that went on in the lead-up to the 'historic' meetings of December 19, 1997, which sticky-taped the two sides of the game back together, was bloody breathtaking. I wasn't going to be invited to be part of any board or committee that might run the thing. I wasn't wanted and Souths weren't wanted.

What had gone on for two years leading up to that meeting appalled the huge majority of people who had any feeling for rugby league. In that regard, the lack of protection or protest from government – state or federal – on the 1995 News Limited–backed raids on the game, and the subsequent events that culminated in the axing of Souths, was nothing short of shameful. But no surprise. Politicians have never shown a lot of ticker when dealing with things that might rattle the cage of a Packer or Murdoch. Confronted with power, influence, media empires and big money, most pollies tend to think about self-preservation. From Howard, Beazley, Carr and Chikarovski there wasn't a yelp, publicly. The silence was deathly, and disgraceful.

When swim coach Gennadi Touretski hit the headlines after anabolic steroids were found in a safe belonging to him in early 2001, Prime Minister John Howard came out swiftly in defence of the Australian swim team. He aligned himself with them, declaring them squeaky-clean, wonderful sports men and women. It was a classic example of political opportunism. When rugby league was bleeding in the mid '90s, nothing was said.

I remember December 19 well, out at the Sydney Football Stadium. Neil Whittaker and Ian Frykberg had done some sort of private two-step all year, trying to put together a 'deal'. There had been too much secrecy and it had been very hard to find out the real story of any progress made. But there was a sense of desperation among some to get a deal done – *any* sort of a deal.

For years some of the clubs had lived the lie that everything was alright financially, refusing to face up to the problem of inflated player payments. I would suggest, though, that even more of the desperation existed on the News Limited side by December 1997. It was burning bonfires of money, daily, on the game; it needed an out. Luckily for News there were more than enough ARL clubs wilting too (having overspent to buggery) and desperately in need of a rescue operation. Rupert Murdoch, riding in with bucketloads of cash, was seen as the great white hope.

At the SFS that day, Whittaker and Warren Lockwood, president of the NSWRL, brought all the club presidents and chief executives into a room and spelled out the reasons why we had to join forces with the Super League clubs in a 20-team competition in 1998. All the club boards were present at the ground and after the initial briefing, each club was allocated a private box. In the Souths box, we decided we'd vote against. Souths weren't in anyone's equation. I knew that to put my hand up that morning was to vote for my club to be eliminated from the competition before long. I didn't believe that what was being proposed was in the best interests of South Sydney Football Club, or its people. I felt we were entitled to stay with the 12-team competition under the ARL banner. We weren't about eliminating anyone, and we sure weren't about eliminating ourselves; but we knew that a 'yes' vote to what News Limited was seeking meant exactly that.

So we went back to the combined meeting and voted no. And so did Balmain, a fellow foundation club. Their later capitulation to an unwanted merger with Wests was a pretty bloody weak effort, but at least they were solid that morning, while all around wavered. I remember Balmain president John Chalk ringing me at home after the meeting. 'I'm with you all the way, mate,' he said. 'We'll stick together . . . we'll fight this fight together, all the way.' Oh yeah? In 1999, the Tigers were gone. Their true fans remain filthy about the way they believe they were conned into the Wests merger. As for us, we had travelled 92 years along the premiership track with the Tigers since 1908, and stood side by side with them in resisting the proposed Frykberg–Whittaker deal in 1997. At the first sign of pressure they had turned their toes up.

Former NSWRL chairman Tom Bellew, then boss of the Gold Coast Chargers, made probably the most telling point at the meeting: 'What concerns our club is that we are handing over our destiny to be determined by a company whose directors we don't know, whose power and functions we don't know in detail and who will be deciding, on criteria we don't yet know, our futures as clubs.' Yet clubs rushed to put up their hands and News Limited got exactly what they wanted on that December 19 morning.

The arrangement was for a reduction from 20 teams to 16 in 1999 and a further drop to 14 – the 'magic' number – in 2000. There was no doubt at all now that Souths were under the blow-torch. It was quite clear that day that some sort of deal had been done between News and the Packer organisation. This was the formula clubs bowed to: 'We're going to be partners, now this is what we want you people to do to make sure that we get what we want.' And clubs that were once so loyal to each other, and to the traditions of a great game, went right along with it. I didn't hold back when the media asked me what I thought of it. 'Anyone who doesn't think Rupert Murdoch has won this war is kidding themselves,' I said. 'This is a win for Super League.' The Murdoch papers trotted out bullshit headlines such as 'It's party time'. As far as I was concerned, there was no reason to party. Jack Gibson referred to the game as 'still in intensive care, still under sedation'.

The ironic thing was that despite the way I feel about the Murdoch mob, I believe they showed more genuine loyalty to their clubs than 'our' mob did to the ARL clubs. In the main, News Limited continued to strongly back and support its Super League 'foundation' clubs (although outriders like the Western Reds (Perth), Adelaide and the Hunter Mariners got sacrificed in the deals done), while the ARL clubs were pretty much thrown to the wolves. Look at the list:

Gold Coast – kicked out, financially sound
Souths – kicked out, financially sound
Manly – merged
Norths – merged
St George – merged
Illawarra – merged
Wests – merged
Balmain – merged

Talk about a shame file. That's eight ARL clubs who are either gone, or who have had their identities changed forever. If anyone tries to tell you the December 19 deal was a fair and equitable arrangement, just draw their attention to that.

On that fateful day, only two clubs stood strong: Souths and Balmain. Both of us voted against what they were proposing.

The rest collapsed or jumped gleefully. Before long one of the two was to succumb to the lobbying and the pressure and go meekly into a merger. It wasn't us. The people driving it tried to bluff us after the meeting, telling us that if we didn't sign the document agreeing to a 14-team competition in 2000, we wouldn't be taking the field. We initially called their bluff. 'If you want to cancel a game, well, go ahead and cancel it,' we said. 'But we'll be there to play.' The pressure was still on us to sign when we turned up at Ericsson Stadium, Auckland, in our opening round game of the 1998 season. There were threats about the game being called off, but I told our CEO Darrell Bampton not to sign. We played – and won. Eventually, on advice from our lawyers when we got back home, the document was signed. We decided that under the threat of money being held back, which would mean not paying our players, it was better in the circumstances to sign. With our reluctant, last-minute signing we attached a letter stating that we retained our right to sue if we were dropped from the League and that we had complied with the signing 'under duress'. In late '99, NRL chairman Malcolm Noad went public on the document in yet another tactic to put pressure on us to merge.

Soon after the December '97 meeting, a story appeared in the Murdoch *Daily Telegraph* under the headline: 'Souths high on list of clubs to be cut'. It was another of many indications of the agenda: rugby league without the Rabbitohs. And when we bought big to try to strengthen our position, secure our future, almost immediately there were people running around saying 'Souths can't pay!' Well, of course, we always could pay – as we had done for the past 90-plus years and will continue to do in the future. Yeah, we spent a fair bit of money in 1998–99, but unlike some others (Norths, for example), we didn't go beyond our means. In 1999 the papers guessed we had plunged $5 million into the campaign to build a winning side, and they were close to the mark.

With the extra influx of money from the Juniors and the

pressure building up because of the criteria that would be used to judge clubs, we went to another level with our spending and team building for season 1998. The decision was made at Souths to spend up to an extent, to hit it pretty hard and try to have a successful year. We had the money from the Juniors and the clock was ticking. This, after all, was to be a crunch year leading towards the season when clubs would be cut from the competition because of the dictates of an outside force. The mob now running the game, the NRL, bowing to the wishes of their News Limited masters, were hellbent on reducing the numbers of teams to 14. And we were in their gunsights. By South Sydney standards we bought big, but within budget. The Juniors were involved now and we wanted to show them we could run the darned thing to a budget, as we had always said we could. We bought a string of players – Tim Brasher, Chris Caruana, Julian O'Neill, Mark Carroll, Terry Hermansson, Sean Garlick among them – and I've gotta say, I thought the purchases were okay really. And we bought a coach, Steve Martin; he proved to be a stubborn bloke and the season was pretty close to a disaster in the end.

Martin was a coach without a job when we picked him up. I can tell the story now that Mark Murray (currently coaching Melbourne) could have had the job after we had trimmed it down from a field of about 11 applicants. One day, when we were getting close to a decision, I asked him for his 'best price' – and he gave me a figure which was still well above what Martin was chasing. It put Mark out of the running. Murray subsequently told Jack Gibson, who was supporting his bid, that he would have been quite prepared to negotiate. ('Why the hell didn't he give us the bottom-end price, the price he would have taken?' I asked.) So we gave the job to Martin and in the end he turned out to be a big disappointment to us.

Martin was a product of what the game had become, an organisation which excelled in creating individuals who considered themselves bigger than the code. We told him he'd have to work with selectors, and in the beginning we gave him selectors who would guarantee him a reasonably free hand in his wishes for the side. Then, as things deteriorated, we put in selectors who we knew were strong enough to oppose him if necessary and provide some balance. Under Martin, the season deteriorated. We started '98 promisingly, with a win over Auckland in New Zealand, then lost 13 of our next 14 games. Team harmony sank. By May, the team was falling apart, with players declaring the coach 'unapproachable' and 'intimidating' at a meeting held at Redfern. John Sattler called it a 'bloody embarrassment' when Norths beat us 42–8 and there was talk of an open revolt by the players, with newspaper leaks, and Martin 'under siege'. Martin's approach was far removed from that of his predecessor, Ken Shine, and he admitted publicly then that he would have to change his style. We stuck with him in the short term. 'We are happy with the coach for the moment,' I told the media. But it didn't get any better.

Finally, Martin resigned, after we had stood him down and appointed Craig Coleman as caretaker coach. Martin made all sorts of accusations about being 'sacked', and the newspapers reported his departure that way ('Martin gets the flick'). But he wasn't sacked. It all ended acrimoniously in court, with Martin chasing a huge amount of money. The settlement figure can't be mentioned, but I can say that we were quite happy with the way things went. I don't want to say much about Martin; he doesn't rank highly with me. I'll just say this: I wonder if he's earning the same sort of money now that he could have earned from us? He got a very fair deal.

A story in the *Daily Telegraph* in January 1998 set the theme for the two years that followed. Under a headline, 'Souths fight to stay alive', journalist Tony Adams wrote: 'It's a sad indictment of the state of rugby league that the game's most successful club has been earmarked as among the first to be cut down for 1999.' He was, of course, talking about Souths.

The writing on the wall couldn't have been clearer: we had failed to secure a single representative on any of the boards or

committees responsible for shaping the game's future. We bat-
tened down the hatches. In a joint media release with Souths,
Juniors chairman Henry Morris announced: 'We're going to
fight with every last ounce of breath in our body.' The fans
showed what they thought about tradition when 28,310 of them
turned up to watch us play Saints in the annual Charity Shield
game. But it was mainly downhill from there. In May a story in
the Murdoch *Sunday Telegraph* declared: 'If the NRL stick with
the criteria they officially released last Friday the Rabbitohs are
next to no chance of standing alone in the 14-team premiership.'
The selection criteria, built on shifting sands, was made up of
three steps: the basic criteria, the qualifying criteria and the selection criteria, which covered such things as crowds, competition
points, gate receipts, profitability and sponsorship. In my view it
was full of holes, and never anywhere near a level playing field.

In the wake of a Souths Juniors' decision regarding financial
support on July 7, 1998, the media wrote our obituary. Included
in the headlines were 'End of the road for Rabbitohs', 'Club must
merge or die', 'The death of a tradition' and 'The end of an era'.
In the lastest step in the long-running saga of the Juniors and us,
Henry Morris had announced that the Juniors had knocked back
a business program we had put forward and that the $1.5 million
a year support of Souths would finish at the end of 1999. 'We just
haven't got the bugs bunny [money],' said Henry. The media had
me 'fighting back tears' after the meeting and, yes, I was very
upset. But the headlines suggesting we were finished were a little
premature. Suddenly the word 'merger' was right back on the
agenda, and even I talked of the possibility, although I never saw
it as a fair dinkum solution – unless it was us taking over some
other joint.

The only sort of merger that had any appeal to me for South
Sydney was the sort of one that St George put together with
Illawarra: Saints kept their colours, their name and their identity.
I don't think anyone in the game doubts that they are in the
driver's seat. I would not be part of anything that was less than a
'takeover' for Souths. Having said that, my position at Souths has

always been that if there is a group of people within the club who sees it differently, and who can get the required number of signatures (100) to call a special meeting, then I would not resist that. And if the members at that meeting voted for some lesser merger arrangement, then I would accept that. I would wish them well, and then walk away.

In the wake of the Juniors' decision, merger rumours, stories and occasionally even fact, appeared almost daily in the newspapers. Cronulla's Peter Gow 'generously' hopped in, stressing that any merged (Souths–Cronulla) team would have to play out of Shark Park and be called the Sharks. The Juniors had an information session with Cronulla, and Bernie O'Neill and Ray Furse from our club met them subsequently too; but despite forces working to push it, such a deal was never on as far as I was concerned. The talks that took place never had my blessing. On June 11, 1998, I told the media: 'Souths have no desire to talk to Cronulla or anyone else until we see if we can stand alone.' The News Limited papers were happy to fuel the merger possibilities, especially the *Daily Telegraph*. Mergers, after all, were in line with the News/NRL desperation to get the competition down to 14. Balmain's Daniel Munk said his team would be happy to talk. Even Penrith were mentioned as possible merger partners for Souths.

Relationships between the Rabbitohs and the Juniors sank to a low ebb after their decision to end funding. In the *Sydney Morning Herald*, Roy Masters called it 'The Great Rabbitoh Schism', and wrote of 'war' between Henry Morris and me (which there never was). I likened us to 'beggars' trying to get money out of them, in the wider interests of the district; Peter Frilingos wrote of Souths as a 'smoking ruin'. I even raised the possibility of calling an extraordinary annual general meeting and taking on Morris for the chairmanship of the Juniors, even though it was not something I wanted to do. My view was simple enough – that we *would* die as a stand-alone club without the continuing support of the Juniors.

It had been a stinker of a season: a 5–19 record for a team which had the ability to do far better; ongoing dramas with a difficult coach (and then a pending court case over his departure); growing pressure from the people who owned and ran the game to corral us into a merger; and the possibility of no further sponsorship support from our backers beyond 1999. These were times about as hard as any that a South Sydney team has ever faced.

11. Bali to Dubbo: A Bad News Odyssey

> At times football heroes have fallen short of our expectations in their personal lives, but is it fair to put players on a pedestal, a position they never requested, when all they really asked was to be judged on the basis of how they performed on the field?
>
> *The Jack Gibson collection in* Played Strong, Done Fine

THE END OF 1998 through to the beginning of the 1999 season was an awful period for South Sydney, at a time when the News Limited noose was tightening on us, and we were desperately working to get everything right. We copped some of the worst publicity the club has ever had because of the bad behaviour of some of our players first in Bali, in November '98, and then in Dubbo after a Country Carnival match in February '99. Some of the headlines were shockers, particularly the *Sun-Herald*'s approach to reporting the alleged rape of an Australian tourist in

Bali. The newspaper's treatment of the story gave the impression that Souths players, who were called into a police line-up, were involved in what took place. As was proven at the time, they weren't. But there was trouble elsewhere on that end-of-season tour too, including fights between Souths players in the Barong Hotel at Kuta Beach, incidents that found their way into the headlines. It wasn't good. The timing was bloody dreadful.

Some of the new breed of South Sydney players had gone away representing their club at a critical time in its history and done some dumb things. I wasn't there and I won't defend for an instant what took place. But I will say this: in rugby league I have been seeing and hearing of similar things from other players from other clubs for donkey's years.

In both the Bali case and later in Dubbo, when Julian O'Neill was pinpointed as the culprit, there was more than a little hypocrisy in many people's reactions. Some of those within the game who were feeding on what took place – and fuelling it – had been on overseas trips where far worse things have gone on than what took place in Dubbo. And I'm not defending that either. It was plainly a disastrous start for the club in 1999, a year which we desperately needed to be a good one for us.

I'm not about to revisit the damned Dubbo thing in detail. Anyone reading this book will have read the story over and over, considering the way the Sydney newspapers hammered it in February–March of 1999. A drinking session in a Dubbo motel room after a Friday night match against Wests led to some disgusting and unacceptable behaviour including the smearing of faeces on towels and elsewhere and the 'trashing' of the room. Furious when I heard the news, I told the media: 'What happened in that room was absolutely disgusting. They were the acts of animals, not human beings.' Andrew Denton, as angry as anyone about the Dubbo incidents and the shocking publicity it had drawn, said it for many fans: 'Souths are going to have to have one hell of a season to recover from this and survive, on top of everything else that has happened.'

I can't say too much more about what went on up there,

because there's a court case still pending. But I'll say the one thing I know: that alcohol is always behind those sort of things. It was in Bali, and it was in Dubbo. I've seen plenty of it over the years. I wasn't in Dubbo, but what took place raises a question for travelling sporting teams: when does the duty of a manager or director stop? Should he be around checking the rooms at 2 or 3 in the morning? At that time in 1999, we shared the ugliest headlines you've ever seen with North Sydney club, who grabbed their own share of the action when four of their players were involved in a nightclub fight in Wagga Wagga.

Julian O'Neill, having something of a chequered past, got nailed with the rap at Dubbo. The accusers said it was him. *He* never said it was him. Maybe that old player's code of silence was involved – and Julian was to hint at that later. But he never gave anyone up. He copped it, went to ground for a while, and then set about trying to rebuild his life, with the club's help. I do question the decision of the motel to sell alcohol to players all through the night until 7 in the morning. Why *wouldn't* they be unruly? Should the motel not share some responsibility? I was of the belief that when anyone is intoxicated, licensed hotels and clubs had to refuse to sell that person any more alcohol, or be open to liability.

I'm pleased we stuck with Julian, despite my anger at what happened in Dubbo. One day I'll be able to tell the full story on all that. As a club we handled the issue the best way we could. Despite the media hysteria we didn't go for the overkill and lobby to have the boy banned from football for life. We suspended him from all football activities, fined him $10,000 and took our time in further examining all aspects of the matter. To cut him off would have meant an almost certain end for O'Neill in view of his previous record (sacked by three clubs, suspended by a fourth). For one, I didn't want to see the bloke finish up as some bum on a street corner. So we paused and considered, and then offered him a lifeline. Thankfully, the NRL backed us in that decision. The club helped put some things in place for him rehabilitation-wise and we adjusted the contract he had with the club so that the incentives for good money hinged absolutely on good behaviour. It was all down to him, to grab the lifeline, and save, and re-build his career. He responded, and as I write these words, Julian's career is still going strongly. In the wash-up I know we did him a great favour.

We certainly didn't contemplate doing what was subsequently done to John Hopoate by Wests Tigers in 2001, when he was pressured into quitting the game, although it proved to be a brief 'exit'. Despite the uproar, we didn't throw Julian to the wolves, we got him counselling for his drinking and arranged for him to see someone about redirecting his life, and rebuilding his image. It's been good to see him sustain and build his career from that point. I mean, what went on at Dubbo was pretty bloody degrading and I'm sure anyone who was involved regrets it. In the interest of balance I think overkill now (as in the case of Hopoate) is out of kilter when you consider the many things conveniently forgotten in the past.

What Hopoate did was silly and disgusting, and dumb. But we now know that the Wests Tigers mob, including the coach, Terry Lamb, got a great laugh out of it and so provided some encouragement to him. Again it comes back to the poor state of leadership in the game. At a well-run professional club someone surely would have stepped in right then and said: 'Hey! Cut that out. You're going to get seen on TV and the whole club is going to be in trouble.' But it was 'funny' and he was getting away with it, and no-one stepped in, so it went on to the fateful conclusion.

Hopoate was just a poor silly player who did something stupid. And everybody was so righteous about it afterwards. Rugby league can occasionally bring out the worst in people. I thought of a conversation I heard in a dressing room one day years ago – two players talking shockingly about each other's mother. Their mothers! I looked at them then and I thought, you blokes are kidding. And when Hopoate's career appeared to be at an end, I thought again of some of the things I had run up against, and of the hypocrisy and selective double standards that have existed in rugby league.

When it comes to the behaviour of football teams on tours, I can tell you that in touring with representative sides I saw things that I had never seen a glimpse of when South Sydney teams were away together. I saw some bloody disgraceful things, friggin' *dreadful* things. Again, a lot of it comes back to weak leadership. For example, I couldn't imagine that any team that went away under Jack Gibson's control would ever go over the top in their behaviour. Any player who did would be on the next plane home. Just like that. But football teams are not easy things to manage and soft management has allowed many unsavoury things to go unpunished over the years. When I was touring, I was accused of being a goody-two-shoes because I wouldn't cop some of the things that went on. My answer was, 'No, I am just a little bit older and a little bit wiser.' My view on it is this: if you've got blokes representing their country overseas or their clubs away from home, you need the right kind of ambassadors, and if they aren't prepared to be that, then they should be sent home. Rugby league, because of the 'old mates' act, has never been tough enough to do that.

I remember a nasty incident when I was on tour with the Australian team in England. A woman walked up to a group of us because we had Australian tracksuits on and struck up a conversation. Her daughter was in Perth, it turned out, and I was saying what a nice part of Australia that was etc. etc. when someone else stuck his head in and said: 'Well, what do you want us to do, f— her?' It was humiliating. 'Please don't take any notice of him . . . he's drunk,' I said, trying to placate her. I'll admit that at times it was embarrassing to be an Australian on tour.

There are different ways of 'playing up' and I suppose over the years, football teams have found most of them. Often it's just fun, and acceptable. But when it comes to things like crapping in someone's bed, it goes way beyond the bounds of human decency. I recall a day in Paris when a young French girl who spoke fluent English got on the Australian team bus to get some autographs. She got off the bus in tears, the poor thing, because of what had been said to her. It was bloody disgraceful. I wonder how the culprits would have reacted if someone had done it to their missus or their sister.

And I remember at breakfast one morning on tour one of our forwards, Ray Higgs, told me he owed me a smack in the mouth. Ray was a Queenslander and the pair of us had clashed in the interstate series that season. I said to him, 'Well, it'll be the quickest boomerang you've ever shot.' And I stared him right in the eyes. He did nothing after that. But there were things on tour that were done to some people that weren't put on others. I think they got to know me – that I draw the line on what I think is funny – and they tended to leave me alone.

Rugby league is played by strong, fit young men, some of whom will occasionally run off the rails. It will never change. Off-field incidents and misbehaviour continue to happen in the game, despite the so-called 'professionalism' that the Super League revolution was supposed to bring. I think the game is at a particularly dangerous period right now, producing a breed of young men who are hugely overpaid and hugely publicised. And because they are 'full-time professionals' from an early age, their lives are not normal ones. They move within the confines of a football club, with not much contact with the real world outside. I know that clubs are trying to balance aspects of the artificial lives that today's players lead. And so they should if the game is to produce reasonably rounded individuals, ready for the working world when their football days are over.

In this chapter discussing players' off-field behaviour, I should return to a theme mentioned throughout the book – rugby league's greatest problem, that of clubs overpaying their foot-ballers. Suddenly, because of the speed of the game and the television image, raw teenagers just out of school are becoming full-time professionals. The game fills their pockets with money and as a result of that, along with the spare time they have as non-workers, exposes them to temptations like gambling and drugs.

In my view the whole thing would be in far better shape if

we had players who worked, and for whom football was no more than just one part of their lives. Rugby league has created a rod for its own back in the money it has poured into the pockets of players in the 1990s and beyond. And it gives little indication that it has learned the lesson.

Today they'll take a talented kid straight from school, put him on a big-money contract, line him up with a TAFE course or two as a gesture to 'doing the right thing'. But it's *not* the same thing. When I started football, I used to bank two quid a week, determined to gradually build it into something. Now these kids can walk straight out and buy a $25,000 car. It is unrealistic; it is not the real world. And it is doing these young men no favours.

The whole bloody game is overpaid. We've got under-talented CEOs getting more than the prime minister and pumped-up, ego-driven coaches, who should probably at best be ordinary $50,000-a-year members of the workforce, earning $500,000 and $600,000. In the big picture, none of them are giving value for money.

And in this era of hugely inflated payments, the whole thing is propped up artificially, with the game never having a ghost of a chance of genuinely earning back what it pays out. Now and then you get a 'joke' announcement which points out the folly of what is happening, such as Parramatta Football Club announcing a 'profit' of $150,000 on one recent season's activities. In the background, glossed over, lies the small matter of $8 million or more injected by the leagues club to pay the bills and create the 'profit'. And the bloke who runs that place, Denis Fitzgerald, wants to have a shot at *me* as a 'poor businessman'! (I suppose anyone who takes $8 million out of a licensed club and puts it into a football club to produce a $150,000 'profit' is entitled to have an opinion on poor business practice.) I would like to have seen Fitzgerald take over the Souths Sydney Leagues Club and the Football Club at the time I did.

There should be an inquiry into what the people who run the game are getting. I can assure you that they pay themselves bloody huge wages, and yet no-one wants to pull them into line.

And it's not as if most of them are running successful organisations – far from it – they're in charge of debt-ridden, struggling, poorly run outfits. Most wouldn't last 10 minutes if they used the same methods out in the real business world.

When the young blokes go off the rails, as players inevitably do, they are crucified. Look at Craig Field and Kevin McGuinness from Wests Tigers in 2001. When they got into trouble with drugs you would have sworn they were mass murderers, judging by the volume of publicity they got. The media, being what it is, sensationalises such things spectacularly in the interests of selling papers and getting ratings, then defends itself by saying, 'We have an obligation to make people aware.' Well, why don't they make people aware of who the drug *sellers* are? I am not condoning what the two Tigers players did. There should be no drugs in sport. But surely there is a better way for the game to get that message across to youngsters than destroying two people it helped create. If the game hadn't handed someone like Craig Field the money it did – hundreds of thousands of dollars – maybe he would have had a job, maybe he would never have got embroiled in gambling or drugs. Honestly, with what the game has done to itself, it's amazing there is not more trouble than there is.

Back in 1990, I first sent Craig Field on in a first-grade match, against St George. The boy had a lot of ability back then; he's always had that. But he's a product of modern football and with some of them you reap what you create. In Craig, we created a young man with plenty of money in his pocket and no work ethic to get up at 7 in the morning and come home at 5 in the evening like a normal person. Out of all the codes, we (rugby league) have probably been the greatest destroyers of youth. We have largely had the wrong people running football and football clubs – and they have set the wrong examples, laid down the wrong guidelines. They have a lot to answer for. And so too do the player managers who have lived so well off the fat of rugby league's madness since 1995.

The time after football is the big worry for young players – and it is a game that can end very suddenly indeed for the blokes who play it. For every Brad Fittler, who has never had a normal working life and who, I read, is going to be turned into a TV commentator when he finishes playing, there are maybe 50 who will be discarded and somehow have to make their own way – after being plucked out of the workforce for seven or eight years, and having lost the foundation period of their working life. The game has a bigger responsibility than it has been inclined to tackle so far: to make sure that the kids finish with something positive for the future. It's a damned shame to see a bloke who's struggling and to think, gee, he should have come out of football better than that. And there are plenty of those.

There are exceptions, of course, there are stories of young blokes from Alan Jones's favourite thoroughfare, 'Struggle Street', who have grabbed with both hands the opportunities that rugby league has presented to them. Despite having stubbed his toes more times than he should have, Darrell 'Tricky' Trindall is one example. Well advised through his career, he's one of the quiet success stories of the game. He has invested wisely and well. Tricky's big chance in life – maybe his only chance – was rugby league. As a young Aboriginal kid from Redfern, he started well behind scratch, but took the advice he was given, used the natural talent he had and managed to negotiate the hurdles that he now and then put in front of himself. As a result he'll leave football in good shape financially.

The Trindall example represents one of the greatest success stories of all associated with Souths over the years; one of a number of indigenous and ethnic kids who have gone through the club, taken their chance and earned enough money to put a deposit on a house and get a start. In my own case, league gave me the chance to be a waterside worker and to work up to my own business.

It's in this way that South Sydney typifies what a good sporting club can do for its district. And I would suggest that in this age of rampant drug availability, such clubs are more vital than they have ever been to society. Clubs like Souths give young men opportunity, and provide a sense of unity, place and purpose.

They can drag kids away from the chaos that can confront them elsewhere and give them a sense of self-worth and hope. A good football club is an endless production line, bringing young men through the process, and helping shape them as better citizens and productive contributors to the community.

Yet in the game of rugby league we have a financier (News Limited) and a head body (NRL) that are about *reducing* opportunities for young men. At the Red & Green Ball held at the University of New South Wales in May 2001, Alan Jones estimated that the News Limited–NRL policy to shrink the competition, cut clubs, foster mergers and reduce the competitions that underpin the first grade costs 500 young players a year their chance to play premiership football. There is no greater indictment on the men running the game than that.

I have the fragment of a memory from my childhood, probably around the time when I first starting playing football, of a saying that once money came into football, it would kill the game. The game is now sailing close to that prediction. The question for league is: is there anyone in any sort of position of control in the game with the balls to truly address the problem? Is there anyone who's even going to try to reduce player payments? Unless they do, clubs will die. And what happens to rugby league then?

12. Into the Trenches

Rugby league clubs are like churches; many of us have one to which we feel we belong. We never go – but the moment it is threatened we rise in protective hordes.

Peter Corrigan, British journalist

TIME, THE GREAT HEALER, got us through the Bali and Dubbo incidents as we headed into 1999, arguably the most important season South Sydney had ever faced. This was crunch year; the year that we would live or die. But the same thing nagged me that had nagged me for seasons now – I was sure we were marked for extinction on some secret agenda that existed in the minds of the blokes now running the game.

I knew the behaviour problems hadn't helped the cause, and when the NRL talked of a $100,000 fine as punishment for the troubles that had occurred, my suspicions were confirmed. After all, $100,000 was a vast amount to a club in our position (although in the end, we paid nothing). The game's leaders were still hell-bent on a 14-team competition, reducing it from 1999's

17, even though public opinion everywhere was overwhelmingly that 16 was the preferred number. Radio station 2UE ran a poll on it, got a huge response, and came up with 90 per cent in favour of 16. The funny thing was that 2UE's weekend football program, after having made such a fuss about the poll suddenly went deathly quiet and barely mentioned the pro-16 result again. The support for Souths from 2UE, the city's top rating station, came almost exclusively from areas away from football. Alan Jones was wonderfully supportive throughout, and so was drive-time announcer Mike Carlton. I had some early doubts about 2UE's afternoon man John Stanley, but Stanley's support for Souths strengthened too. Sports Director Peter Bosly who was losing his own club (Norths) was also very sympathetic to the cause. There was a flicker of hope when ARL big guns Michael Hill and Colin Love came out in print in favour of a 16-team set-up, Hill backing it up with a workable blueprint. The idea disappeared down the gurgler without trace after that. News Limited wanted 14 . . .

2UE's Ray Hadley went along cosily with that plan, especially after he had gentled NRL chairman Malcolm Noad through an interview on May 9, following up a face-to-face story with Noad that had appeared in that morning's *Sunday Telegraph*. Hadley was as soft as butter on the 14-team issue, notwithstanding the fact that 90 per cent of his listeners had just indicated that they favoured 16 teams! He kicked off by mentioning the fact that Michael Hill was taking the 16-team proposal to an NRL board meeting and continued, 'Based on the article this morning in the *Sunday Telegraph* I would tend to think that he's perhaps wasting his breath.' Noad agreed, of course, and that's pretty much the way the interview went.

Much was made of the 'contractual arrangement' – that the 14 total was locked in because 18 or 20 clubs had agreed to certain things at the meeting of December 1997. What absolute bullshit! Already a number of agreements from that meeting had been changed, or not carried through. (For example, there was agreement early on that no one person would be on both the

NRL Board and the NRL Partnership; Ian Frykberg was on both. News Limited said it would divest its interest in all but one club . . . we're still waiting on that.) It was a cheery little interview. 'Have a good day down at Bruce Stadium,' said Ray to his new mate Malcolm at the end. 'I'm sure Kevin (Neil) there will look after you.'

Hadley, the bloke who had screamed and shouted in support of the ARL against Super League on *The Footy Show* back in '95, had lost me by that time. Later in 1999, I wrote him an open letter in my 'By George' column in the *South Sydney Bulletin*. Hadley had bagged Souths extensively on a Saturday afternoon show in September, supposedly based on 'mail' provided by a Souths insider, and had got things wrong. I hit back, pointed out some truths and told him that many people believed they had detected bias in his comments regarding Souths. None of it was helpful. Hadley was then the voice of rugby league and, while his anti-Rabbitohs stance might have pleased some at high levels in the game, it didn't go down well with the many people who cared about South Sydney. One of Souths' respected long-term officials made the following comment in a letter written to me in late 1999: 'Unfortunately the bias does not end with the criteria. Some of the questions asked of Noad, Frykberg, Whittaker and Co. by prominent sporting commentators have been absolutely sickening.'

We knew we would have to pull out all stops if we were to have a hope of surviving, and we revved up for the season as probably no Souths administration had ever done. We played it hard; at one stage I threatened to hand our juniors over to Randwick Rugby Club if the planning rationalisation (i.e. the axing of Souths) went ahead. In early March 1999, I wrote an open letter to Souths fans which, to the surprise of many, ended up as the major item on the back page of Rupert Murdoch's *Daily Telegraph*. It got there via a sort of challenge, with us saying: 'Look, this is newsworthy, but we know you won't publish it.' But they did, and that was good, and appreciated.

Generally their approach to me and the things I did through

the years of battle had been more along the lines of making me, and anyone I was involved with, look like village idiots. We've convinced them that we're not that. But whether it was conscience, or whatever, they gave my letter a great run in '99. The letter was a cry for help and support. 'After an off-season of dramas and adverse publicity,' I wrote, 'I urge you all to send a powerful message to the NRL, that you're not prepared to let South Sydney die without one hell of a battle.' I called to fans for their support, their cheers, their presence at matches, and promised an exciting Souths year. 'Save Souths' was the headline.

Under coach Craig Coleman, the football team went on to show that Souths' heartbeat was still strong. We had some great days, only faltering when the League outed our best player, Darrell Trindall, for seven matches. (Was that part of the deal too? I have wondered since.) Despite the fact that this occurred at a critical time of the season, round 12, we remained in finals contention until round 20. I was at the game and Tricky's tackle on Newcastle's Peter Shiels didn't draw any criticism from the crowd, the ref or his touch judges. Yet they managed to trump up a grade two 'reckless high tackle' charge and dump him for seven weeks. At that time Tricky was leading the season's major player awards, the Dally Ms, as player of the year – that's how good his form was. It was a disgraceful decision notwithstanding the fact of his previous judiciary record and it brought an avalanche of calls of protest on talkback radio. The previous week Super League loyalist Matthew Ridge of Auckland had been suspended for only one week longer after facing three separate serious charges, including one of gouging.

So much that had happened off the field had been driven by motives unconnected to the playing of pure football that it would be naive to think that some of those motives didn't carry onto the playing field too. Take Souths' 1999 season and the suspension that derailed us midway through. We were sailing along pretty well, then all of a sudden we hit a decidedly rocky road. Strange, that.

And from 1998, the first year of the reunited competition,

some of the refereeing of games has caused an amazing amount of talk around the traps. Some of the things I have heard from remarkably strong sources would curl your hair. None of the rumours are good for rugby league. Above all else, people just want a game that is fair dinkum, a level playing field.

One early game in 1999 hammered home the true message of what rugby league should be about. On March 27 we went back to the game's old headquarters, the Sydney Cricket Ground, taking an ancient rival, St George, with us. We drew a crowd of 15,324 on a Saturday arvo, and the game and the occasion were just fantastic. At halftime at the most famous ground in rugby league, as teams from the two most famous clubs took a break, Morry Anthony read his great Souths poem. 'You kill the seed, you kill the game. Don't let us disappear!' he pleaded. His last verse resounded around the ground: 'So let's all band together now, And with one voice propose, Long live league, long live Souths, Up the Rabbitohs!'

It was a marvellous afternoon, showing how good a game rugby league is and showing how *especially* good it is when you mix it with tradition and old rivalries. But the wolves were already at the gate. We had 14 players coming off contract, the rumour was that we were to be cut, other clubs were waiting to pounce on them . . . and how were we ever going to keep young stars like Craig Wing if we had no guarantee about the future? The NRL gave the other clubs a free shot at our players.

The 1999 season was geared towards the search for South Sydney success on and off the paddock as we endeavoured to build our case in the face of the NRL's criteria. In April we appointed a management team, Complete Marketing (described by the media as 'high-powered'), to support the cause. The Juniors provided seed capital of $240,000 to fund the new initiative. The team was headed by Bernie Lange, a successful businessman from Adelaide (and former AFL Adelaide Crows director), and included Paul Keogh (ex-PBL), Mark Colley (Adelaide Crows) and Angus Hawley (IMG). Lange stepped in as Souths chief executive, with

Darrell Bampton switched to general manager of football services. They were very vocal about Souths being a fantastic marketing label and, in the beginning at least, seemed to be enthusiastic and genuine about Souths having to remain a 'stand-alone' club. Their approach was totally new ground for Souths and I must say the marketing plan they put down, targeting hugely increased membership and annual sponsorship, looked at first glance sensational, if optimistic. It had never been done in rugby league before but had a solid basis in another sport and we were all hopeful.

They talked a good game, Complete Marketing. Best thing I've ever heard, I thought when they first came in and delivered their submission. Our deputy chairman, Bernie O'Neill, to his credit, was more sceptical. 'Hey, it just doesn't happen like that, George,' he said to me not long afterwards. Because of the new deal and the changes that needed to be made, we had directors who were going to lose their jobs and were far from happy about that, and others prepared to get off the board and move aside for this new group, who just might save the club. It was a big call. We had what I believed was a good board in place, a people's board, but it was such a struggle.

Others no doubt saw the board as 'old style' and 'old rugby league' and believed that in a rapidly changing game, we had to change too. The position was this: in terms of 'modern management practice' we may not have been the fanciest-run organisation. But how does 'modern management practice' stand up anyway when you consider the atrocities of HIH, One.Tel and plenty of others in the '90s? The fundamental thing was that we had *always* made the finishing line in paying players and paying our way, and we had done it without outside help. The money from the Juniors had arrived only in recent times. We had stayed afloat for 92 years, we were okay financially, contrary to mischievous rumours, and we had been frugally run, because we had to be. Okay, we weren't flash. But we were a non-profit community club and we got the job done.

Back then we were between a rock and a hard place, with

'Number 14 Group' (or 'Group 14'), a team of high-profile Souths supporters who had thrown their weight behind the campaign, urging us to make the decision to try a new path. Group 14 also set up a sub-group, the Millennium Team, designed to formulate a plan which would guide us into the new century. I doubt that any other club could have matched the 'muscle' and experience represented by Group 14, started in July '99, by Martin Lissing, Jerry Lissing and Steve McDermott, who came up with the idea of getting all the high-profile people at the club working together. Most of the people on the Group 14 list were on board already, as supporters of the club. The following were start-up members of the group, whose aim was to add muscle to the battle we were waging, to unite people in the club and to pursue something that we all believed in – that Souths should not only survive, but be one of the most successful clubs:

Businessmen: Martin Lissing, Jerry Lissing, Steve McDermott.
Politicians: Laurie Brereton, Deirdre Grusovin, Anthony Albanese, Charlie Perkins, Ron Hoenig, Vic Smith, Nick Greiner, Eddie Obeid, Michael Gallacher
Media people: Andrew Denton, Ray Martin, Don Lane, Mike Whitney, Mikey Robins, David Tapp.
Professionals: John Brown (KPMG), Michael Porra (sports marketer), David Bloom (QC), Mark McCulloch.
Sporting world: Wayne Harris.

Other prominent people joined later (officially and unofficially). The name – 'Number 14 Group' – was something Don Lane had first brought up many years before, the concept being that there were 13 players on the field, and the fan was the all-important 14th member of the team. The group of high-flyers added profile to the team and the club, especially so when keen Souths supporter Russell Crowe brought his mate Tom Cruise along to a match.

The board basically handed over the management of the club to the new marketing team for a time, and I supported it, probably without too much conviction, because I thought (well, hoped) that maybe it was the only way we could save our football club. I always had my doubts though. They were bringing in proposals that weren't the tried-and-tested football administration formulas that I had known. I was never too comfortable with the new approach that seems to be part of football these days – the bullshit marketing and the fluff. After all we had real things at Souths: the most famous jumper in the game and a tradition of success over 92 years that no other club could match.

I was never comfortable either with 'the Millennium Plan' that eventuated from this new deal at the club. I came to believe that much of it was pie in the sky. And when they asked me in the witness box at the big court case in 2000 whether it was true that I believed it unachievable, I could only be honest and answer 'yes', but that I had gone with it because I thought they *might* be right. My honesty probably didn't make our task any easier. Others on the board had more faith in the possibilities than I did, and I went with their view. Despite my misgivings about some of the people involved and aspects of what was being proposed, the fact was that during the long court case before Justice Paul Finn when we were required to prove that the money pledges were in place, Souths delivered the goods, notably so when Channel 7's Kerry Stokes came on board with big support, something that no doubt was not pleasing in the slightest to News Limited or the NRL.

To this day I don't know if it was the right decision to change things at the club the way we did in April 1999. But my firm belief now is that whatever board with whichever administration approach was in control, we would have been exactly where we are today. There are those at the club who would argue that we wouldn't have had a case to fight if we had stayed on the same track. We had been pencilled in for exclusion and that was always going to make it tough.

Sydney had been through a football war, featuring the two heaviest hitters in the Australian business world, Packer and

Murdoch, and looming over every other sport was the shadow of the Olympic Games, which were approaching and shaking up the sponsorship scene like nothing had ever done before. The marketing job was always going to be a huge challenge. But Bernie Lange's group were declaring that they were going to give us 25,000 football club members! That was the stated target. And the eventual outcome? Well, by the time they left we had built up from 500 to around 3500 and really strained to get that far. By the end of 2001 membership was in excess of 17,000.

We made progress in '99 though; by May crowds were up more than 100 per cent on the previous year, and we had signed a $600,000 major sponsorship deal with Downtown Duty Free. In late July, Henry Morris announced that the Juniors would extend their $1.5 million a year sponsorship of the Rabbitohs until the end of the 2002 season. At the same time Morris slammed the NRL for its failure to include junior development in the criteria that would decide the future of clubs. 'It's absolutely scandalous,' he said. 'It makes you think there's a conspiracy. Why wouldn't you include the life's blood of any club?'

Within Souths' changing structure there was an edge to proceedings from very early on. In the interests of the greater good of the South Sydney RLFC, three solid blokes from the old board, Ray Furse, Stan Browne and Tony Henderson, stood down to make way for representatives of the Group 14 new breed, then at an extraordinary general meeting, the remaining five members resigned, opening the way for Group 14 members to take their spots. No sooner had Lange and co. organised that with my assistance than Lange marched me upstairs at the club on the night the change took place and set me up in front of the media. 'George will be resigning in a couple of weeks,' he said, on the record (*What!*) This hadn't ever been mentioned, and I was filthy. I fumbled around the best I could. 'Yes, if these people can get everything in shape I'll be looking at moving on with the other board members,' I told them, or words to that effect. When

I came downstairs I was fuming. I bumped into state politician and board member Eddie Obeid, a member of the 14 Group and one of the blokes pushing this new deal, and I said to him: 'Look, if that's the way you blokes want to do friggin' business I can tell you I won't be doing any business with you. I don't mind being told I'm not wanted, but I don't need that friggin' idiot upstairs to be saying it in front of the reporters.' I gave Bernie Lange my resignation in writing the next day.

In the letter I called the events of that night 'disappointing and embarrassing' to me on a personal level, writing: 'I feel it could have been handled in a more respectful manner taking into consideration the way in which I have served this club at board level for more than 10 years.' Board members gave me strong support – and refused to accept my resignation. In quick time it was Lange who went, not me.

The next day, Lange wrote me a letter apologising for what he had done, expressing his hope that I would stay on the board and displaying what seemed sincere remorse. 'I can't undo the damage. I can only genuinely seek your forgiveness,' he wrote. But the alarm bells were sounding loudly for me and on reflection now, I can't get away from the thought that this new mob never stopped working in their efforts to roll us, and set up a different agenda, that is, a merger, for Souths.

They weren't in place a week and a half before Lange told us: 'We're bankrupt . . . we can't make it.' I explained to them, 'We're a non-profit operation . . . we're virtually broke at the end of *every* year!' And solicitor Ron Nathans, heading the Middletons, Moore and Bevins team, was pushing the same line, effectively putting the fear of God into us, that we were insolvent and had no choice but to roll over. It was a battle from that point on. 'We're not insolvent,' I told them. 'I don't see where you're coming from.' Increasingly I suspected some sort of conspiracy.

My theory today about what took place is this: the Lange mob came in with these high-flying plans of support and professional help and were genuine in that, but when they realised they weren't going to be able to achieve what they had set out to do, they switched course and started to push the joint-venture line. In their minds was the thought that they'd land the management and marketing job for the 'new' merged club; perhaps they'd been guaranteed it.

To be fair to them, we (the board) had appointed Ron Hoenig as our nominee to consult with and work with the new marketing group. At the start I had full faith in Hoenig – but, as became progressively apparent, Hoenig strongly supported the idea of a merger with Cronulla. You can only imagine that his views were firmly conveyed to Lange, Colley and co., as were those of Middletons, Moore and Bevins who believed that we were insolvent, couldn't win a court case and leaned towards the merger option too. Some of those were in writing, so Complete Marketing was getting some inaccurate messages, which no doubt changed their view of us. I am sure they were also being told (wrongly) that the Juniors, who were funding them to the tune of $240,000 to support our cause, wanted a merger for Souths. That was bullshit, even though the Juniors had looked into various options.

A letter from my files, sent in November '99 to our legal people, captures accurately how I felt by that stage about what had been going on within the club. After expressing my discomfort 'from the start' with Complete Marketing, I wrote:

> In my view, from the very instant they became involved they were most determined to change the structure of the board – not to represent the club to continue as a member of the NRL and to develop sustainable revenue streams from marketing based programs as they were engaged to do.
>
> . . . In my opinion Complete Marketing failed to bring any significant sponsorship to the table. In my initial meeting with Bernie Lange and Mark Colley they suggested that maybe $9 million in marketing could be achievable considering they had done something similar with the Adelaide Crows.

> . . . They were very critical of the club's management
> structure from day one – but in my opinion they didn't
> leave our office in good shape at the conclusion of their
> contract and were very disappointing.

Things happened in a great jumble that year. One of the best was
a chance meeting I had with a city lawyer and Rabbitohs supporter, Nicholas Pappas, at a big Souths fundraising function in
the Bennelong Restaurant at the Opera House, where Alan Jones
delivered an impassioned speech about how stupid and unfair the
NRL's criteria for membership were. It was a time when we
were under great pressure, with insolvency talk and pressure on
us to merge. 'George, if I can be of any assistance to you, contact
me,' Pappas said to me in a brief exchange. 'I've got a pretty fair
idea of what's going on and the thing you've got to do is do your
financial numbers.' He pressed his business card into my hand.

Nicholas turned out to be a great and committed fighter for
Souths' cause and with a couple of other young legal blokes,
Rowan Darke and Andrew Christopher, became absolutely vital
to our struggle. I invited Nicholas and the others to a forth-
coming crucial meeting at the club in October 1999 and that's
when they joined the fight to keep us alive.

Spurred by Pappas's comments I told Nolene and called Bran-
don Punter, our very capable young financial controller at the
football club, then made a further call, to Henry Morris at the
Juniors. 'Henry, I need you to do something for me,' I said. 'Can
you pay us the $1.5 million a month early?' 'Yeah, I can do that,'
he replied. The money bought us time and strengthened our
hand against those crying 'insolvency'. No, we weren't insolvent
and hadn't been and, yes, we had a business plan.

Hovering in the background right through this unsettling
period was the suggestion that a merger with Cronulla was the
best and only option for us. We were never consulted on any
other basis. Signing players was ferociously difficult because the
NRL would give no guarantee about our future. Who'd sign for
a club that may not exist? So back in '98 we had to sign blokes

for three years, including 2000, not even knowing whether we were going to be there.

The problem with sporting club mergers is that you lose the identity of the clubs involved. For all the bullshit that is talked, any merger is a brand-new identity and unlikely to be any more than a pale shadow of the clubs it represents. There's only one way to make a merger work: new colours, new emblem, three directors from each club and an independent chairman. Then you've got a *new* club, but you've also lost just about all that you had. I think mergers are a poor solution. The only deal that would have ever have suited me at Souths was a 'takeover', with Souths preserving everything it had.

In the game now there are different shades of mergers. As discussed, the St George–Illawarra merger is in fact a straight takeover by St George. Illawarra worked out from the word go that they had no money, not much bargaining power and by doing a deal they could at least retain some small part of their identity. But the club really is St George; it is not a merger in any way and if Illawarra got an even shake in that, I'll stand on my head. Andrew Denton summed it up in typical style when he observed that the Illawarra club were represented by no more than the socks the players wore. Balmain pretty much ate up Wests in their mid 1999 merger deal, although not quite to the extent of the St George–Illawarra arrangement.

To merge is to give up your history. My team is the South Sydney Rabbitohs. We comprise the entire South Sydney district; the clubs, and pubs and homes and the parks where kids in red-and-green jumpers kick footballs around. The colours belong to the district. When a bloke from New Zealand rang me one day later on, interested in 'acquiring' the colours, it registered deeply with me: 'Strike me dead . . . these colours are *ours*, they don't belong to the Auckland All Stars or the Canberra Raiders, or anyone else.' And when it came to the push for us to merge with Cronulla, the fact was, there was nothing in it for Souths. Without the artificial propping up of Super League/

News, the Sharks would probably have been broke, a club with an uncertain future.

Incidentally, among the shocking things the game's new leaders and owners have done is to make the 'home' colours of the majority of teams almost unrecognisable. And they can change from year to year, in line with trends overseas whereby football clubs change their strips yearly so that fans feel obliged to go out and buy the new one. Those things are sacrosanct. I have nothing against having different home and away strips to strengthen the marketing, but the colours should be left with their traditional designs and strength.

In '99 when various forces were trying to railroad us into a merger, Easts' Nick Politis rang me at home one morning and advised me to take the arrangement that was being offered. 'What's going on, Nick?' I asked him. 'Have you done some sort of a deal with them?' I let him know where we stood: 'Nick, you look after Easts and I'll look after Souths. How does that sound?' And the only times that NRL chief executive Neil Whittaker wanted to talk to me then were about Souths merging. It was always: 'Have you given it any consideration?' My answer was always: 'No, I haven't.'

Blokes like Eddie Obeid, who became increasingly strong pro-merger for whatever reasons, blamed me for 'destroying' the deal with Cronulla. The arrangement with the Sharks was going to be this, and it was going to be that, he told me, and if it *had* been the way it was spelled out to me, I wouldn't have objected too much. The bullshit I was being given from within our club was that the merged team would be called 'the South Sydney Sharks', playing in red and green. The club would be run by a nine-member board, five from Souths and four from Cronulla. But as I found out via the *Sydney Morning Herald*'s Roy Masters, the proposed merger was no such deal at all. It was close to a takeover. 'I would be lynched if I gave up our colours and gave up Shark Park,' Cronulla president Barry Pierce told Masters. 'Any talks would have to be beneficial to the Sharks and the game in the Sutherland Shire.'

The Cronulla rumours were always close that year. Now it was official that what was being offered to us was to be the lesser party in the merger. I thought of everyone who had come in and said Souths were going to be in the driver's seat in any deal done. It just wasn't true. I'd love to see the NRL minute books and see exactly who – from Souths – attended the meetings that were held. I wasn't privy to any of them. I was left right out of the loop. Justice Finn raised that issue in the later court case we fought. In the witness box I made it very clear that I had certainly been 'left out', as in this exchange. Mr Marr: 'You weren't told that Mr Walker [of Lang Walker] had said he was only prepared to sponsor Souths if they merged with Cronulla?' I answered, 'No, I was not privy to any of that, sir.'

I was on the outer when it came to a few things around that time, including when our mob went to the Juniors and asked for an extension from the three years of the sponsorship agreement to five years, as well as extending the business plan to five years (which was the requirement under the NRL criteria). They put the business plan to the NRL without me voting on it, or approving it. I was left right out, although I had been part of the previous board which passed the three-year plan.

There was a merger agenda at Souths at that time, alright. Blokes were off talking to Cronulla. And I know for sure they were off talking secretly to News Limited and the NRL too (although confirmation of that only emerged a little later). One player in the whole thing had regular contact with the NRL and News Limited's Ian Frykberg. There was the smell of a deal in the air, and it didn't smell good. There was no doubt in the world they were being told: 'It's you for the chop . . . you'd better do something about it.' Getting close to the crunch, they were in a state of near-panic and that's why the merger agenda came to the top of the pile. As was relayed to me at one stage from a News Limited source, Souths were seen as 'unfashionable'. Can you believe that? What garbage.

The pressures for us to merge came in different ways. Even the former NSWRL and ARL chairman Kevin Humphreys, long since gone from any official role in the game, came to me and declared, 'You've got to merge this club.' I told him straight I didn't see it that way at all. I was not surprised to hear later that Humphreys was a powerful influence in Balmain's decision, one rumoured to have been manipulated by strong outside forces, to get into bed with Wests, and a decision that many solid Balmain folk are now ruing.

By the middle of 1999, panic was in the air as the clubs under merger pressure – Norths, Manly, Penrith, Balmain and Wests – jockeyed for position. At Souths, the sixth club under threat, there was no panic, although there were ongoing developments and emerging differences of opinion that threatened to undermine us. An extraordinary general meeting voted to split the leagues club and football club. Within our club there were pro-merger and anti-merger factions and relationships progressively declined in our administrative dealings. I called a meeting at one stage and declined to invite the club's acting CEO, Mark Colley, for whom I had increasingly little regard. We were very different kinds of people and we clashed badly. Colley wrote a scathing letter to Henry Morris which was subsequently trotted out in court. It took me to task for my 'lack of professionalism', etc.

At the next board meeting at Souths Leagues Club on October 20, Mark Colley and Paul Keogh from Complete Marketing went in heavily with the insolvency story, quoting the KPMG solvency review. No doubt they were presenting the messages preached by the likes of Ron Hoenig and Ron Nathans, head of the Middletons, Moore and Bevins team. 'We've got to take heed of our legal representatives,' they said, raising the question of personal liability being lumped on the directors.

'We're not broke and I won't be part of rolling this club over,' I told them. 'You will have my resignation in the morning.' As I got up to walk out of the meeting, board member and ALP state parliamentarian Deirdre Grusovin rose. I continued, 'Whatever we do here tonight, it's got to be unanimous. Nobody is getting me to vote South Sydney out of the competition [because that's what the decision being called for meant]. Nobody . . . and we're not bankrupt.' Deirdre stayed on her feet: 'George is right,' she said. 'We can't do it.' Colley went white.

The Complete Marketing group cut their ties with the club a few days later, with Mark Colley writing that they'd felt 'increasingly uncomfortable' with the overall process of managing the club over the last two months (September, October 1999). 'It is our view that given the overall outcome of the deterioration of our role within the club we will need to conclude our professional association.' They wished us every success in the continuing battle to remain part of the competition as a stand-alone club. And the fight went on.

It was a time of deteriorating relations at the club. In truth, Complete Marketing's management was effectively 'gone' well before that final step. The relationship between me and them by then was at zero rating. And our board? Well, they were inclined to believe the solicitors pushing the insolvency line more than they were inclined to believe me. And there was concern among them about the line being pushed, that they were personally liable if the club fell over. Understandably, these scare tactics made the wives of some otherwise staunch directors very uneasy. It was only me sticking fast that eventually changed their minds. (I won't recount here who put their hands up, but I know at one stage that night I was the only person on the board adhering to the belief that we weren't broke.) And I knew that if they were going to merge the club, I was out. After that I insisted that the power had to go back to the board of the football club. This took the power away from Complete Marketing, and they were near enough dead in the water. I learned a valuable lesson: that all football club business and negotiations had to go through the chair.

After that night in 1999 when I got up to leave the board meeting and Deirdre Grusovin intervened and played her role in steadying the ship, there was much speculation over who was ready to sink Souths. I know only one thing, if I hadn't got up to walk out of the meeting, declaring that they'd have my resignation in the morning, then it would all have been over.

Nicholas Pappas showed his qualities at meetings at the club amid the dramas of October 1999, when the insolvency scare campaign and merger option were being strongly pushed. Concerned with developments within the club I invited along Nicholas and some other like-minded legal men to a meeting requested by representatives of North Sydney's fight for life and organised by Nolene. Norths were in an even worse position than us; they had already been told they hadn't passed the NRL solvency test. Norths' hope was that some sort of combined fight involving them and Souths would help the cause. Ron Hoenig was prominent at that meeting, outlining the grim scenario that Middletons, Moore and Bevins was pushing. Hoenig's agenda by that time was strongly pro-merger (with Cronulla). That night a couple of legal blokes tagged me after the meeting. 'You can't have that company of solicitors representing the club, with them trying to tell everyone that the club is gone,' one of them told me. 'You should look at changing your legal team.'

At the October 20 meeting – one Pappas remembers as a night of 'doom and gloom' – Ron Nathans of Middletons, Moore and Bevins told the meeting there was no prospect, in his view, of Souths ever succeeding in any court fight against News/NRL. It could cost $10 million and be a waste of time, he said. The advice couldn't have been any grimmer, and heads were down all around the room. Nick told the ABC's *Australian Story* program on August 2, 2001, 'There was an unbelievable sense of gloom in the place. I remember seeing tears in George's eyes and Andrew Denton with his head in his hands. I felt at that moment, at my very first board meeting, I was witnessing the death of Souths.'

Nicholas Pappas told the meeting that night about how he had been a Souths fan all his life and now here he was at his first board meeting at the club, and there were people talking about throwing in the towel and putting the jumper in a trophy case. He pointed to the people from financial experts KPMG, who had been talking about the club's 'insolvency', and asked how that was possible when the club had $1 million in the bank? The club's solicitors were starting to look very uncomfortable around this point. 'We've got to do this properly,' said Pappas. 'We've got a duty to our members, a duty to our supporters and a duty to the history of this club to investigate all the options properly.' Nicholas spoke for 10 minutes or more, and at the end of it, heads were lifting. It was an important moment in the whole thing, a turning point. The fight was now on.

Right through the whole struggle I fought hard for what I believed in and I made some friends, and lost some friends. There was bitter argument at times. Anyone who shot a brick at me . . . I shot it right back. But, in saying that, I believe that just about everyone at our club involved at a high level genuinely wanted what they saw as being in the best interests of Souths. All cared for the club. But for the ones who wanted me to be no more than a chauffeur, just driving them towards the result they wanted, they picked the wrong bloke. The channels were always there to challenge me, if they had wanted. Nobody chose to do that. I consider my fight vindicated by the transcripts of the 2000 court case (not to mention our eventual victory in July 2001). In the narrow world of the law, if ever there was a case that right was right, it was ours.

In recent times I've never been quite sure where I stood with Souths' boards. Probably some of them thought of me as a hindrance. I am black and white in my beliefs, and that's most likely a problem for some. But I do know about running football and football clubs. We had nine tough years of keeping Souths involved while we tried to build the base of a successful leagues club, only to be undermined by the government decision to give pubs poker machines, and in those nine years we got into financial trouble just once. And as soon as that happened I put a full-scale audit on it. When we won our battle I said that if some people currently on the board didn't like the way I operate and the way I like things done, then they should stand a ticket against me and let the members decide. I fought hard with some on the new board as I did with some on the old board. But I will say this: we were not gypped by anything done by a South

Sydney board of directors, we were gypped by the way the League decided to judge its criteria. That was never going to be a level playing field, and through 1999 the pressure built on the vulnerable clubs – the ones whose books had been marked.

When Balmain crumpled, and allowed themselves to be talked into a questionable merger with Wests in late July 1999, the Tigers did something inexcusable. They demanded an NRL guarantee that there would be only 14 teams in 2000, despite the huge public support for 16, and despite the fact that such a call would effectively gun down one of their 'mates' – us. I was furious and I told the media that their attitude was virtually one of 'stuff Souths!'

'Their call for 14 teams is virtually calling for the NRL to axe clubs like Souths,' I said. 'I can't help but wonder what motivates such a turnaround from a one-time ally. The call for our removal is inexplicable. Balmain and Souths after all stood shoulder to shoulder in condemning the takeover of our game.' I wrote to Balmain chairman John Chalk and told him exactly what I thought.

By then, news of North Sydney's disastrous financial situation was starting to leak out, and despite the efforts of the Save the Bears group, Norths were lurching towards an unwanted partnership with Manly. The politicking going on in the game then was amazing. A big issue for the NSW Labor Government was Grahame Park in Gosford, a ground into which they had ploughed $12 million, Gosford being a marginal seat. The government had a vested interest to make sure the ground was used in a big way: it wanted an NRL side there. So did News, to capture the potential pay TV market. Norths were heading there on their own, but managed to administer themselves a financial uppercut which left them $6 million or so in the red and on the ropes, and Manly were struggling too. The agenda was to prop up two lame-duck clubs at the expense of Souths. I made a suggestion to Eddie Obeid that we would be prepared to play six games per season at Grahame Park and six at the SFS if we were successful in the criteria process. The NRL immediately knocked that on the head.

The North Sydney–Manly merger that eventuated (they became the broke and under-achieving, and now defunct, Northern Eagles) was a sporting scandal. Norths contributed strongly to their own downfall with a 1998 season in which club management threw caution to the winds and ran up a $6 million deficit, mainly on player overspending, in their desperation to secure the Bears a sole franchise at Gosford. The blokes in charge probably qualified for worst single-year management performance in the history of the game. But for all that, Norths were dudded, brought down by agendas that had little to do with football.

Under the chairmanship of Ray Beattie in '99, Norths took a huge punt. The theory doing the rounds was that under the criteria that the NRL was putting together, any team finishing in the first five that year would automatically be selected in the final 14. So Norths threw money around willy-nilly, relocated to Gosford, but finished up having a losing season, and at the end of it, confronted a debt level for a single season that was almost beyond belief. I suspect that Norths always thought deep down that they had a 'security blanket' in the wealthy North Sydney Leagues Club, a club well run and producing whacking profits each year. Along the way too they received what they believe to this day to have been a 'nod and a wink' from NRL boss Neil Whittaker that they would make the cut and head on to Gosford to stand alone as a regional club.

Two outside factors were strongly in play in what happened to the Bears. Firstly, the pressure was right on the NRL: there had to be a team up at Grahame Park, because of the $12 million the State Government had spent, added to the Federal Government's $12 million. Secondly, Manly, down on the peninsula, once wealthy and still influential, had hit the wall hard financially. They were looking like they might miss out on the cut and were searching for a saviour. They had a trump card in Ken Arthurson, a bloke who was well connected, shrewd and capable of playing the political game.

Norths weren't interested in a merger, and especially not with

Manly. The pair had been bitter northside rivals for half a century and for anyone who knew anything about rugby league, to have them as partners was bloody ridiculous. It always was. It came as no surprise in August 2001 when it was announced that the Northern Eagles, close to broke, would be closing their doors at the end of the season, with Manly to reclaim the licence. But, as I said, there were much larger forces involved. Norths shifted to Gosford and set up offices there. And I'm sure that even despite their collapsing season in '99 they thought they'd be okay as a stand-alone club, that Norths Leagues would support them as a one-off gesture to secure their future. After all, the Bears had come through a 10-year period of achievement in which their performances had been the club's best in history, even though they hadn't won a premiership. And they had always had the luxury of something Souths could never rely on: a wealthy leagues club to bail them out.

But at the moment of greatest need, that support was gone. Powers-that-be in the League wanted Manly to be part of the ongoing structure so suddenly the merger was on the drawing board. The second leg of the double came when the Norths Leagues Club, enthusiastic backers of the football team over the years, suddenly dug their heels in. With the leagues club's support there is absolutely no doubt that Norths could have gone to Gosford, become a genuine home team, playing 12 games a year on Grahame Park, and made a success of it. But at the critical moment when they really needed their licensed club to underwrite them, the licensed club went missing. No deal, they said.

There was a huge campaign afoot to hustle Norths into an unwanted merger, and the appointment of an administrator at the club at the start of October '99 was a key event, and questionable in its timing. Within hours the administrator, Max Donnelly, had released his report to creditors, recommending a joint venture with Manly and was soon on national radio outlining this merger as the only option. It was all despicable. Sure, the Bears had been grossly irresponsible for one season, taking a punt on making their future plans absolutely secure, and coming unstuck. But they didn't deserve what happened to them, the fait accompli: they'd be railroaded into a marriage they didn't want with Manly, who weren't that keen either. Norths' claims of a wealthy consortium ready to back them went unheeded.

When the deed was done Ken Arthurson's quote pretty well summed up the feeling: 'If you are going to get rooted, you might as well lie back and enjoy it.' I can understand the Norths Leagues Club saying, 'Look, this can't possibly continue, but we'll bail you out for just one year, give you the chance. If you get into strife up there, so be it.' But for the leagues club to dump them cold . . . it was bloody awful. I believe that News Limited was in this up to its neck, despite assurances that it was at 'arm's length' from such developments and leaving it all to the clubs to sort out. The merger leapfrogged Norths over us.

In the end Manly were saved – well, sort of – easing the pressure on a faltering leagues club. North Sydney were dudded spectacularly and lost their identity. Gosford didn't get a home team – six games a year doesn't rate as that – and neither did Brookvale. And the NRL got a lemon, two clubs who didn't really want to be together and who more often than not played that way. And within a year or so the pot of gold provided to the merged clubs was pretty well gone, lavished on $500,000-a-year footballers, and the club had to slink back cap in hand to League HQ for a refill of at least $1 million. There is no greater indictment of the NRL's lack of administrative nous than this decision which saw this ugly partnership swiftly head towards collapse. Oh yeah, there is . . . they kicked Souths out.

On August 29, 1999, we played our final premiership game of the year, against Parramatta at Parramatta Stadium. They beat us 34–16. Before the game a Parramatta newspaper advertisement for the match asked: 'The last Eels v. Rabbitohs match?' Were we to assume that Parramatta knew something we didn't? The ad was disgraceful and distasteful, another sign of the fallen standards and the disintegration of the old quality of 'mateship' in the game.

Making life more difficult then was a shocking fumble by the ARL that had the effect of further building pressure on vulnerable clubs. Someone at the ARL (and no bastard ever came clean and said it was his fault) 'forgot' to invoice Channel 9, Optus and News Limited for monies due – $15 million in total, $1.5 million to each club, including us. Ken Arthurson called the blunder 'appalling and incompetent'. I think he went a bit light on them. All eventually paid what was morally owed to us, although there was reluctance in some cases. The withholding of the money was a gun at the heads of clubs like us. With us, we had to take News Limited to court before we finally got the $500,000 it had pledged.

We were under siege. There was $1.5 million due and we had our solicitors and our CEO telling us we were broke because this money was hanging in the balance. On that basis they could have gone to every ex-ARL club in the competition, and they would all have been in the same boat! I have some suspicions about the ARL 'blunder', although maybe it was just that – efficiency not being a big feature of central rugby league administration – and I know for sure that it helped increase pressure on us, pressure to crumble and take the merger option. We even had blokes from Group 14 telling us to vote to merge. Anyhow, Packer paid his share of the money owed to us and the others eventually did too, although we were still suing for the News Limited money during the big court case in 2000. Despite propaganda to the contrary, before we fought the Federal Court case, we had $1.8 million in surplus funds . . . which we progressively depleted with the court costs.

On September 23, 1999, the ABC put to air its outstanding and moving *Australian Story* program on the club, telling of our plight, our fight and our determination to keep going. It was a great, emotional piece of television, a tribute to producer Helen Grasswill, a non-football person who had been impressed by Souths' contribution to the community on many levels. She saw the club as something that gave people hope and purpose. The program struck such a chord with ordinary people through the land that within two hours of it going to air more than 100,000 hits were registered on the ABC's website, and the Souths' computer crashed under the strain. The *Australian Story* piece, along with the continual strong campaigning being conducted by Alan Jones and Andrew Denton, built up the pressure on News and the NRL not to cast us off. There was clear evidence by then that, even if it was a little late in the day, Souths now had a vigorous management and marketing program in train. After we were cut, the admired ex–ABC broadcaster Caroline Jones, who had a working connection with *Australian Story*, contributed a poignant and powerful commentary piece in support of Souths for the *Sydney Morning Herald*, 'A Murrurundi girl's note to Murdoch', addressed to Lachlan Murdoch. She wrote:

> It might help if I explain a few things about Australians, so you can understand why people are saying they hope you rot in hell. Strong words but, you see, you've trampled on a thing that matters to people. We can hardly find words for it but it's something to do with meaning and a deep sense of belonging. It's deep and real, something we know in our guts.

This is how the piece ended:

> There are some things here that money can't buy, though it surprises me to say it. When you do a thing that makes Australian men cry, you know you're on the wrong track. And the way we see it, what's the point of being the richest kid in the world if people like George Piggins say you're a mongrel? It's a terrible thing to be called. I hope this will make things a bit clearer for you. All the best for your future.

The article touched a deep chord with a lot of people. The depth of passion displayed in *Australian Story* and later in Caroline Jones's letter should have been enough to warn News and the

NRL off. It should surely have registered that a community asset like Souths lives deep in the Australian psyche. To tamper with it, as they were doing, was fraught with danger. But I can only imagine that the attitude by then was head-in-the-sand, and that the advice from within the NRL to News continued to be poor. In the wake of such a reaction they didn't waver. On Monday, September 27, 1999, a couple of weeks before our fate would be decided, 2UE's John Laws interviewed the NRL's Ian Frykberg. The interview was a real Dorothy Dixer, kicking off with Laws's matey opening line, 'G'day Frikkers.' It included the following excerpts:

> *John Laws:* Is Souths the team most likely to be cut in the criteria next month?
>
> *Ian Frykberg:* Well, we have a board meeting later on today and we're going to be given figures from this committee which is chaired by Ernst & Young about what the latest in the criteria is. Until that happens I don't really know, but certainly one of the danger clubs.
>
> *JL:* Yeah. When you look at yesterday's grand final and you look at the success of the merged team [St George-Illawarra] you'd wonder what all the fuss is about really. I understand loyalty and club loyalty but I suppose, as I keep saying to people, it's better to partially survive than totally disappear, isn't it?
>
> *IF:* Well, I think that's correct. The fact is everyone involved in rugby league knows about the emotion that's involved with teams that have been there since day one and it gives no-one any pleasure to be sitting around at a time when hard decisions have to be taken. But the fact is, there are a number of clubs which do not have the financial ability to continue into the future. Now . . . club directors at some of the clubs haven't yet told their members . . . um . . . Souths is one of the clubs that is struggling financially.
>
> *JL:* Have they told their members?

IF: Well, I don't think they've told their members the full story.

The interview continued in that vein, with Laws guiding Frykberg through NRL policy ('Is this cast in stone now . . . this 14-team business?'), giving the NRL director the chance to expand on the party line. It was Laws at his warmest.

He wound it up this way: 'Ian Frykberg, who is the director of the NRL and a good fella and a clear thinker. I can sense he understands there is emotion involved in all this, as I certainly do . . . But as somebody said to me the other day, "What would you do if the Bulldogs [Laws's team] had to merge?" Well, I mean, I'd cop it if it meant survival. It is better to be partially here than totally gone, isn't it?'

Two days later there was a most unusual turn of events.

Soon after 10 o'clock on his morning show, Laws opened by reading the poem 'If'. It was the time of the 'Cash for Comment' inquiry with commentators such as Laws and Alan Jones under investigation and in the papers. Laws continued:

> I am told by one newspaper, who correctly will remain nameless, that the story is bubbling around town that I interviewed Ian Frykberg on my program the day before yesterday because I have an arrangement with the NRL. When are you people going to give up? I wouldn't mind an arrangement with the NRL – I mean, they could do with a bit of help next year. I wouldn't mind that at all. I would be very happy to promote the NRL as I was happy to commercialise Super League in many ways within the radio industry, and outside the radio industry.

He then went on to explain why he had talked to Frykberg: 'Frikkers is an old friend of mine and I have great affection for him and great regard for him as well.' After addressing another issue, there came the nub of it:

The rumour was that I was supposed to be supporting the NRL or Super League. I supported Super League when it was around and I did it by way of commercials bought and paid for by Super League and recorded by me for radio stations whenever they wanted to use them. And I also provided them with feedback from my listeners, as to the feelings towards Super League. As you can imagine, I was not often the bearer of glad tidings because nobody was too happy about it at the time. But there were many reasons I was interested in Super League and I wanted to do a bit to give them a hand. Because I felt that at the time of the arrival of Super League, football was headed in the same direction as cricket was when Kerry Packer intervened there. Ah. He intervened brilliantly in cricket. It went through a difficult time, but ultimately it benefited and I figured the same thing could happen to League . . .

Now, at the risk of sounding annoyingly honest about this – there are a couple of other factors involved, one being that I happen to work for the Murdoch group. Mr Murdoch is one of my many . . . well, the Misters Murdoch . . . are bosses of mine. I've got many bosses. And given that I've had an association with them for about 15 years, I trust that we would have developed some mutual affection there.

Secondly, I believe there were benefits in Super League. And I felt very strongly that some of the radio stations for which I worked were extremely selective in their comments. I wonder if the snipers checked to see if their motives were totally pure.

But thirdly and most importantly is Ian Frykberg. Now I've known him for years, and I've got great affection for both he and his wife. He's a terrific fella. And Frikkers said to me one day, 'Lawsie, do you really think Super League's getting a fair run on radio?' Well, when I stemmed the hysteria, I gave the honest answer, which was no. And he said, well, if we buy ads, will you give us a hand. And I said, 'Yeah, if you buy them.'

Laws then spoke of a document: 'I have here a document, right in front of me – and it simply says "Super League Propri-etary Limited" and "Richard John Laws", which is me, "endorsement agreement". Now if you'd like a copy of this Mr Ackland [Richard Ackland, then fronting *Media Watch* on the ABC], I'll give you a copy. You don't have to get it by devious means.' He then quoted clauses from the document, which included the following:

• The reading and embellishment of radio commercials live-to-air by Laws. Said Laws: '"Embellishment" means I have a bit of fun with them, as you would hear me have fun with every commercial I do on a day-to-day basis.'
• The personal endorsement of Super League by Laws on the program. Laws explained: 'In other words I would tell the truth and say, you know, I think Super League's doing the right thing. Because I did believe they were.'

Laws concluded by offering the contract to 'any newspaper or television station listening to me'. He mentioned the *Sydney Morning Herald* and the ABC by name. 'There's absolutely noth-ing sinister about it, it's all there,' he said. 'And I am very happy to give it to you.'

This was an extraordinary piece of radio, considering that there had been no previous public awareness of Laws's special deal with Super League. It had been flushed out, almost by chance, by a journalist's simple enquiry after the Frykberg inter-view. The journalist had been aware that Laws had had a commercial link with Super League club Penrith, but no more. Word of the questions being asked, and at a delicate time, nudged the broadcaster to go the whole hog and disclose his wider Super League ties.

On September 28, 1999, it was all out in the open. News leaked from an NRL board meeting to the Murdoch papers *The Australian* and the *Daily Telegraph* was that South Sydney and North Sydney had no chance of being ranked in the 14 under the selection criteria distributed to clubs. Considering where the stories appeared, they had to be right. On October 2 (in the *Daily Telegraph*) came the further news that Souths had passed the 'basic criteria' but still remained likely to be the team cut. The final decision was now just 18 days away.

Clubs were judged, and allocated points under six separate headings under the criteria which decided the future shape of the NRL competition. The categories were:

Crowds (home)
Crowds (away)
Competition points
Gate receipts
Profitability
Sponsors/other income

Under the headline 'How criteria worked' on the fateful October day that the 14 teams were announced, the *Daily Telegraph* explained the criteria to readers – complete with positive spin on the contentious and never-explained 'weighting' in some categories:

> The clubs were assessed at two levels. The first level, called the basic criteria, examined playing facilities, administration, solvency and development. North Sydney, for instance, was deemed to have failed at the first level with their 'profitability' figure of six points.
>
> The second level, called the selection criteria, rated the clubs on crowd support, competition results, sponsorship and finances. In being scored in the various categories, the team achieving the best performance was given 20 points, the second best 19 points and so on. But

that is not the final score as you see it [the *Daily Telegraph* published all scores].

To give a fairer assessment of each club's performance, statistics experts advised that 'weighting' be added to various categories. For instance, it allowed for fairer scores to be given to clubs which finished below a rival on the final competition table, but had the same number of premiership points.

Although they were still assessed with the other clubs, the exceptions to the overall process were Brisbane, Newcastle and Auckland, who were part of a 1997 agreement which granted them a licence to the 2000 competition irrespective of their points scores in the selection criteria. In return the three clubs had to show proof of a five-year business plan and minimum revenue of $8 million.

The NRL used independent accounting and legal experts to monitor, collate and verify all data. The rules of the criteria were first issued in May 1998 and finalised in September of that year. There have been no changes since.

As a club we weren't about to flinch in the face of the threat presented by the criteria or the merger agenda carried around by some within the ranks. Our campaign message was straightforward: 'Keep 16'. I did my best to turn the pressure back on News Limited and the NRL as crunch time approached. To kill Souths, I told the media, would be akin to cutting Lassie's throat. To me there were just two questions: would Souths be tough enough to maintain our stance, and was the NRL tough enough to kick us out, knowing the damage that would do. And whenever I got the chance I repeated what became almost a mantra for the club: that we had paid our way for 92 years notwithstanding the struggle it had been at times. We had provided opportunity for young men and a continual focus and enjoyment for the district. We had a *right* to be part of the elite competition. 'We would rather die on our feet than grovel,' I told them. 'I am not going to run a side for Murdoch. If we can't be in the premier competition I'd rather see Souths pull their colours out and put them in a glass case.'

As October 15 approached we decided to take our cause to the streets, planning a monster rally five days before decision day to drive home our message. In putting it all together and promoting the message, we had powerful and crucial support from Alan Jones and Andrew Denton, both of whom in the strongest terms alerted people to the injustice that was just around the corner for Souths. As Denton said: 'If the NRL want to kill South Sydney they're going to have to shoot us right between the eyes in broad daylight before the public and then explain before the public why they did it – because their fingerprints will be all over the gun.' Channels 10 and 7 were solid too, obviously sympathetic to our side of the story.

We were by then fighting against the odds – a man down – but fighting on. The man was our great front-rower John 'Lurch' O'Neill, who had finally succumbed to cancer and died in August. Even on his sick bed John was fighting for our cause, willing Souths to live as his own life ran down. I'll tell you about him in the next chapter.

13. My Best Mate

Into my heart an air that kills
From yon far country blows:
What are those blue remembered hills,
What spires, what farms are those?

That is the land of lost content,
I see it shining plain,
The happy highways where I went
And cannot come again.

A.E. Housman, A Shropshire Lad

JOHN O'NEILL'S DEATH from liver cancer in August 1999 at the age of 56 united South Sydney club in grief, and, in its own way, his passing delivered a message to rugby league's new rulers about how deep, fundamental and genuine are the passions that this game generates. This was not about pay TV or 'product' or some false view that league was a business more than a sport. This was about things that were far more real: a good and decent and tough country bloke who had turned himself into a champion rugby league player, and joined a club he had grown to love. The club and its people loved him in return. And on the day of his funeral a huge crowd filled Sydney's St Mary's Cathedral and spilled far into the square beyond. There were people from all walks of life and I'm sure the big bloke would have been looking down and thinking, what's all the fuss about?

I remember the first time I ever saw him, back in 1965, at pre-season training at Waterloo Oval. There was John, another country bloke, Jim Morgan, and Ivan Jones, and I recall one of the group I was with saying: 'Get a load of the bush boy haircuts.' John and I became mates over the years, more so from 1975 when he came back to Souths after his spell with Manly.

He was always a Souths bloke, really, although he played his heart out for Manly and was a huge factor in them winning their first and second premierships. Even when he was over there we'd see plenty of him and if any of us – Ronny Coote, Bobby McCarthy, Gary Stevens or me – were having a barbecue we'd always invite John. He coached at Souths in 1977, when I was captain, and our mateship grew stronger still. I think in the end, coaching became John's worst nightmare. He was working like a navvy in his building business and he found coaching a lot more stressful than he thought it would be. Realising that, John went to see Jack Gibson. It was John who brought the most successful coach in the game to the club in '78.

John O'Neill was a great mate of mine, and Nolene and I were never far from him and his wife Clare and his daughters, Michelle, Julie and Cindy, in his long and brave battle against cancer. I will never forget his courage as he wrestled with pain worse than any of us could imagine. As a footballer it was never John's way to give up and he was like that through his long illness, making sure that things were right for Clare and the girls and the grandkids, John, Dean, Jessica and Ryan, before he let go. He lived way past the life span the doctors originally predicted, and I have no doubt it was his care for his family that kept him going. I had never before experienced what I did through those long months. All of us who were alongside John felt privileged, although saddened, by the knowledge that we were going to lose a great friend.

There are many stories I could tell about John. All who bumped against him in life have those. Some are too personal, and I choke up when I think of them. I recall a day when the families were down at Lake Conjola at the properties four of us had built there – John, Gary Stevens, Ron Coote and me. It's a glorious spot, three kilometres in through rugged bushland, and all of a sudden you merge through an opening onto a beautiful lake. It was a day fairly late in John's life. He and I had driven into town to pick up some horse food and as we neared home he spotted his little grand-daughter Jessica, playing alone out the front of his house. 'Let me out here, will you mate?' he asked me. 'I'll go down and play with her for a while. I'm not going to be around much longer and I'd like to give her some of my time.' I sat there in the truck and watched him walk across the reserve. He was a frail figure by then, and especially so for those of us who knew him as the tearaway front-row warrior in the thick of it in battles for Souths and Australia, cutting a dashing figure as he powered through the rucks.

'I would like to have one more horse ride,' John said to me one morning down at the lake. John's son-in-law Peter Markham and I saddled the horses – I had recently bought a new Appaloosa – and I said to John: 'This horse is bombproof. It's supposed to be such a good horse, it's not funny.' So John took his horse and I hopped up on the Appaloosa. 'Are you right to get up, mate?' I asked him. 'Yeah, I'm right,' he said, and somehow with great effort dragged himself into the saddle. We rode down behind the properties and came to a place where there were a couple of donkeys in a paddock. For some reason John's horse just rolled – pulled his forelegs up, and rolled over. John managed to hop out of the saddle. 'This bloody horse is mad,' he said. The horse recovered its feet and John went to get back on, but he had used up his energy and couldn't do it. I dismounted to give him a heave-ho up, and when I put my hands on his backside, there was just skin and bone. With him safely in the saddle I went to get back on my bloke and was half in the saddle when the horse spooked and took off. Without me. I came straight off the back and hit the ground hard. It knocked the guts out of me. I honestly couldn't move for about 15 minutes, then I gradually came good. And, above me, I could hear John O'Neill's familiar laugh. 'Bombproof, eh?'

He loved horses and riding and kept it going as long as he possibly could. Finally, late in his cancer, there was a day when he took a bad fall from his horse and good mate 'Thunder', and broke five ribs. I drove him back to Sydney as smoothly as I could and the pain must have been terrible as he lay on the back seat. But, even with cancer closing in on him and the five broken ribs, he was not sorry for himself. All he said was: 'Shit, it hurts.'

'I've had a great life,' he would often say. 'I'd do it all over again.' And I can still see him lying on his bed in agony, and arguing on the phone with some builder about a job that was underway. I'd think to myself, 'Why is he so worried about that when he's so close to the bloody end?' John had the answer, and I understood: 'I have got to set the missus and the kids up. I don't want any loose ends left.' Right to the end he was like that, focused on getting it all right for the family, making sure that the future, which was not going to be his, would be good for them. He was such a hard-working bloke. One of the regrets of those who knew him is that he didn't ease off a little bloody earlier and enjoy what he had. Right to the end he was so appreciative of the things happening around him and worried about others. 'We can't expect you to keep mowing the lawns,' he'd say when I'd go to his place to do that. Afterwards, no matter how crook he was, he'd lift his head from the bed: 'Thanks, mate.'

On the bad days he would occasionally say things like, 'Mate, I'd be better off dead.' But then, long after the medical men had told him he'd be gone, he'd keep going, running his business from his sickbed when he could barely lift his head off the pillow. It was remarkable to see.

The motivation, always, was his family. From the north-west plains town of Gunnedah, he'd met Clare, from Tambar Springs, when they were both about 16. They had built a life together, built a closeness that few have. Late in his life, when he'd tell her, 'When I'm gone, you get someone else, and enjoy yourself,' she would look at him and say dryly, 'Yeah, Mick [the pet name Clare had for him], I'll go and put an ad in the paper if you like.'

The tradition of Wednesday night dinners continued fairly late into his illness too. We'd been doing that for 20 years or so, and we kept it going. We'd seek out vegetarian places to help him with his continual trouble with his stomach and I'd say to him: 'C'mon, mate, we'll go for a walk,' and we'd often leave the girls there at the restaurant and go for a stroll and a yarn. We still go to dinner Wednesdays – Nolene and Clare and Joyce Churchill and me – just about always to Souths Leagues Club.

John was a funny big bugger and when you had him as a friend, he was a friend for life, as his old mates from Gunnedah could testify. He was as close to them when he was a star foot-baller and successful city businessman as when he first left the town to try his luck in Sydney. He had time for everybody. When I think of him, I think of a bloke who never lost his country qualities, but was very 'South Sydney' too. Friendships meant a lot to him, and he would go out of his way to make sure they were sustained: the Gunnedah crowd, football mates from tours, the blokes at Souths he had played with.

He died at 56, a young man still. The cancer was probably the only thing that ever got over the top of him. And I think he tried just about everything to beat that too in the way of natural therapies. Clare took him to clinics in Melbourne and his youngest daughter Cindy would go all over the place to get him the right organic foods to eat.

In many ways a bloke like John O'Neill is at the heart of what this book is about. He loved the game he played and loved the club that gave him his opportunity. He played his football rough and tough but afterwards it was drinks and laughs all round. It was the reason he was so well liked. A third strand was his wonderful lifelong work ethic. He loved a game of football, loved a game of cards and a beer or three with mates. There were many Monday mornings when no doubt he had a sore head, but I doubt there was a Monday when he wasn't out there getting stuck into the work. He was 'old' rugby league, a product of the way it used to be – a game that brought together blokes from different clubs and different places, all of them mixing and growing in the experience of playing a game which was just part of their lives. But an important one.

I won't forget John Bernard O'Neill. He was my best mate, a giant in so many ways. I can see him now standing on a table at some club in Hawaii on a Souths end-of-season trip, singing 'The Teddy Bears' Picnic' and going through all the actions, and laughing that big laugh of his and enjoying himself about as much as anyone possibly could.

He was a great bloke and a great rugby league bloke, and he's much missed at Souths and plenty of other places. John died when his club was under the greatest threat of its long existence. And he died worrying about that.

14. Rabbit Cull

The sheer emotion of what is happening in Souths is a microcosm of what is happening in many working-class communities in Australia. What was held dear and what bonded people in terms of family and loyalty seem to have gone from the workplace and from many institutions. Sport was one of the last vestiges that people held on to . . . and if you strip away 100 years of meaning and identity played out through sport, it can really cripple a community.

Graeme Cole, lay chaplain

NEIL WHITTAKER, WHO LIKE me had played hooker for a foundation Sydney club, was the bearer of the news on the infamous day they dropped South Sydney, Pride of the League, from the premiership after 92 seasons. 'George,' he said on the phone when I took the call at Souths Leagues Club, 'they've cut you.' It was 1.54 on the afternoon of Friday, October 15, 1999. 'The dirty bastards,' I replied. Whittaker just happened to have been handed the filthiest job in Australian sporting history. He was a pawn in a bigger game. 'I'll see you in court,' I said. I was surprised that it was Whittaker who had done the dirty deed rather than NRL chairman Malcolm Noad. 'If you're going to pull someone's house down,' I told the media, 'you would think they would have the balls to knock on the front door. Instead they send the messenger. We mightn't have much money compared to them, but we've got more class.'

As a bloke, I quite liked Neil Whittaker. But Whittaker, as chief executive of the NRL, and coming from the ARL side of the fence, was charged in 1999 with the duty of seeing that South Sydney, along with all the other ARL clubs, got a fair crack of the whip. But when you looked deeply into the criteria that had cost us our place in the game and realised that some clubs were judged under very different practices of accountancy to Souths, suddenly you couldn't think anything other than that Whittaker had failed dismally in his duty of care to Souths. It was his job to make sure that all was above board and fair, so how did he allow Souths to be treated in such a way? And if the blame today lies with him, it lies too with anyone else from that background on the NRL executive board – Hill, Politis and the others who went along with what News Limited wanted. They just palmed poor old Souths off, and they know it. In Whittaker's case I think he started out trying to do the right thing, then finally got swept along with the tide and decided not to resist. Yeah, they all let us down, Whittaker and the ARL blokes. In the end it became a matter of all NRL sides against one club. Us.

That night, the news that we were 'gone' dominated television and radio. On Super League criteria we had run 15th on 73.75 points, with Penrith rated 14th (120.25). The TV images were of Newcastle chairman Michael Hill sitting on the end of the line alongside News Limited's Malcolm Noad and Whittaker at the media conference that followed the killing. Hill was in a curious position. His club, Newcastle, was in a shaky financial situation and he had made a fair bit of noise earlier that year in favour of a 16-team competition, although he had gone quiet on that. He had said to me one day how much he had respected the strength of my position, and my loyalty. 'When I get on this thing [the NRL], I'll make sure Souths' interests are looked after,' he promised. A Newcastle reporter on the day we were cut asked him the question: did he believe the accusation that he had red-and-green blood on his hands? 'No,' said Hill.

By evening, Souths Leagues Club was awash with tears and beers. The news that we had been booted out was no bolt from the blue; nothing that we hadn't expected. But the anger simmered and I called for calm as there was talk of a march on the NRL headquarters at Fox Studios. The signs had been there for everyone to read: people trying to send us bankrupt by withholding payments due; newspaper speculation in the right places; and big pressure on certain board members to force us to merge. We hadn't been in a fair race. I thought Justice Finn in his later judgment pretty much backed that up: what had been done to us mightn't have been against the law, but for sure and certain it had been unfair.

I tried to find the words as I faced a media army: 'They've killed the greatest club on earth,' I said. 'But we owe it to our fans to give it our best shot. The fight ain't over yet . . . we'll have our day in court.' I couldn't hold back from hitting out:

> I don't want to see rugby league die, but some of the people in it are another matter. I hope the bastards rot in hell. This used to be a game in which it didn't matter if you were black, white or yellow. It didn't matter if you were Catholic, Protestant or whatever. You were united in league. Taking Souths out has destroyed the hopes, dreams and lives of so many people. They've stuffed the little bloke. It's amazing. In four or five years they have managed to ruin 90 years of history.

Journalist Norm Lipson, who was in the fight all the way, summed it up when he said, 'The one bright spot that many people in South Sydney had in their miserable lives was their football club. What is their life without that?'

Henry Morris, standing at our shoulder in the fight, didn't hold back either. He declared it the 'most sinful day' in the history of rugby league. 'The NRL can get nicked as far as I am concerned,' said Morris. It was a tough day and night and emotions ran high at the club. There were people crying all over the place; something had been ripped from their lives. My motivation to keep fighting has always been those people, the true Souths people who deserve a football team, and the kids who deserve something to aspire to in their district. At the heart of all this are the people who haven't got much in their lives – people for whom life has been a pretty stern battle without too many trimmings and for whom the local football team was the one shining ray of enjoyment come the weekend. These people haven't got farms, they haven't got yachts or speedboats or flash cars. For many of them the enjoyment of life was following their football team in the winter, and going to the beach or the park in summer.

Seeing men in their sixties weep openly is not an easy thing to contend with. But I saw plenty on that night in October. It weighed pretty heavily, I can tell you. There were wreaths and fresh-cut flowers strewn all over the foyer of the club. It really was a wake. A football club chairman represents a lot of people, all the way from the business people who support the club and the game, to the more affluent supporter who watches as comfortably as he can from a reserved seat, to the ordinary, dyed-in-the-wool supporters who'll sit out in the rain and cheer for their team. This last group is the one you really fight for. In the *Bulletin* a few days later, Catherine Lumby wrote that the cutting of Souths unleashed 'an earthquake on the sporting world'. As the fury grew, another journalist observed that 'by taking out Souths, Rupert Murdoch and American-born Lachlan have hit a nerve in the Sydney psyche that neither fully understand.'

People who supported us hurried to cancel subscriptions to Foxtel and to the *Daily Telegraph* and *Sunday Telegraph*, and declared they would never fly Ansett (in which Murdoch had a stake) again. Longtime Souths fan John Ireland, president of the Sydney Catholic Club, had to fork out a $100 cancellation fee to get Foxtel out of his house. It was a small price to pay, said Ireland.

Being excluded was a strange feeling – something I couldn't get at physically and take by the scruff of the neck. It was apparent that the only course left was to go to court. I had no doubt we would fight on. Remembering the dismay of that long day and night, I know now that for us to have kept fighting – not knowing what the final verdict would be – at the very least provided some grieving time for people. The passing of time gave people a chance to move on from the initial kick in the guts, in better shape to move on to something else in case the NRL and News Limited ultimately got their way with Souths.

By October 15, 1999, we had built a great depth of awareness and feeling within the population about the injustice that was about to be done. To our supporters, Rupert Murdoch was Elmer Fudd, 'always trying to shoot Bugs Bunny'. Many ordinary Aussies, football fans or not, saw us as part of a much bigger picture – a society in which economic rationalism and corporatisation and globalisation had already had a crushing effect on many. We had stirred the fire in many people and the huge downtown Sydney rally billed as 'Reclaim the Game', five days before the decision, was the key event in all that. This was a terrific day. John Sattler sang 'Glory, Glory to South Sydney'; Alan Jones sent a powerful message from France; and the speakers included Ray Martin, Andrew Denton, Mike Whitney and David Hill of 'Save the Bears'. 'We will exist as long as you people continue to support us,' I told the gathering. The marchers included the wonderful 95-year-old Albert Clift, and 78-year-old Tom Wade, son of an original Rabbitoh, 'Sonno' Wade. The media came up with vastly different crowd estimates, with the *Daily Telegraph* picking the lowest figure (15,000). What a surprise! The *Illawarra Mercury* and the *Newcastle Herald* went for 50,000, the *Sydney Morning Herald* for 20,000 (although 50,000 in a later estimate). Before everyone arrived at the Town Hall the police were talking 35,000. I know only this: I stood on the steps of the Town Hall for at least 15 minutes, waiting for the crowd to make its way up George Street, and there were an awful lot of people. I think you can only be guided by the opinions of those who had been to lots of demonstrations and rallies over the years, back to the Vietnam days, and the general estimates of the crowd that day from these people were in the vicinity of 30,000–40,000.

It was a shot across the bows of the NRL and News Limited and an issue that under normal circumstances would have been seized upon by state and federal politicians. From all of those areas there was mostly silence. Probably, if we'd marched to Fox Studios, Murdoch territory, as had been suggested, they would have had the dogs in and the army and the coppers there to belt us.

We only ever had isolated individual support from politicians. Never was there any suggestion of our plight becoming a larger political cause, despite the 40,000 that day, and the 80,000 at the next march. We had some lip-service support, even from Howard and Beazley, via letters sent to us, but never any more than that. Rupert Murdoch was too big to buck. Rupert was wielding the axe over our necks and they were all terrified. The politicians knew as well as I did that for Murdoch and his cronies to take rugby league away from the people of South Sydney was a disgrace. They knew they should have stood against what had been done, but most of the pollies cowered.

There was the occasional honourable exception. Deirdre Grusovin, the NSW ALP member for Heffron and a member of our board, was really solid throughout with her support; and her brother, Labor's shadow minister for Foreign Affairs, Laurie Brereton, was with us all the way, marched at our rallies and attended our functions. The ALP member for Grayndler, Anthony Albanese – also a board member – really stood up to be counted with his hard-hitting speech in Federal Parliament as he introduced a private member's bill after we had been cut – a bill backed by Bob Katter, Gary Hardgrave, Alex Somlay, Arch Bevis and Tanya Plibersek. Laurie Brereton seconded Albanese's motion, which among other things called for 'the NRL to include South Sydney in the 2000 competition'. Albanese's speech was strong and to the point, but gained little attention in the media. In part, he said this:

> When sport becomes simply corporate business, it alienates those on whom it relies for support. Indeed, this debate goes to the very heart of the alienation which people are feeling about our society. We are told that we are being emotional, that our human interaction, relationships and historical links do not matter. These ignorant corporate executives do not understand that sport is about loyalty. It is about passion and emotion. Local institutions such as South Sydney form the fabric which binds people together and makes a cohesive society. A society is not made up of individual pay TV subscribers.
>
> Whilst money cannot buy respect, News Limited and the NRL have the opportunity to earn respect by doing the right thing and listening to what the members of the public, the consumers, are saying.
>
> Like the working-class people who support them, South Sydney have always paid their way, unlike teams such as Melbourne and Cronulla, which would be insolvent were it not for News Limited. People from this proud tradition know how to fight in parliament, the streets and in the court. We will fight as representatives of those who had their hearts broken on 15 October. It is the courageous men and women who shed tears that night at South Sydney Rugby League Club who own the game, not the faceless men who have red-and-green blood on their hands.
>
> There are a lot of ordinary Australians who long ago tired of those who speak of rationalisation and product. They have been waiting for something to fight for. South Sydney has given them that and George Piggins has given them that leadership.

I'll never forget the two rally days we had in downtown Sydney when people of all colours and creeds came together to march and support us. I doubt there's ever been a better example in Australia of the way sport can bind people in a shared cause or a better example of how a sport, and a famous club like Souths, can contribute to the multicultural mix. At those rallies we had people from a big range of ethnic backgrounds. The Greek community in particular have been wonderful supporters – people underestimate how strong Souths are in the city's Greek community – as were the Lebanese community throughout the fight. Both groups put on big fundraising nights for the club and raised huge amounts of money. Jim Hanna, a Sydney journalist, a member of our Lebanese support group and a Souths fan since 1972, wrote a moving article in June 2000, conveying what Souths meant to him:

> I was born in Lebanon and grew up in Toowoomba and western Sydney. I have never lived in Redfern. Yet the South Sydney Rugby League Club remains as much a part of me as my Lebanese heritage. Souths is where Jewish and Arabic people sit together, share a drink or a meal and celebrate the things they love (like Souths). We embrace Souths, because Souths embraces people regardless of their race, colour or creed. Souths is about much more than rugby league. Souths is one of the few remaining places that represents a set of values and beliefs that people say they still believe in, but too few seem to live by.

There were many Aboriginal people there at our rallies too, players from their community having been a big part of our club. Alan Jones told the story later of how an Aboriginal mother had come up to him that first day and asked the simple question: 'What will our kids do now?' Charles Perkins said on the radio one day: 'South Sydney encouraged Aboriginal people to be part of it. It was a community thing really, not only for Aboriginal people, but a lot of migrant kids moved in the direction of South Sydney in terms of their emotions, their relationships, their geography.'

One of the great things about rugby league is that it has always been open to all races, all religions, people from all walks of life. Eventually, as Australia continues to change, there's no doubt we will have the Chinese and Vietnamese playing the game too. A football club is a sensational way to blend young Australians from different backgrounds together.

Our fighting fund received an unexpected and emotional boost on the death of one of the great guys of our club, Tom Brock. Tom was the best club historian in the game, by a mile, and a wonderful worker for Souths over a long period. In the wake of his sudden death in 1997 came the totally unexpected news – he had left the club $200,000.

The October '99 rally was the culmination of a huge amount of work and creative effort. The amount of unpaid toil that went into the events that funded Souths' fight is extraordinary, reflecting better than anything else how important many people think the club is. We had concerts, carnival days and rallies – kicked off by a big 'Keep 16' press conference at the Sydney Cricket Ground in September '99 – special football days, country trips, and Red & Green Balls at $100 a head. The huge 'Save Our Souths' fundraiser at Darling Harbour, organised by Ray Martin and attracting a crowd of 1750, with hundreds turned away, hit the headlines when Russell Crowe paid $42,000 for the timekeeper's bell from our first year, 1908, when we played Easts at Birchgrove Oval. A wonderful old man, Albert Clift, then 95, who had been Souths' timekeeper for 40 years, donated the bell for auction, and what a fine gesture that was. Albert had had the bell as a cherished possession for much of his long life, the outstanding single treasure in the remarkable Souths museum he built at his home at Mascot. But he gave it up because of his love for his club, and his determination that it would live on way past the end of his own life. And Albert dug far deeper into his treasures than just the historic bell. He brought in for auction an autographed football which had belonged to Souths' legendary second rower of the 1920s and 1930s, George Treweek, plus a premiership blazer won by another famous old Rabbitoh, Eddie Root.

At the rally there were people from so many other clubs headed by Newcastle, who were great supporters throughout the battle. There were many people from the merged teams – Balmain, Manly, Wests and Norths – and probably just about everywhere else. It wasn't just a Souths crowd, although the predominant colours were red and green, it was a disenchanted *rugby league* crowd. The message it sent out couldn't have been any more powerful. Undoubtedly there were people there who had no direct interest in rugby league at all. They just cared about the principles involved. Like the huge crowds that had marched across the Harbour Bridge for the cause of reconciliation, they were there because they wanted to right a wrong.

Back at the leagues club after the first rally in 1999, a supporter came up to me, placed a cheque in my hand and walked away. I glanced at it, and couldn't believe my eyes. I took it over to Nolene for confirmation. 'How much is this for?' I asked. It was as I suspected – a cheque for $5000. It came from a bloke named David Francis on behalf of his family. When Nolene went over to thank them for their generosity, David's wife told her that she had saved the money for new curtains for their house. When Souths had been kicked out, they had held a family meeting and decided that the curtains could wait – that the future of their football team was more important.

The support we had throughout the fight was fantastic. Sometimes it arrived in unexpected places, and at unexpected times. In April 2001 I badly burned both my legs in a stupid accident (i.e. throwing petrol on a fire) while burning-off at our place at Lake Conjola. Driven to Milton hospital with my legs hanging out the car window to ease the pain, I was rushed into casualty, and past a bloke waiting there. I remember his words: 'George, I'm a Manly supporter, but you can go ahead of me. And if you get back in . . . I'm going to be a Souths supporter!'

In the *Sunday Telegraph* of October 10, the day of that first big rally – which had been confidently tipped to be the biggest sporting protest event in Australia's history (and it was) – the only mention of the upcoming march came extremely briefly in a story featuring the thoughts of Balmain CEO Daniel Munk. Munk, hardly a household name in rugby league, gave Souths a tongue-lashing: 'Souths should wake up to themselves and form a joint venture with Sydney City or Cronulla rather than become extinct like Newtown'. Newtown of course were not 'extinct'; they had lived on after being cut from the premiership in 1983. We had supported them to the tune of $150,000 per season plus provision of accommodation for several years. When we were kicked out of the competition that arrangement ended and John Singleton managed not to acknowledge what Souths had done for 'his' club when he trumpeted some new deal with Auckland.

Daniel Munk, eh? He was a former employee of Denis Fitzgerald up at Parramatta. At a KPMG lunch that I had attended a good while before, at which they had picked me out to be guest speaker, I spoke about football's place in the community, how important the team was to a place like South Sydney, and how I believed there was a strong case for all licensed clubs and pubs in a district to provide some support to the major football club because that club represented 'the community' that supported it and made its money. The theme seemed to go down well. But Danny Munk, who was at the lunch, made it very clear that he wanted to empty his football club, Balmain, right out the door. Danny undoubtedly had ambitions to become one of those guru CEOs of a leagues club, and is probably a pretty capable bloke in that area. I wish I had a recording of the lunch. He was emphatic that Balmain Leagues Club didn't need its football club and that things would function a lot better without it.

And here he was lecturing us in the *Sunday Telegraph*. His opinions that day counted for nothing with me. But I *can* understand the attitudes of blokes like him and others at leagues clubs when they see the unchecked spending of football clubs suffering from tunnel vision, clubs hellbent on trying to buy a premiership, and bugger the consequences. The leagues club might need some refurbishment work – and at the same time they've got the football club wanting to run out and give some player (or *players*) $700,000 a season for three years. Under the NSWRL/ARL the game never got close to arriving at a system of balance by which guidelines were in place so that football clubs couldn't send the leagues club broke. And yet the support for football was still there, as it must be under the charter of the leagues clubs. I always reckoned a 60–40 system would work – that a leagues club would be obliged to put at least 60 per cent of its clear profits back into the club itself, and the welfare of its members. A maximum of 40 per cent would go to running football and sport in the district. That sort of 'cap' would be a happy medium. But blokes like Daniel Munk need to be reminded now and then that there wouldn't be a Balmain Leagues Club without rugby league. He mightn't have wanted a football club, but you can be sure that the people of the community did.

Getting Souths' case across via the media was always difficult. Except when pressured, Murdoch's News Limited outlets were inevitably going to be very selective about reporting South Sydney, because our fight and our struggle to stay alive didn't suit the company's agenda. I had an example during the writing of this book.

One of News Limited's *Sunday Telegraph* writers, Cameron Bell, rang me up for my point of view. I took Cameron through some of the shocking anomalies of the whole thing, the specific details which could leave only one conclusion – that under any fair dinkum commonsense judgment some clubs had been given cosy runs while others, like Souths, were obviously in the gun. I didn't hold back. Then I said to him: 'I'll tell you now, son, what I've just said to you – do you want to have a little wager about your chances of getting it printed?' 'I'd like to think I can,' he replied, although he declined my invitation for a bet. The story never appeared, as I knew it wouldn't. It would always be that way anywhere in the world, I suppose, when a media organisation owned a sport. As Andrew Denton put it, 'A public game has become privatised.'

My experience with Cameron Bell was pretty much the norm. There was an occasional 'gesture' to Souths when the pressure was on, such as the decision to print my open letter in the *Daily Telegraph* in early 1999, but it was erratic, as if a response to a twitch of conscience now and then. The ongoing story of Souths' fight for life was never given a full and consistent treatment by the media. Even the Fairfax media went surprisingly quiet at the start of 2001, rarely paying any attention to the ongoing Souths story. And especially as the year unfolded (until the Federal Court decision), the News Limited press chose to pretty much ignore what we were up to, no doubt pretending we weren't there in the hope that we'd go away.

I'm not an expert on the media, but I would imagine the period since 1995 featuring the blatant pro–Super League line that the News Limited press (headed by the *Daily Telegraph*) peddled during the early months of the fiasco, represented a low point for the Australian sports media. What was published at times bore, in my opinion, no connection with fair or balanced reporting. Some people in the print and electronic media sold their souls; they threw their principles out the window. Others jumped the fence, sniffing the breeze on who was 'winning' the battle at the time, exploiting them if they could, before moving on. They have to live with that. Such people will never again have my respect, or the respect of countless fair dinkum people in rugby league.

Probably the most infamous example of media bias came when the *Telegraphs – Daily* and *Sunday –* chose to virtually ignore our first big rally and march in October 1999. The *Sun-Herald* of October 10 ran a full-page article; the Saturday *Daily Telegraph* carried nothing on the upcoming Sunday march, and the *Sunday Telegraph* ran nothing more than that snide passing mention above, quoting Balmain's Munk having a go at Souths.

Senior sports journalist and league historian Ian Heads, at the time writing for the *Sunday Telegraph*, felt strongly enough about the paper's decision not to run any preview story on this, the biggest protest in Australian sporting history, to resign, preferring after 35 years of writing about the game to walk away to other things. Heads wrote subsequently of the 'disrespect' he felt the two *Telegraphs'* stance represented to a great Australian sporting club. The story of the march led the evening news bulletins on TV, having been the biggest story in town. The *Daily Telegraph* the next day covered the march on page 44; the *Sydney Morning Herald* reported the rally on page one. Andrew Denton said later that he believed the *Telegraph's* stance to virtually ignore the rally was the 'turning point'. On *Australian Story* in August 2001 he said, 'I believe that was the moment when News Limited lost the battle. It absolutely hardened our resolve, there was no question we were being done over.'

That we weren't judged in the same way as other clubs in 1999 is beyond question. That's one reason we headed into court – to get answers on that. The best chance for victims of an injustice, which is what we were, is to get their message across in the media. But there was little help there, and why would there be when a media organisation that opposed you owned the game? In the situation Souths were in you have to depend on media outlets to help you, but some of them just went about closing us down. I couldn't get our full story into the papers so the public could form its own opinion. Alan Jones pushed very hard on our behalf, but he was one voice. Jones's anger showed out in a brutal interview on October 18 in which he really carved up NRL chairman Malcolm Noad.

Virtually as soon as the decision was announced to cut Souths, the pressure was back on us to form a joint venture with Cronulla. The usual forces were at work. But as far as I was concerned, nothing had changed. The deal had to be on their terms, said the Sharks' Barry Pierce. From Cronulla's point of view the deal hadn't altered: it was their colours, their home ground, their name or nothing. It was nothing, I said. I had no doubt their major interest lay in snaring Souths Juniors' talent and money. The Sharks incidentally had finished fifth in the criteria ratings, but only because News Limited had filled the pockets of this struggling club with money.

My belief was that it was more honourable to retire our jersey than to give in to some half-baked 'partnership'. Group 14 member Andrew Denton backed me, declaring that the sort of 'merger' proposed was effectively a takeover. Said Denton, 'It's like having someone burn your house down and rape your wife and then say, "Oh look, come and live with us, it'll be alright, mate."' I was of the opinion that if Souths could not win legal action then we should retire the colours. I felt it should stand as a lesson down the ages for all who follow that there are some things that money and corporate thuggery cannot subdue or buy.

But opposing forces were then at work on our board. At the time we were dropped from the competition, the board comprised: Ron Hoenig, Eddie Obeid, Deirdre Grusovin, Martin Lissing, Steve McDermott and Michael Whitney. Hoenig and Obeid, operating in tandem, were increasingly pro-merger, but on October 22, they resigned from the board, realising they were out of step with the wishes of other board members and the rank and file. Hoenig and Obeid issued a joint statement, describing our stand-alone stance as an 'escape from reality'. Their departure united our board, and we soon ended up with blokes like Anthony Albanese and Dominic Sullivan, the mayor of Randwick, on the board, and both very strong and solid supporters.

There were carefully orchestrated attacks on the club via the media, and this time from Souths-aligned men like Michael Cleary and Don Lane. If both believed so heavily in the line they were pushing, that we should do a sweetheart deal with Cronulla, there were avenues through the club for them to express that belief. But they chose to go to the News Limited media (or did the media go to them?). In the *Sunday Telegraph*, Cleary said, 'We're lucky at this stage to have anyone [i.e.

Cronulla] prepared to pick us up. If they want to save the club, amalgamation is the only answer. I'm a strong believer that 50 per cent of something is better than 100 per cent of nothing.' Lane's words appeared in both the *Daily Telegraph* and *The Australian*: 'The path Souths are travelling is ridiculous. What good would an injunction [the one we were seeking to get us back into the premiership] do? And who is going to pay for the litigation?' Pushing the merger-with-Cronulla angle hard, Lane took a swipe at me: 'George isn't a hero. He's a blockade. He has set himself up as the martyr – I think he likes that position. They're going to kill the club.' Lane did the media rounds in an assault on the club and its pledged stand-alone position. In an interview with Stan Zemanek (2GB), Lane called me 'obstructive' and again pushed the merger line hard. He also called our lawyer Nicholas Pappas a 'cowboy' – a derogatory and stupid remark. Via his commitment, determination and skill, Nick was to emerge as one of the true heroes of the whole battle.

With Cleary, I wasn't that disappointed or surprised. Back in 1967 I had played in the same football team as him, 16 or 17 games, and he probably didn't even know I was in the side. What he thought of me or Souths was of no great account to me. I was a fair bit more disappointed with Don Lane though, who had been a Group 14 member on our Millennium Committee. He had been close to the club, especially earlier on. He had been in my home. What he did was disgraceful and I likened it to 'a king hit from the blindside'. Lane knew as well as anyone there were correct channels, club channels, he could go through to put his belief to other people.

Both he and Cleary were entitled to their opinions, but I wasn't going to be a puppet for them or anyone. It's so easy to fire off verbal bullets as they did, jump up and down and make a noise. But were they prepared to get any more involved than that, were they prepared to get their hands dirty and follow through on what they were proposing? No. The same applied to anyone who fancied the merger path: get the signatures required, call a meeting and test the water with the rank and file.

Not one of the pro-merger mob did it, and without that step I sure wasn't going to be shoved around by them.

Merger speculation, fuelled by the desperation of the NRL and its backer to push the red-and-green colours into some sort of a deal as public anger grew, came with the regularity of the rising sun in 1999–2000. I think at different stages the media had us linked with everyone but the North Pole Numbats. We were going to Cronulla or to Easts or to Adelaide or to Gosford. The fact was, we weren't going anywhere.

And on our exclusion, there was a different slant to the pressure to merge: the 'attraction' of playing in first division, while retaining our name and colours, was always being dangled in front of us as an option by the NRL. As far as I was concerned, it was no option. The first division was a disappearing competition, with no profile. I don't think we would have attracted a cracker in sponsorship – even Souths Juniors had a clause whereby they could pull their money out of that. We would have had an income of around $250,000, and we'd be playing against sides like Parramatta, valued at $4 million or so. To compete on a level playing field would have been difficult; did we really want to be part of a competition which was light years away from the premier league, where South Sydney rightly belonged? We would have become like Newtown, wiped out by the League years ago but still bravely fighting on in a minor league. The Souths jumper deserves a lot more than being trotted out at some prelim game before a few hundred spectators. Frank Cookson and sections of the Juniors pushed the first division and merger options but, thankfully, didn't have the numbers.

Behind the axing of South Sydney of course stood the 'criteria for entry' that the NRL, along with auditors Ernst & Young (to whom the League paid a small fortune), had come up with. We had run 15th in the ratings and, for whatever reason, the powers-that-be had decided that there would be only 14 teams in the competition. The criteria was supposed to judge clubs equally and fairly, but as I will explain further on when I relate my personal views of the court battles we fought, it never even got close to that. The League and News Limited sold out on a principle that had existed in rugby league for most of its life – a level playing field. The NRL produced criteria that killed off Souths.

When you read the court evidence, as you will, you'll read of the things that other clubs were able to put forward under the criteria, then you'll read of things such as the money contributed by Souths Juniors to the Rabbitohs ($1.5 million per year) that *wasn't* allowed to be counted in our favour as sponsorship revenue. News Limited/NRL unsurprisingly denied throughout that there was anything untoward. NRL chairman Malcolm Noad insisted: 'There was no doctoring . . . because I know it *did* not happen. We had independent advice from Ernst & Young who worked for more than 2000 hours on the criteria with a committee of senior NRL executives, Whittaker, (David) Gallop and Mark Powell.' Noad, whom I'm told was a handy rugby league player in the old Journalists' Cup competition, said he could understand the emotionalism of Souths' plight, but that the club was not unfairly treated. 'If the inference is "was Souths targeted",' he said, 'then the answer is unquestionably no.'

News Limited pushed ahead with its 'magic' 14-team formula, even though it knew that in doing it a very substantial part of the rugby league community would be disenfranchised. The ARL had wanted 16 teams, News Limited 12. The pair of them eventually settled on 14, although many people believed they would cut it to 12 eventually in line with the News Limited preference. We had never been pencilled in on the old Super League competition models and there was no reason to think that had changed. I'd bet money that the name 'Souths' did not appear on any of their blueprints.

It became apparent in court later that lies had been told by some of the other clubs and that the NRL had believed those lies. It believed others, but wouldn't accept our figures. Yet it is now a matter of history and record that our figures stood up under Federal Court scrutiny. It just added weight to the truth that already existed: that they made a bloody awful decision in tipping us out of the competition. Where was the justice? A mob puts rules in place, then shifts them around and decides it will count money contributed in relation to some clubs and not in relation to others, and plays with words like 'gifts', 'sponsorship' and 'grant'. Whatever term was used, the Juniors' money was cash supporting Souths; it was going to pay our way. So why shouldn't it have been counted? They were heading towards a preferred outcome, that's why, and the rules were drawn that way.

There was only one fair way for the whole thing to be conducted: everyone should have been privy to the details of everyone else's criteria. We should all have been able to analyse the Auckland $2 shelf company and the Melbourne $2 shelf company. And when it was demanded that we must all have $5 million income guaranteed per season, we should have been put completely in the picture. Where was the money coming from? Was Murdoch going to continue to prop up some clubs with millions of dollars while others were getting nothing at all? After all, the December 19, 1997 agreement among the clubs had said that News would in due course reduce its interests to just one club. It had also promised 'transparency'. It was never put on the table, any of it. And you don't have to be Einstein to work out why. There was always a hidden agenda – who they wanted in the competition and who they didn't. No doubt they hoped they were going to get away with it without anyone having the balls to take them to court.

I will never believe other than that we got dudded on an NRL criteria which was built on a questionable base and given 'weightings' which were never fully explained. Things were changed to suit their ends, not ours. We should have been 14th qualifier, and in that case we could have carried on as a viable and highly competitive football club. I think any fair-minded person reading the transcripts of the court case would agree they vindicate my belief. If there was an Australian law in place for 'rightness' and 'fairness', we'd never have been out of the competition.

The key question was never addressed: how do you gauge a successful club? Through the criteria, they tried to present us as dinosaurs. Our grants from the leagues club had totalled $2,722,500 in 15 years, yet clubs like Parramatta (Leagues) had far surpassed that in a *single* year. We had been in the competition for more than 90 years. We had always paid our players. We'd run last a few times and first a few times – a few times more than any other club, incidentally. We had provided entertainment to the people of the district and opportunity for its young men, through good times and not so good. We had been there to add something of quality to our district. To me, that's success. Rugby league clubs like Souths have provided a way of life to people – a club to go back to and to socialise in, a chance to be close to the players – and the chance to be part of an atmosphere that's created only by sport.

The mob who took over the game were motivated by trying to create 'profit', and failed miserably. But even if they had been successful they would have missed the point of what sport is about. It's about creating friendship, mateship, community pride. If you've got a good club there's this fantastic aura . . . it becomes the hub of the district. The people of South Sydney claimed South Sydney Football Club as their own. They didn't want to see it die because of Rupert Murdoch or anyone else.

There were some terrible things done right through the Super League period and its aftermath, and the way some of the clubs turned on Souths like we were rats in '99 and beyond was one of them. You can throw some of the ARL clubs into that. I came away from 1997 not having much feeling for or opinion of some of the blokes involved with them. It got even worse in October 1999, when other ARL clubs effectively 'ganged up' on Souths.

When we were initiating court proceedings, which could have had the effect of disrupting the 2000 competition, stories appeared of other clubs prepared to take legal action against us. An anonymous club CEO was quoted in *The Australian* and confirmed that likelihood. Earlier I had written to two of our (formerly) traditional ARL clubs, Balmain and St George, asking them to withdraw their threats of legal action should there be a 16-team competition. Balmain didn't even bother to answer and St George replied that they could not do what I requested, for legal reasons. I told the media that my respect for both clubs had gone.

In the wake of our axing from the premiership, there was no shortage of 'advice' from former allies. 'For God's sake, George, don't love your club to death,' said John Chalk. And Danny Munk chimed in: 'With all this court stuff all they're doing is organising a very expensive funeral. They will die a lingering death.' I treated the comments with the contempt they deserved. Balmain club, after all, had meekly given away their tradition and their colours of 92 years, and dumped us in the process, after agreeing to stick with us 'all the way'. They had to live with that. The sweet irony of it was that they had qualified 14th under the criteria and could have stood alone!

Leading the anti-Souths charge and a new true believer in the Murdoch way of doing things was Parramatta CEO Denis Fitzgerald, an official who was not popular among the rank and file. Fitzgerald and I traded verbal blows more than once. In late 1999 there was a meeting of club chief executives and presidents at a hotel in Mascot when we at Souths were full steam ahead to fight the NRL over the decision to kick us out. Fitzgerald got up at this meeting and announced, 'I think anyone who takes the NRL to court hasn't got one bit of decency or care for this game in them.' 'Denis,' I said, 'I've got one question for you. If Parramatta got shot out of the competition, can you sit there and tell me you wouldn't go to court on behalf of your members, that you wouldn't fight for them? Just a yes or no answer will do, Denis.' And you know, he wouldn't answer the question. He just sat there. Didn't he want the game's new masters to hear his answer? Or was he perhaps one of the chosen ones with a guarantee that his mob wouldn't be chucked out because he had sucked up? As far as I'm concerned, Denis has always been there for Denis.

When we were cut, Fitzgerald even said he didn't feel sorry for Souths: 'They've had the opportunity for two years to form a joint venture and they have chosen to look backwards, not forwards.' Fitzgerald also decided that a personal attack was in order: 'When I played against George Piggins in the '70s he was a hard, tough and uncompromising forward, but he was neither skilful nor clever. George displays those same qualities as an administrator.' On October 17, and with some glee I would imagine, the *Sunday Telegraph* lined us both up for a full-page 'head-to-head'. Denis took a further swipe at me via a story about General Custer (who died with his troops at the Battle of Little Bighorn); he urged the merger with Cronulla, and declared: 'We need to accept the NRL's determination of the 14-team competition for the year 2000 and effectively and enthusiastically promote the new, more competitive premiership.' Spoken like a true believer! My version of the way it was got a little more personal. I didn't (and don't) think much of Fitzgerald, and certainly don't need his lectures. I ended this way: 'I remember a bloke once saying to me about the treachery surrounding the whole rugby league battle: "George, the more I understand humans, the better I love my dog." Denis, let me simply end this by saying that every time I see your name in print, I have this terrible urge to walk my dogs.'

In the midst of the anger and disappointment at what had been done to the club in October '99, a fierce determination emerged to fight to the bitter end. There began days of hard work – a chase for the clues in a paper trail which left no doubt that we had been seriously duped. Our lawyers had told us that we couldn't win a court case. That of course was like a red rag to a bull to a club like South Sydney, so used to jumping hurdles and tackling adversity. On the day after we were booted out of the competition there were remarkable scenes in the club's boardroom, with a small army of workers sifting through piles of papers from within the club and boxes of clippings and material brought in by sympathetic supporters from the Newcastle club. Barbara Davis, a great supporter throughout the Souths fight, and her friend Dee

Collins made the trek from Newcastle to bring valuable material. Dee had collected boxes of newspaper clippings from the ARL v. Super League court case and these, once sorted and classified, became the basis of our search for the paperwork we needed. The quest continued to find further background material to begin a court challenge. Nolene and I were there all day along with Jim and Peter Lahood and their wives, the Lissing brothers, Martin and Jerry, Norm Lipson – the hard-baked Sydney journo who was such a loyal and staunch fighter right through the whole thing – and plenty of others.

The big paperchase had been largely sparked by the ABC journalist Helen Grasswill. When she had been preparing her *Australian Story* program, we gave her access to Souths' financial records, in fact to all our paperwork. We had nothing to hide. Then, as it turned out, to satisfy ABC lawyers as she prepared the program, Helen had to dig into the records of some of the other clubs, seeking further information to support contentions some of our people were making. On the day we were kicked out of the competition she was genuinely shocked; the decision to axe Souths didn't add up in any way with what she had found out in her investigations. That same day she told us bluntly: 'You can't fight this unless you've got documents.' The proof was there for the finding if we could dig deep enough. Rumours had been circulating about the financial standing of other clubs. We knew deep in our hearts and our guts that the financials of the other clubs added up to a crock. But we had no concrete evidence. We also had the problem that documents that should have been in our own files were missing.

So, the search began. It continued all the next day, then the next – at home – as Nolene dug out and searched through all the boxes of papers I had brought home from meetings in the previous 10 years. Luckily, I'd kept copies of most things. Nolene became the focal point of the operation in the days ahead and the phone rang non-stop. There were plenty of people keen to help, and we turned up vital information on clubs such as St George–Illawarra and Penrith which became part of our court case. The sight of Nolene surrounded by all the paper drove home to me what a terrific ally she had been through the whole fight. She never took a backward step and was just great at harnessing people and information.

We sought help wherever we could. We even went for a long shot and contacted US media billionaire Ted Turner, owner of CNN and the Atlanta Braves baseball team, seeking support. We were aware that Turner was no fan of Rupert Murdoch and employed the help of Russell Crowe, who made contact with one of his mates linked to Turner, Burt Reynolds. We subsequently sent a brief proposal and a Souths merchandising pack. Like most long shots it didn't come off, but these were desperate times, calling for desperate measures, and it was worth a try. The lampooning of our move by Ray Hadley and fellow commentators on 2UE's 'Continuous Call' brought the station a stinging letter from Dr Jim Lahood. He wrote:

> It may sound 'far fetched' and unbelievable that Ted Turner would spend any of his money on an Australian rugby league team, but I dare say that five or six years ago the suggestion that Rupert Murdoch would have spent hundreds of millions of dollars on the game would have been met with similar disbelief. Your parody portrayed the South Sydney guernsey as good only for washing cars. Clive Churchill and John Sattler thought enough of the guernsey to suffer the agony of broken bones to further its glory. When you belittle Souths you belittle everything that is great in sport. When you ridicule the desperate measures that the people who love and cherish Souths would go to, to preserve their family, you do yourself and your radio station a great discredit.

The Commonwealth Bank helped the fundraising fight by agreeing to scrap transaction fees on donations and we kicked off a Reclaim the Game appeal, seeking public support. In another move, we shifted our legal power from the hands of Middletons, Moore and Bevins, who in the main had been disappointing in their attitude to our struggles to 'stand alone', and appointed Nicholas Pappas to head the team to handle the coming court battle. I was also not happy with the stance taken by Ron Nathans, head of the Middletons, Moore and Bevins team, who was strong in pushing the 'insolvency' aspect of KPMG's assessment of Souths.

I was also unimpressed when an assessment by the firm on our financial standing – one with which I disagreed strongly, incidentally – was 'leaked' suspiciously to the Sydney media on October 20, a few days after we were cut from the competition. Their opinion was strongly against us taking on the NRL/News Limited in court and described us as being in a 'somewhat perilous financial position'. The leaking of the report (by whoever it was) to a media ever-ready to stick the boot into us was a treacherous act. On the same day that happened, News Limited agreed to provide every ARL-aligned club – except Souths and Norths – with the $500,000 in outstanding funding. They held a gun at our heads. The money would not be handed over until we signed an agreement that the money would be used to discharge 1999 player contract obligations, but to get the cash we would have to unconditionally release News Limited from any claims we may be considering over the 14-team competition (i.e. legal action). I refused to give such an undertaking.

We played hardball as best we could, going about our business quietly and then dropping the occasional bombshell in the press. Near the end of that turbulent October we threatened to wind up the cash-strapped ARL if they didn't arrange payment of the $1 million funding that was due to us (from News Limited and Optus). After all, it was originally the ARL's fault that the money hadn't been paid owing to that shocking administrative stuff-up. But there was a large moral issue too: News and Optus *knew* they had agreed to pay the money. Now both were leaning on a technical hitch. It was pretty atrocious business behaviour in my view. Just because some blockhead had failed to send an invoice didn't take away from the moral obligation.

Every day brought a new development. Our young star Craig Wing, who was described as 'the hottest property in Australian football', pledged to stick with us to the bitter end, although in the circumstances that unfolded we eventually cleared him to leave so he could pursue his career. I'd like to think that his heart stayed with us.

In late October David Moffett arrived from rugby union ranks to take over as the new CEO of the NRL. Moffett rang me one day and came over to the nursery at Eastlakes for a mag. I told him straight that we were getting the short end of the stick. Moffett said he wanted to find a solution, wanted to find an acceptable way of getting Souths back into the competition, as he didn't want the game dragged through the courts. I told him that I knew how to fix things up, and that if we had all been judged under standard practice of accountancy, Souths would have run 14th, and Penrith 15th. I suggested then that we get a taxi together and head out to Penrith and explain to Roger Cowan (Panthers boss) that there had been an error in the accountancy procedures. I offered to call the cab but Moffett declined.

'We're wasting our time, aren't we?' I asked him, and made it very clear that I was not giving up, and that I was not interested in mergers. The game had a new chief executive, but nothing had changed.

Our hopes for the future of the South Sydney Club now hung on a single thread: litigation. Only one thing was certain – we would fight on.

15. Our Day in Court: Round One

> You've trampled on a thing that matters to people. We can hardly find words for it but it's something to do with meaning and a sense of belonging. It's deep and it's real, something we know in our guts.
>
> *Caroline Jones, open letter to Lachlan Murdoch,* Sydney Morning Herald

THE COURT BATTLES that we fought at the end of 1999 and midway through 2000 to try to save South Sydney were as dirty and devious as anything I had ever been involved in, far tougher than any 80 minutes of football I had ever played. With their crafty tactics and dummies and frequent eruptions of foul play, the courtroom stoushes were as fiercely contested as any grand final. I came away from them amazed at how remote the law was from the real world, and from the hopes, dreams and beliefs of ordinary people. We got rolled in the first two battles. And shouldn't have.

The tough stuff was 'on' from the word go. On the November day in 1999 when we filed papers in the Federal Court, seeking a mandatory injunction against the NRL which would compel them to include us in the 2000 competition, the NRL chose to publicly announce its 14-team draw. It was as if they were saying: 'There – get that up you!' Our claim was they had breached the *Trade Practices Act* and that the NRL criteria did not treat all clubs equally and fairly. Legal action and tactics and the search for evidence dominated our lives at Souths. We were fighting on two fronts, tackling the ARL and News Limited in the Federal Court at exactly the same time we were chasing, via the Supreme Court, the $500,000 owed to us by News Limited.

In this time of intense pressure and fight for survival, one-time allies deserted us. All but three clubs – Newcastle, Canterbury and North Queensland – signed affidavits supporting the 14-team competition and kicking us in the teeth. The clubs rolled over and gave News Limited exactly what it wanted: documents which claimed that for us to be put back in would be detrimental to the competition. All these clubs signing letters sticking the knife into Souths. There wasn't one that said, 'Hang on, we just can't do this to Souths.' And some of the blokes involved, I'd played football with them, known them since I was a kid.

Cronulla's chairman Barry Pierce said in his statement that Souths as 15th team should not be part of the competition because we'd ruin the neat two-round home-and-away system and cost them money. Cronulla spoke of marketing strategies and a whole lot of other things about season ticket holders, but not one word about how Souths might be good for the game. For other clubs to accept quietly that Souths hadn't made the cut, and that's the way it was going to have to be . . . I could live with that. But for them to actually sign documents saying that Souths *shouldn't* be in the competition was unbelievable. It was like living your whole life with your brother, then writing secretly to a judge and asking him to put your brother in gaol. It really made me think about where I was going with this whole thing. And I thought if it wasn't for the club and what it had meant to the district, and if it wasn't for the people who wanted that club to live on, I could so easily have walked away. When those documents appeared I knew that I couldn't care less if I never went near any of those people who'd signed them again. And in court, some of them turned on us too.

Sometimes, it was the little things that kept me going. I was in the bank one morning with my mum, and a kid standing next to me tugged my jumper. I soon became aware that the boy was a deaf mute. He pulled a pad out of the bag he was carrying and wrote me a message. It said just this: 'I am a supporter.' I can tell you, I got a lump in my throat. Then he looked up at me and mouthed the words 'Thank you.' I took inspiration from kids like him, and from blokes like Roger Harvey, who is blind but who never missed our home games, trundling along with his radio, taking in the vibes of the crowd and screaming his lungs out for the Rabbitohs. Roger's mum used to take him to the matches. If our game happened to be the one being called he'd listen on the radio, otherwise his mum would be the broadcaster of what was going on on the field. After his mother died, a group of our supporters took it on themselves to make sure that Roger still got to the football. They picked him up at the home he is in, in Lewisham, drove him to the game, and drove him home afterwards. And *that's* what football clubs are all about. The effect of our exclusion from the competition on people such as Roger and so many others was nothing short of devastating. I think too of the father who couldn't bring himself to tell his mentally handicapped son who loved the club that Souths had been kicked out; instead he played the boy videos of old Souths games.

Earlier in 1999 the majority of the clubs had signed a long-form club agreement, which specified that the NRL competition would be made up of 14 teams. The five clubs who didn't sign were Souths, Balmain, Wests, Newcastle and Sydney Roosters. There were occasional bursts like that of what added up to support. At the Souths' fundraising dinner in '99 three clubs took tables: Canterbury, Wests and the Roosters.

Later in 2000 the 14 members of the NRL Club Council, which had Denis Fitzgerald as its chairman and supposedly reflected the independent voice of the clubs, was asked to sign a document reiterating its support for a 14-team competition. Sydney Roosters, to their credit, chose to abstain while every one of the other 13 signed. Predictably, Fitzgerald himself rejected a 15-team competition. 'My view is that we maintain 14 teams – or go less to 12 – not go up,' he told the *Sunday Telegraph*. That put him on the record as wanting to kill off more clubs, and to destroy more opportunities for young men wanting to play rugby league. The stance of the 13 clubs who signed was laughable. Only days before, many followers of these same clubs had joined the second big Souths march, which jammed the centre of the city. But they knew they were going to sign the document. Some of them had already been back to the keepers of the purse, News Limited, for financial refills. They should have been ashamed of themselves; all knew that Souths hadn't been dealt with fairly under the criteria. The Roosters were walking on eggshells because of another factor: in the wake of them signing the affidavit before the court case, the Souths Juniors threatened to ban their small selection of junior teams who played in the Juniors competition. The Roosters wanted to keep good relationships with the cashed-up Juniors and the great depth of young football talent that existed there, particularly if the Rabbitohs disappeared forever!

Meanwhile, we worked furiously hard to raise the money it would take to bankroll what we were trying to do. The highlight of all that effort was the Save Our Souths fundraising dinner at Darling Harbour in mid November at which Russell Crowe dug deep and bought Albert Clift's bell. In all we raised $330,000. Later when Crowe was in Sydney promoting the movie *Gladiator*, he was asked at a press conference what General Maximus would have done to save the Rabbitohs. This is what he said: 'This may sound puerile to non–sport-loving people, but this has really changed my attitude to this city. I always thought it was a right you could always have – that you could follow your football team in your dotage. People made a decision to end that and I really resent it. It sucks.'

The first hearing before Justice Peter Hely in courtroom 21C, 20 storeys high in that big building on the corner of King and Macquarie which I got to know so well, was like a mini-preview of what was to come in the boots 'n' all case six months later. Hely, bespectacled and quietly spoken, had been a QC for News Limited in the original ARL v. Super League hearing. He asked us if we had any objections to him hearing the case. We said no. We had no reason to believe that him being there would go against us in any way.

Chasing the injunction against the NRL to compel Souths' inclusion in the competition for 2000 and beyond would get us back in, and mightily embarrass the NRL. The head of our legal team, Chris Gee QC, hammered home key points, stating that the criteria for membership of the NRL was 'patently unfair'. Within the criteria there was 'weighting' for various categories that was never explained. Inevitably that 'weighting' did not favour our case. Ex–Super League clubs had been allowed to include large multi-million-dollar settlements from News Limited under 'profitability' while for Souths' the $1.5 million per year funding from the Juniors (for three years) was not accepted as 'sponsorship'. This was to be a sticking point throughout: the red herring about whether the Juniors' commitment to us was a 'grant' or a 'sponsorship' – as if it mattered – while huge payouts from News Limited/Super League to clubs were accepted as okay under 'profitability'.

And while the Souths Juniors money had been rejected as 'sponsorship', monies from two other leagues clubs (Brisbane and Wests) *had* been included as acceptable sponsorship. Henry Morris's written declaration that the Juniors' $1.5 million was a legitimate sponsorship deal appeared to count for nothing. The other mob preferred to play with words: 'grants' versus 'sponsorships'. The point *was* that if the $1.5 million per season from the Juniors had been accepted by the NRL as sponsorship and the extraordinary one-off Super League settlements excluded from 'profitability', a reallocation of criteria points on *that* basis had us way ahead of Penrith in 14th place. We would have been in the 14, alive and kicking and entitled to a five-year licence and $2 million in funding.

NRL finance manager Ed Farish conceded as much on the same day that Penrith chief executive Mark Levy told the court that his club had received a $9 million Super League payout from News Limited, and that it was 'part' of his club making the cut. Penrith had received $13.5 million in funding from News Limited in 1998–99, including the $9 million for the current year. In a normal year, the Panthers grant had been in the vicinity of $1 million from the leagues club. So there it was, right there. News Limited argued that its settlements of huge amounts to the ex–Super League clubs was balanced by the ARL's payout to its clubs. This was absolute bullshit, the ARL handout of (Optus) money being a mere pittance by comparison.

And this was the cruellest part of all: that it was so obvious the criteria had been shaped in a certain way to favour the clubs that were wanted in, yet that approach didn't count in the eyes of the law, as the court initial judgments were to prove. Yep, our opponents could manipulate things unfairly to specifically *exclude* us and *include* others, but that injustice wasn't worth a zak under the law. This court case and the next were not in any way about right and wrong; they were about the technicalities of the *Trade Practices Act*.

It brought into the open a bigger question: the ability of the law to handle corporate assaults on community assets. Such things as the importance of the club to the local community was not taken into account – and that's outrageous.

To me, it's an amazing situation that under the law covering business transactions there is no implied (or automatic) obligation to be fair. What the ARL and News Limited had done in their partnership was a private arrangement, and the obligation for the arrangement to be a fair and principled one wasn't there. One of the legal people explained to me that the law divides transactions into business transactions and consumer transactions. Consumer transactions have all these consumer remedies of fairness, but this (the birth of the NRL) was a purely private business transaction. There was no implied obligation to be fair. Under the way it works I can cheat you – I can tell you this is the best business you could ever buy, that it's worth millions of dollars – and when you find out it is worth nothing after buying it, there is no redress purely on fairness grounds. You may be able to sue me on misrepresentation under the *Trade Practices Act*, but that is very, very hard to do. The problem for us was that there was no express term of fairness in the contract Souths had with the NRL, the one signed on legal advice we received soon after the start of the season.

I've gotta think now that that was an oversight back in early 1998, a bad miss in the sort of supposedly 'expert' advice we were getting at the time. I have no doubt that if we'd been working then with our current legal team, letters and documents would have been drafted differently and no-one could have come back and attacked us. Because of the lack of any written 'fairness' arrangement, the law was saying to us now: 'Unless you can convince me there was an obligation to be fair I can't do anything about it.' To me it's a bloody long way removed from the old Australian way, where you'd shake hands on something, and the unspoken arrangement from that point was to act in a principled and fair way.

In a similar spirit, there were some bad things said and done in that first court case, as in the second. The contribution of one-time St George CEO, then NRL communications manager, Geoff Carr made me boil. In a statement read to the court, Carr declared that if we were reinstated we would almost certainly finish last, and that we should sit out the season. Thanks for the advice, Geoff. St George CEO Brian Johnston went even further. In his statement to the court, Johnston said that his club stood to lose $50,000–$80,000 in sponsorship and $118,000 in gate takings if they were stripped of a home game, which would happen if Souths were reinstated in a 15-team competition.

Under cross-examination, Johnston went on to goose himself.

His basic message was that for Souths to come back in would be bad for the game. But he had to admit – because it was true – that St George's biggest game of 1999 was against Souths, when we drew a record crowd of 28,310 to the Charity Shield game on February 21. The fact that it was an old ARL ally, Saints, putting in the slipper in court really hurt. Johnston tried to make the point that St George had merged with Illawarra for the good of the game. But, in fact, one of the really fair dinkum reasons was that St George's home ground, Kogarah Oval, did not fulfil the requirements of the criteria. Geoff Carr was to involve himself still further. On the eve of Justice Hely's decision a few days later he told the media that a favourable result for Souths would represent an 'absolute nightmare'. A 15-team draw would create 'all sorts of difficulties', said Carr. The NRL certainly favoured 14, but despite Carr's words, the fact was that a workable blueprint for a 15-team competition *did* exist and was tabled during the hearing. Later, in mid 2001, the model had to be dusted off and brought back into play.

I had always liked Geoff Carr, and thought of him as a good St George man. But for him to get up in court, as he did, and say that Souths' presence would be detrimental to the competition was despicable. I suspect the supporters of St George, a club which had played shoulder to shoulder alongside Souths in the competition for all those years, would have thought exactly the same of him.

The Saints, the second most successful team in league history and a traditional rival of Souths for so many years, disappointed me throughout. In September 1998, Saints decided to merge with Illawarra, the two clubs putting their hands out for an $11 million funding package and a seven-year licence. But what St George did not have to do was to put the slipper into Souths. By the time of the court case they were long since on the record as threatening legal action if the competition was not reduced to 14 (that is, if teams like Souths, Balmain and Wests *weren't* killed off). Wests made the same threat after doing their merger deal. And Brian Johnston went on radio in support of 14 teams at a time when he was sitting comfortably on the NRL board, supposedly representing his ARL 'mates'. Now he was up there in the court case, undermining our position.

Phil Gould flew back from holidays to answer Carr's unhelpful in-court claims that we would 'finish last' and that our matches would be lopsided. 'I find it a bold statement, to say the least,' said Gould, who argued that 2000 could be a stepping stone for bigger things for our club, and that for us to sit out the season would leave us greatly damaged. The club *would* be competitive in 2000, he said.

Late in the case we had news of support from 'high places'; nine Australian Catholic bishops had signed a statement of support for the Rabbitohs. The press release was couched in these terms:

> Recognising the important part of sport in the Australian psyche and the grand traditions of South Sydney over 92 years, the under-signed Australian Catholic Bishops support the retention of the club in the national Rugby League Competition. In doing so, the Bishops seek to be a voice for countless Australians who lament the loss of valued institutions at the hands of corporate giants.

Earlier, one of the signatories, Bishop Pat Power, auxiliary bishop of the Archdiocese of Canberra and Goulburn, had offered personal support, declaring that marching with us at the October 1999 rally was 'one of the most memorable days of my life'. Bishop Power wrote: 'So much of what Souths stands for is *people power*. . . While Souths are excluded from the competition, rugby league will fail to be the people's game and will continue to lose its popular support. The message is clear: "Give the game back to the people by allowing Souths back into the competition".'

In Sydney, Catholic priest Brian Rayner delivered successive Sunday sermons in the South Sydney district deploring what he suggested was the lack of moral responsibility in the NRL's decision to cut the competition to 14 teams. He told his congregation: 'The scriptures, of course, don't mention football mergers and the like, but they do speak about greed and the preoccupation of some people to accumulate wealth to the detriment of others. They speak of our obligation to be mindful of the needs of the poor and the disadvantaged.'

The case finished on December 3, 1999; a relief for our loyal supporters who had rolled up each day to sit through the often dry legal argument. Throughout it all, our coach, Craig Coleman, tried to hold it all together on the playing side, running a group of 'faithfuls' daily at training. Coleman was continually in touch with a range of players and remained optimistic that we would be competitive – 'stronger than last season' – if we got the nod. But when it came to playing strength, we were on a knife's edge. A successful judgment from Justice Hely would guarantee us a place in the premiership, to kick off in February, with the full court hearing to come hard on the heels of that.

But in a few whispered words at 12.30 pm on December 8, Peter Hely dismissed our application for readmission to the 2000 premiership. It took a couple of minutes or less, a barely audible judgment backed by a 34-page document. 'We're gone,' said Henry Morris. Justice Hely's reasons were as follows:

• The 'real risk of substantial financial loss to other clubs' if we were admitted.

• It could not be predicted that Souths could compete in the 2000 competition without the $2 million grant that the NRL was to pay the other 14 teams.

• He declared the club 'verging on insolvent, if not insolvent'.

• He was not satisfied that Souths would be able to compensate other parties for losses sustained if the injunction was granted, and Souths ultimately failed in their claim. 'Souths' financial position and its ability to perform its undertakings as to damages has always been an issue in these proceedings,' the judgment said. 'The balance of convenience is heavily against the granting of the interlocutory relief sought, no matter what sympathy one may feel for Souths.'

The view from the legal eagles was that Hely had been fair under the law and had not had a lot of room to move, because the club couldn't put up the required financial sureties at that stage in the event of losing the full hearing. None of that of course addressed the moral rights and wrongs . . . which were clearcut.

But Justice Hely provided glimpses of hope, such as when he declared that our Trade Practices claim was 'seriously arguable'. But the result was shattering all the same. I honestly thought we were odds-on; I thought we couldn't get beaten. Emotion spilled over in and around the courtroom as our supporters struggled to come to terms with another smack in the mouth. At one point a group of them ringed the NRL lawyers in an angry confrontation. In *The Australian*, journalist John Mac-Donald, who had cast an eye over the day, wrote, 'Football had nothing to do with it. This was business. All the emotionalism counted for nothing with the bean-counters.' The headline writers went for the jugular: 'The day South Sydney died', 'Rabbit chop', 'South Sydney slaughtered', 'Kicked out' and 'Souths king-hit in court'.

From this case, some things shone like beacons:

• We had been treated unfairly and differently in comparison with other clubs.

• If the $500,000 withheld by News Limited had been available to us under the criteria, we would have qualified 14th and there would have been no court case. None involving us, anyway.

• If the $1.5 million a year from Souths Juniors had been accepted as a sponsorship and the Super League settlements excluded from 'profitability', we would have been in the 14. There are rumours that the NRL at one stage had indicated to the Complete Marketing people that the money *would* be classified under 'sponsorship', but if that's true, there was certainly a big switch in opinion somewhere along the track. During the hearing Henry Morris confirmed this via a note still in the files:

'Mark Collie [sic] told me quite clearly that the NRL had accepted our money as sponsorship.' I understand that Colley had been led to believe that this was so, and it wasn't until late in the day that the sponsorship was heavily questioned by the NRL.

• Souths would certainly have been the 14th team *if* News Limited hadn't introduced a brand new team (Melbourne, announced in September '97) into the competition, for 1998, *after* the ARL–Super League deal had been done in December 1997. News owned 70 per cent of the new team with an indication that they would reduce their involvement. The new team was then given a super-cosy and highly questionable run through the criteria (as discussed in the next chapter). A certain number of teams in 1997 had agreed to future arrangements in the competition and another club – completely uninvolved in that process – had then been added to the mix.

• The criteria that decided the life and death of clubs was based in the main on just *two* years in the duration of a competition that had been going for 92 years! And those two years came during and after a period of the greatest turmoil in the game's history, a period which had crash-tackled the game and left it in disarray. The only criteria clause extending over a longer period related to competition points, for four years from 1995 to 1999.

• The criteria failed to take into account 'junior numbers' – something at the heart and soul of the game, representing its future. Souths were particularly strong in that area (via the excellence of the Juniors' extensive competitions) so the category was not included. The 'weighting' put on the various criteria categories remain a mystery to this day. It seemed clear to me that the weightings applied to the various categories were there to help provide a conclusion that had already been decided upon. In court they could never explain the weightings, apart from the weak explanation that various things were rated more highly because they were 'important'.

Consider those points. The whole criteria thing was full of holes, and we identified a stack of them at Souths: the criteria were established and controlled by unknown people who offered no transparency to the clubs; different clubs were treated differently under the criteria (for example Auckland got a cosy run); there were different versions of criteria categories; the criteria were judged by people with vested interests, that is News Limited and certain individuals with club affiliations; the criteria demanded a five-year business plan, yet the NRL itself had no five-year business plan; the lack of market research involving the decision to go to 14 teams. The number 14 was just something 'the boys' decided, against overwhelming evidence that league fans were happy with 16. Then there was the constant speculation that Souths would be cut 'under the criteria', smoothing a path via the media for what eventually happened, and the falsification of crowd figures by some clubs.

I was advised by our legal team that we had gone closer than most had thought likely to getting the injunction under Justice Hely. We won on the first of the two tests: that there was a serious question to be tried in our challenge to the NRL, but lost on the second, concerning the general 'balance of convenience'. The question was: by keeping Souths in, were other parties going to be prejudiced? Because it was not only News and not only the NRL but the *clubs*, or most of them, saying via their affidavits that our inclusion would be the ruination of the 14-team competition – that was what beat us. And Justice Hely judged that the balance of convenience lay on the other side. We were encouraged by Hely's finding that we had a strongly arguable case; Peter Hely was apparently regarded as a trade practices expert. His worry was that we'd go back in and then collapse financially in 2000.

Back at the club that afternoon and night it sank in: for the first time in 92 years South Sydney wouldn't be fielding a team in the rugby league premiership. For the people at the helm, the night was a repeat of what we had all been through back in October when they cut us. What was happening to a great sporting club was against the Australian way of life and against the principle of a fair go.

Once again we found ourselves at the leagues club, consoling deeply upset people and trying to somehow rescue from the disappointment the necessary spirit and enthusiasm to fight on. There were angry people at the club that night, people who wanted to march in protest on the NRL at Foxtel. That would have only added to our troubles and I called for calm. 'We might be out, but we're not beaten,' I told them. 'Who knows what the future holds? Maybe one day we'll be back.' The NRL was predictably talking 'merger' talk and I quickly shot that down. I also declared I wouldn't watch another NRL match until we were back in. At the club Andrew Denton spoke of the 'Judas-like submissions from other NRL clubs'. 'Souths are not going to go away,' he said. 'Reports of our death during the case were greatly exaggerated.'

Throughout the fight, Denton and Alan Jones provided strength and credibility. I'm sure it has not been easy for either of them. I heard the rumours of them being pressured to 'ease off', 'take a step back', or else. People such as them put careers on the line because of their belief in Souths and hatred of the injustice done to the club. But rarely was there a hesitant step and the club and its fans should be thankful that we had them around – and some other stout-hearted friends in high places too. The funny thing about Jones and Denton, then both breakfast broadcasters on rival Sydney radio stations, is that there is no love lost between them. And yet, in the interest of a greater cause, they were united. The support of influential men such as Jones and Denton and others helped keep our cause strongly up front in the eyes of the public. There's no doubt they helped us considerably; they kept our profile up, and we were fortunate to have them on our side. But it's a reflection on the way of things that an organisation fighting for life as we were needed that high-level support to be in with a chance. I ask the question: Shouldn't the law be enough? Or is it there only for the rich man? Shouldn't it be that the law is the law, and the law is there for all of us as it is for the likes of the Murdochs?

After the Hely decision, we regrouped and made our plans. Eventually, as the disappointment was replaced by renewed determination in the days that followed, there was a unanimous decision: we had to fight on. Within a few days we had decided we would not field a first division side in 2000, preferring to keep our cash for the bigger issue of the court case, although we would field junior rep sides. Craig Wing, suddenly a player without a club, had his say: 'My childhood dream of playing my career for Souths has been taken away.' Before long we gave our remaining four contracted players – Wing, Jeremy Schloss, Chris Caruana and Jason Nicol – permission to negotiate with other clubs. Craig 'Tugger' Coleman was an unemployed coach, but his determination to fight on was never in question.

A *Sydney Morning Herald* editorial the day after the judgment made a telling point: 'The NRL, in fact, has never really given a convincing argument why the Rabbitohs should be thrown out of a competition of which it is a founder member.' The editorial closed with the $64,000 question: 'Is a 14-team competition worth breaking the hearts of the supporters of such an iconic club?'

I had my own say, courtesy of the *Sun-Herald* on December 12:

> Had I really heard evidence revealing that millions of dollars given to Super League clubs such as Penrith was accounted for in such a way that it gave them an advantage over us and meant we could not make it?
>
> Did I really hear the NRL accountant say the money we received from Souths Juniors was not sponsorship – which it was – so it wouldn't count in our criteria points, even though he still counted the other clubs' $9 million settlement from News Limited as profit, which got them a hell of a lot of extra points?
>
> And I wondered whether I'd really heard people from the NRL, who were once pals on the ARL, tell the court how Souths' inclusion would be a disaster. What? . . .
>
> So, Souths were shafted. The question is: why?

In another way, I threw down the gauntlet to the NRL and News Limited, who by now were thoroughly aware of the storm they had whipped up by killing Souths. In the wake of the Hely decision I went on Channel 9's *Today on Saturday* show and offered to resign as chairman. In an interview conducted outside my house, with the blue Pacific Ocean as the backdrop, I said that if News and the NRL would do what the people wanted and put Souths back in, and if I was perceived as the hindrance to that happening, then I would resign immediately. It was a test for them, and an opportunity. But my offer went straight through to the 'keeper, further proof that the cutting of the Rabbitohs' throat was seen as a desired and permanent outcome by them.

It was always the South Sydney way on the football field to be on the front foot. Before long we were that way again off-field, taking enough out of Peter Hely's judgment to know that we had a strong enough case to fight on. At the club, the board was boosted by the addition of federal MP for Grayndler, Anthony Albanese, and the Randwick mayor, Dominic Sullivan, both strongly committed to the cause. Albanese promptly fired a shot across the News Limited bows. 'It's impossible to argue that News Limited have not abused their position in the reportage of this dispute,' he said, declaring that the ACCC could be asked to investigate whether the NRL and News had breached national competition policy. At the press conference welcoming the pair on board on December 16, Dominic Sullivan showed where he stood. 'We will not fall on our swords,' he said. 'You'll have to kill us before we drop out of the competition. We will not roll over for a bunch of spineless, faceless bean-counters. We will be standing . . . we will be fighting.' It was the way we all felt as we headed into the first (or last, depending on your point of view) year of the millennium.

The strength shown by Albanese and Sullivan was not evident in another prominent politician when Henry Morris and I wrote to the member for Maroubra and NSW premier, Bob Carr, seeking his support in helping get Souths reinstated to the competition. Carr in his reply chose to adopt a somewhat moralistic tone, writing unhelpfully: 'Ultimately, just as is the case in any sporting contest, one side or the other will have to accept the independent umpire's decision.' A little later when the premier was in a promotional photo celebrating the arrival of the Northern Eagles at NorthPower Stadium I couldn't hold back. 'Bob Carr is photographed up at Grahame Park [NorthPower Stadium], which will be used to generate profits for the NRL, a commercial enterprise half-owned by Rupert Murdoch. Bob Carr has given him Fox Studios and Grahame Park while me and Henry [Morris] can't get an audience. Charity begins at home.'

My relationship with the premier had been edgy for quite a time. As mentioned, in 1998 I had threatened to stand as an independent against Carr, as a protest against crippling poker machine taxes being planned for imposition on licensed clubs. Belatedly, in mid November 2000 Bob Carr went strongly to bat for the Rabbitohs. In the wake of the 80,000 turnout at our rally, he issued a press statement, making the point: 'The size of the crowd on Sunday sent an important message – a way has to be found for Souths to be included in the competition.'

Our quest in 2000 was for a $2 million war chest to fund the fight. First up was a 'Save Our Souths' family day at Redfern on February 5, organised by Andrew Denton and clashing (by design) with the NRL's double-header season opener at the Olympic Stadium. The day featured a Souths Legends v. Personalities touch football match with H.G. Nelson and Roy Slaven as match-callers in an afternoon of entertainment, leading into an evening concert featuring the likes of Aria award-winning band You Am I, Troy Cassar-Daley, Allan Caswell, Little Pattie and Le Club Nerd. We drew a crowd of 17,000. At Homebush they had 62,000 to see four leading teams play . . . so we reckon it was a moral victory. Ours was a great day. Eric Simms came down from the crowd to kick the 'winning' goal in the touch football match, refereed by Barry 'the Grasshopper' Gomersall and Paul McBlane. The only casualty was me: a ripped hamstring in the Legends game followed by a declaration that I was out for the rest of the season. We raised plenty of cash.

The Souths Leagues Club, not trading well, was in the news then with the distinct possibility that we would reach some deal under which it would be taken over by a wealthy bidder. With their development at Liverpool in a bind, Canterbury Leagues turned their eyes to the licence at Souths, and all of a sudden they became something of a friend. Eastern Suburbs didn't want Canterbury to get the club, so they made a move too. For our own part, we wanted a third candidate, Souths Juniors, to take it over, but they wouldn't commit. That being the case, in my view it had to be either Canterbury or Easts, and to do business would have been a positive move in the circumstances of the time. But my board overruled me; they wanted to put it on hold.

I had the sense that Canterbury's specific interest lay in the licence, and it was Easts who put something to us that was fairer. If they were to take it over they would only do it after the court case had been completed – and the club would remain as 'South Sydney'. Our board wanted the Juniors or no-one, and before I went to the final meeting – well, *my* final meeting – I rang Henry Morris, but it was still no from them. By then, Canterbury were out too. I reckoned we should have taken the Easts offer, but on the vote of the board it was no. They wanted to go back to the Juniors *again*. I just felt we had been running into that brick wall long enough and I wasn't prepared to go on with it any further. I resigned that night, after 10 years as chairman.

It was probably time to go. Friendships had become a bit strained in the ongoing two-way battle to save both the football club and the leagues club. But don't get me wrong on that; I'd love to see our leagues club survive, and if I could help out with a deal tomorrow I'd pick up the phone immediately, call Souths Leagues Club chairman Bernie O'Neill and pass it on. The directors of that club have worked hard for a long time because they care about the place.

The leagues club has felt the weight of a shocking double-whammy in recent times. First came the government's bloody awful decision to give the pubs poker machines. Then when the NRL ousted the football club, it was a big kick in the guts to the licensed club too. People just didn't want to go there much anymore. It was akin to a death in the family; people didn't want to hang around with the body. As the long wait went on to see whether the Rabbitohs would stay alive, enthusiasm started to wane. Going to the club was not what it once had been.

A sense of gloom had settled over the place.

Now and then I would think back to 1990 when I took over as chairman of the club. Back then my dream was to move the club across to Redfern Oval and build a beautiful facility there on a refurbished and modern oval. I went as far as having plans drawn up for the development, and when Canterbury, backed by the Macquarie Bank, came to us with their proposal to take over the club in 2000, they had sketches of what they proposed, and it was sensational. The cost would have been around $40 million. I pulled out the plans we had done 10 years earlier, and they were amazed. They couldn't believe we hadn't gone ahead back then, at what would have been a fraction of the cost. It had been my strong belief (and it never really changed) that we had to get the leagues club up and thriving if we wanted to sustain a successful football side.

Another development we had on the drawing board was a plan to convert the car park and adjoining property into 100 apartments. South Sydney Council passed that initially – and then, I'm told, a highly influential person knocked 10 off the number, reducing the appeal of the building to the bloke who was contemplating the development. He was going to build us a $5 million car park for the club. Finally, he didn't take up the option and the board approached the Juniors again.

As Olympic year unfolded, we worked hard at raising the money we needed. In February came a big boost: the arrival – finally – of the $500,000 Optus owed, the result of a deal brokered with the company by ARL chairman Colin Love. The News Limited $500,000 was still in limbo, but the Optus money was a big kick. We went bush too, playing matches and conducting coaching clinics in NSW country districts such as Orange, Dubbo and Scone. The support out there was terrific, the country people identifying very closely with our plight of being crushed by a corporate giant. They knew about those things. Because of the support for Souths that existed we went out of our way to spend time in the bush with the team over the past couple of seasons. And the country people have been just great. But I've gotta say this: the game gives every indication it's dying out there. We went to centres where, 10 years ago, you wouldn't have fitted the people in for a game featuring a Sydney team, and we found the interest had waned. People hated what had been done to the game and were showing that in the most obvious way – by walking away.

The signs that the game was fading in the bush led me to believe that even if Souths got back in – which I knew would be the best thing that could possibly happen for rugby league – there were no guarantees at all about the game's long-term future. Our fundraising continued in full swing as it had to and our small army of volunteers – the likes of Phil Pike, Marcia Seebacher, Don Clark, Andrew Hanley and Eileen McLoughlin (who has worked voluntarily for Souths for five years in various office roles at the football club) and the very committed and loyal media man Norm Lipson – did a mighty job. They were the greatest group of volunteers any club could hope for. One highlight was the annual Red & Green Ball in May 2000, for which we squeezed 1000 people into the University of NSW's Roundhouse at Kensington, and at which we raised more than $120,000, released a book (*Pride of the League*) and took some painful pleasure from the many scathing words uttered about what the NRL and News Limited had done to the club. The Greek and Lebanese communities both held big fundraising nights which brought in $100,000 in total. A couple of days after the Red & Green Ball, the book-signing session for *Pride of the League* drew a crowd that stretched from Pitt Street Mall all the way down and around into Market Street, as blokes like Jack Rayner, Eric Simms, Bernie Purcell and Craig Coleman signed copies for three hours or so.

At that signing, I met a bloke named Ernie Fairbrother, an elderly man in his seventies clutching a pictureframe. Inside it was a real treasure – a letter from his father, also Ernie, from

Gallipoli in 1915. Ernie Snr had been wounded and from a field hospital had written home to his family in Waterloo. 'How were Souths going?' he'd asked his mum. Could anything make the point more strongly? It showed how much the club had meant, and for how long. There were modern parallels to Ernie Fairbrother's poignant letter in the notes of support we received from soldiers then serving in East Timor, all offering their support for the club and the cause.

We were back in court, familiar territory by now, in April 2000, at a preliminary hearing of the case that would again bring down judgment on our future as a football club. Our legal team filed an amended statement of claim alleging that News Limited had provided tens of millions of dollars in funding and loans to eight clubs and accusing News of 'misleading and deceptive conduct' in the selection of clubs for the 2000 season. The case was not to begin until June 13, but we had fired the first shot.

Our claim was that the criteria favoured clubs in which News Limited had pecuniary interest. The clubs named were Canberra, North Queensland, Melbourne, Canterbury, Penrith, Cronulla, Brisbane and Auckland. For the case that lay ahead we recruited one of the best in the business, Tom Hughes QC, who had appeared for News Limited in the successful appeal to the full bench of the High Court in the Super League v. ARL case. He would be supported by Richard White SC, a trade practices expert, and Nicholas Pappas and his team. We had 'lost' twice now – at the NRL's hands, and in Round One in court – but in the process we had gained leverage and stayed strongly in the public domain. To fight the fight via the legal route was the only hope of keeping South Sydney alive. Once that cord was severed, there was nothing . . . unless the Murdoch-run competition collapsed, or something dramatic like that, which, of course, was not impossible.

We raised our sights to Round Two. As before, it was David versus Goliath. But we knew we had the people with us all the way, and we knew that we had right on our side.

16. Our Day in Court: Round Two

The time has come to put on wigs, it's time to wear
    the gowns,
South Sydney's taking up the fight, and we are back in
    town.
You may think you've won the war, but don't collect
    your bet,
We mean bloody business, mate, you ain't seen nothin'
    yet.

Morry Anthony

WHEN WE CAME BACK to the Federal Court before Justice
Paul Finn to fight the big case in June and July of 2000, they put
me in the witness box for five days. Sometimes it seemed the
main aim of the other mob was just to try and make me look a
bloody idiot. I was in there day after day in the last week of June,
after first taking the block just after lunch on Friday, June 19,
and I answered everything as truthfully as I possibly could. I
didn't try to hide anything. I did my best in what to me was

273

an unnatural, uncomfortable environment. And it was never easy, thanks to the often incomprehensible legal debate that dragged on endlessly. I'll admit that plenty of that went right over my head and I'm told that the proceedings were so complex at times that even the lawyers had difficulty following them. There was no doubt that the other side's tactics were to try to trip me up; they called me a liar and even made an issue of the fact that I'm not a good speller. And, you know, I kept thinking that there was not one thing in my life that I had to prove to people like them. I just happened to have been a person who'd been involved in sport and a particular game, and who played that game and found a better position in life because of it. And here were these people trying to bring me down because of my lack of education. I suppose it's the way the justice system works – that adversarial approach. But I ask: what principles are there in that?

The fact is though, when you tell the truth it's an awfully hard thing to beat. When they were taking issue over the key point of whether Souths Juniors' $1.5 million per year injection into the Rabbitohs was a 'grant' or a 'sponsorship' I was able to shoot *them* down. The failure to include the money under 'sponsorship' in the criteria was a strong factor in us not running 14th, of course. They were trying to say it wasn't a sponsorship, while I was saying it was. Next day I was able to bring into court a document relating to a sponsorship arrangement with Randwick Rugby Club which showed that Ray Furse, our treasurer and former director, happened to use the word 'grant' when referring to a sponsorship. It was just his habit, his way of saying it.

We had gone into the case well cashed-up, as we needed to be. There had been an immense amount of hard work by our marketing people and the volunteer army. In just 10 days, for example, we had sold 60,000 red-and-green ribbons at $2 a pop. We were flat out keeping up with the demand for the famous Souths jumper, which was outselling all 14 NRL club jumpers. In the days before the hearing opened we posted a $500,000 bond to prove we could pay court costs. Needled by our legal action, News Limited had finally come good with the half-million owed to us – and paid to the other clubs long before – with the parties agreeing that the funds would be used as security of costs in the Federal Court case. We would fight the case on two grounds: our claim that the 14-team competition was an exclusionary provision in breach of the *Trade Practices Act*; and the question of the fairness of the criteria, even though we pretty much knew it would be difficult to win on that.

We were suing four target groups: News Limited, the NRL, the ARL and the 14 NRL clubs. I insisted that the question of the criteria had to be part of our attack, even though I was aware of our legal team's reservations about that, that we couldn't win on those grounds. I wanted to make sure we got the thing out into the public arena. I wanted to make the public aware of the blatant unfairness of the criteria, to share with them things we had learned, that some teams were favoured and others were marked for exclusion. We did that very successfully in the case. But fairness, sadly, was cheap currency, as Justice Finn emphasised in his judgment many weeks later when he argued that fairness in relation to the criteria was only 'an objective to be pursued, not a designated, promised or warranted outcome'.

Pursuing the fairness line, though, enabled us to get out into the open some of the documents and startling facts and figures that you will read in this chapter. On fairness, News claimed they had been fair by letting newcomers like Melbourne in. What baloney! They owned 70 per cent of the bloody joint. Make no mistake: the criteria allegedly designed to give a 'fair result' were *exclusionary* . . . not *inclusionary*. News also tried to argue that this (from 1999) was a brand-new competition, unconnected with what had gone before in rugby league. After 92 years of the premiership it was fairyland stuff.

Throughout the 40 days of the hearing, a large group (between 70 and 100 each day, and 300 or so on opening day) of red-and-green faithfuls sat through the long, often mind-numbing sessions of daily debate. Sometimes emotions spilled over. When News Limited's senior counsel Noel Hutley questioned the dedication of Souths fans – 'because fans can change their loyalty' – one of our mob yelled: 'Bullshit, mate!' The media tagged them 'the Bunny Army', and now and then there would be bursts of applause to enliven the dry proceedings. Hutley's false contention flew in the face of the words of our man Tom Hughes QC, who told the court in his opening address: 'Tribal loyalties abound in rugby league. Tribal loyalists, the followers through thick and thin of a particular club, are a distinct and recognisable class. The Souths tribal loyalists have a very distinct ethos . . . they are attached to a club which has produced some of the legends . . . people who are legendary in the code, such as Clive Churchill.'

The complicated legalese and the gruelling day-to-day grind of the court battle is perhaps for another larger, drier book at another time, written by some expert in the law. It is not for this one, which represents my personal views of a life, and the things that occurred in it. Instead, I will begin by giving you two different viewpoints on the case. And there was a third too, just as strong and persuasive, but regrettably never published and existing only as a private document now. At the time of the court hearing, former State of Origin coach Phil Gould, one of the game's great thinkers and experts, submitted a story on elements of the major Souths court case as his weekly column in the *Sun-Herald*. The newspaper chose not to publish. I subsequently read a copy of Phil's story and to me it provided a clear and important picture of just some of the injustices involved in the NRL's preparation for the shift down to a 14-team competition.

But so too did other aspects – details gathered in an exhaustive 'paper chase', and some of the evidence given during the long and gruelling slog of the case:

• Some extraordinary further facts were uncovered when our legal people and researchers pinned down 'the money trail', disclosing the vast News Limited payments to Super League clubs

– revelations which left absolutely no doubt that the criteria could not in any way be considered a level playing field.

• Disclosures, admissions and facts that emerged day by day in evidence given in the court are included, and all add to my conviction that South Sydney had been 'rorted'.

I would suggest that a reading of these two separate views of the case by any reasonable person would confirm the larger truth that a very serious injustice was perpetrated, and raise the inevitable question of how the law could possibly fail to find a way to support that view. An understanding of the sustained anger which has supported Souths' fight becomes clear.

THE MONEY TRAIL: These are public record facts we dug up on the extent of the support given to the Super League clubs. In total they give an amazing picture of the huge financial black hole that News Limited tumbled into when it fell for the 'spin' back in 1995, and the extent of the help that some clubs received.

• North Queensland, Auckland, Penrith and Melbourne did not satisfy the criterion for solvency which was one of the basic criteria for determining a club's qualification to participate in the competition from 2000. (Unsurprisingly Auckland fell over, flat broke, within weeks of the hearing concluding. Eventually, with players unpaid, a new Auckland club structure was put in place, one that was not seemingly subject to the criteria.)

• As of September 22, 1999, Melbourne required additional funding of $3,250,000 to cover a shortfall of revenue against expenses, projected losses in 2000 and player top-up payments. On September 22, 1999, News agreed to contribute additional funding of $2,275,000. There was no requirement to show how the gap between the two figures ($975,000) would be funded or details of loan repayments, despite that being an obligation under the solvency criterion.

• Melbourne required and received funding of $13,439,000

Never Say Die

from News and Super League in respect of the 1998 and '99 years, the two years of the criteria.

• The solvency of Melbourne Storm Football Club Limited depended upon the projected receipt of a 'management fee' of between $9.5 million and $10.4 million between 1999 and 2004 from Valimanda Pty Ltd. The NRL did not seek or obtain any confirmation of Valimanda's financial capacity to pay such a fee.

• Background on player payments, grants, loans or the taking of equity from November 1, 1995 to December 31, 1996 included:
    Auckland: $5,800,000
    Brisbane: $5,500,000
    Canberra: $10,000,000
    Canterbury: $9,100,000
    Cronulla: $6,800,000
    North Queensland: $16,000,000
    Penrith: $8,600,000

• Identified grants, indemnities and sponsorship to Super League clubs of $31,103,347.

• The making of additional payments to the following clubs during the year ended June 30, 1997:
    Auckland: $572,657
    Brisbane: $980,166
    Canberra: $616,178
    Canterbury: $2,287,534
    Cronulla: $1,664,177
    North Queensland: $5,357,712
    Penrith: $2,827,500

• The total of payments to players with Super League clubs, including benefits and travel and accommodation costs, was $27,567,654.

• Funding provided by News or Super League to North Queensland to the end of 1997 season was $29,000,000.

• Brisbane received a grant from News (or NRL Investments) of $9.2 million for 1998–99.

• Auckland would have incurred losses of $9.2 million for that period if not for a grant of $5.6 million and the writing off of $2 million from News.

• Payments made by News or Super League to Melbourne in respect of 'player top-up payments' to September 22, 1999 totalled $5,828,000.

• Canberra, funded wholly by News in 1998–99 and 2000, paid players not less than $7,268,000 in 1998 and budgeted for $6,235,000 for player payments in 1999. News poured $7.5 million into Canberra in 1998 and another $9.3 million in 1999.

• A loan of $4.4 million to Penrith was forgiven by News Limited.

And so it went on; the evidence showed that a heap of money had been made available to the ex–Super League clubs, providing them with the chance to make the criteria, that rules had been bent, questions left unasked and unanswered. The Super League 'settlements' after a period that was difficult for all football clubs were deemed acceptable under the criteria. And yet Souths' perfectly legitimate $1.5 million per annum from Souths Juniors was rejected under the sponsorship criteria, and that decision, allied to the acceptance of settlements to the ex–Super League club under 'profitability', brought us down in the end – just because they played with words. What did it matter? It was money. It all adds up to a scandal of monumental proportions. The other mob claimed fairness; that notwithstanding the vast amounts paid to the ex–Super League clubs, they had taken into account the payments from the ARL (Optus, etc. to their clubs). Utter bullshit! The ARL payments were *minute* compared with the money dished out by News. And they trotted out the line that, after all, *they* had closed down clubs such as Perth, Adelaide and Hunter Mariners. No comparison. These were contrived clubs put together in haste, the last two to give Super League enough teams; probably they should never have opened. Souths had been in the game since 1908, let's remember!

I suppose you've gotta say I'm biased in support of my football team and my belief in the principles involved. But even setting that aside I would find it impossible to come to terms with the statement made by former Super League chief Ian Frykberg, such a big player in the whole thing, during his evidence: 'The principal concern of myself and others was that we needed to ensure that the process was both the fairest possible, and seen to be fair. My fervent view was that no club should be excluded.' Frykberg declared himself satisfied that the criteria were 'fair on all clubs'. I wondered what sort of bonus Frykberg might have received for the job he did.

THE THINGS I HEARD: These are some of the admissions and statements that stuck in my mind as I listened to and observed day by day a passing parade of witnesses. I had no doubt the geographical blueprint for the 'desired' competition had been drawn up in some News Limited bunker long before. My personal belief is that the criteria was shaped to suit that. Some of the things that came up in evidence over the 40 days were never reported and my guess is that this was partly to do with 'vested interests' and partly to do with the boredom factor – the thing becoming *bloody* boring at times – and also because of the difficulties in fully understanding a very complex case. Journos were there some days and not others, and I wondered about that. I remembered earlier things from outside the court too, such as Ray Furse's memory of Roger Cowan (Penrith) telling a meeting of club officials at the Sheraton Hotel, Mascot, that the criteria favoured those clubs that had been rorting the system. This mixed bag of memories and things said is in no particular order of importance, but all of them, I believe, contain the seeds of things not being 'right' and build towards the bigger picture. Collectively they add up to dynamite.

• The admission by Peter Macourt, the deputy chief executive of News Limited, that some fans would be lost to the game if their favourite team (e.g. Souths) was axed from the competition.
• The declaration by Ian Frykberg that he wanted to reduce the number of teams to bring back true 'home and away' contests, followed by his admission that despite having only *one* home and

away–based competition in the previous 13 years, the ARL had been able to run the premiership without inconvenience and with success. Frykberg declared that he didn't know whether one-off payments to Super League clubs had increased their chances of inclusion in the NRL competition from 2000. (He should have rung me – I could have told him!)

• Neil Whittaker's claim that the exclusion of traditional Sydney sides from the competition was a necessary, although undesirable, price that had to be paid in the interests of putting the game 'back together'. (And Whittaker came from the ARL side of the fence!) He was in the box for a long time, and got pretty well chopped up.

• Whittaker's statement that he had lied when he said in late 1997, 'Had we [the ARL] not ended this war, we believe we could always have produced the best rugby league competition in Australia.' Whittaker's original declaration was, of course, right. But in court he recanted, and thus toed the party line.

• Whittaker's honest agreement that certain clubs had enjoyed 'unequal levels' of financial support during the years 1998–99, the two years taken into account in the criteria.

• Whittaker's further agreement that millions of dollars provided to Canberra 'significantly' helped the club meet the selection criteria. Evidence emerged that Canberra, the club bailed out by the ARL years before, would have operated at a loss of just under $7.6 million in 1998, and been insolvent. News Limited then gave the Raiders $7.593 million – resulting in a net operating loss of zero.

• Whittaker's admissions on the Melbourne Storm: that he had been told by the (criteria) committee that the club faced losses of more than $4 million in 1999 without the backing of private company Valimanda, and that he had relied on Ernst & Young to ensure the Storm met the financial criteria (i.e. he had not looked into the figures himself).

• Whittaker's frank admission (as CEO of NRL) that News Limited funding to help former Super League clubs join the NRL's new competition 'didn't sit comfortably' with him.

• The concession from former NRL general manager Peter Jourdain that News Limited funding of some (ex–Super League) clubs could have advantaged them in their quest for inclusion.

• The conviction of our people during the case that Auckland would fail within six months (they did), that North Queensland would be dead in the water within 12 months without a major rescue operation (they were) requiring a News Limited buyout in 2001 to save them when they were millions of dollars in the red, and that Melbourne would be out the door before long (we're still waiting on that). My own view is that Melbourne will die for certain. News surely has little more use for them chewing up the money now that Foxtel has the AFL (from 2002) to attract the pay TV subscribers – which, of course, was always the purpose of the whole episode.

• Jourdain's admission that he was not allowed to disclose the details of News Limited's funding of Super League teams to concerned ARL clubs. Jourdain declared that he never envisaged News Limited would give multi-million-dollar payouts to Super League clubs when he helped to design the criteria for entry into the competition.

• The admission by Richard Fisher of Ernst & Young that Melbourne Storm was selected for inclusion in the competition despite being dependent on $1.3 million of outside funding for its survival. Fisher further admitted that he had made the recommendation for Melbourne's inclusion without information about Valimanda Pty Ltd's ability or willingness to continue the club's funding. Fisher told the court that he would have been 'concerned' had he seen correspondence outlining Melbourne's funding arrangement with News Limited.

From our point of view, Fisher's strong role in the process deserved attention. In 1998 Fisher undertook a marketing assessment of Souths, gaining an intimate knowledge of the working of our club, the internal mechanics and internal finances in the process. That experience was a string in his bow when he tendered for the position (overseeing the criteria) with the NRL. We complained about a conflict of interest: that he had gained a deep knowledge of one club (Souths), which put things out of kilter from the start, because he had no inner knowledge of all of the others.

• Evidence that both the Brisbane Broncos and Western Suburbs were allowed to include payments from their own leagues clubs in their sponsorship submissions to help satisfy the criteria, in contrast to Souths, who were not allowed to include payments from Souths Juniors (which of course was not our own leagues club).

• The other side of that coin: the refusal to accept written declarations (August 6, and September 28) to Neil Whittaker from Henry Morris that the $4.5 million being invested in the Rabbitohs by Souths Juniors was a genuine sponsorship as opposed to a grant. This was an absolutely critical event in the whole thing. The NRL selection committee took the line that the money was for 'operational control'.

• News Limited created a subsidiary called NRLI (National Rugby League Investments) to be a partner in the running of the NRL, on a 50–50 arrangement with the ARL. News Limited owns 100 per cent of NRLI. One of its defences of the *Trade Practices Act* claim was that even though it (News Limited) was the one who may have offended section 45 by entering into an arrangement that was designed to exclude competition, the party that was going to *implement* the 14-team comp was not News, but the NRL. News were claiming this was a completely separate entity, and independent contractor. In fact, this new company was totally accountable to News. It was a completely spurious defence.

• The admission by NRL finance director Ed Farish that the Melbourne Storm needed an extra $2 million to meet its 1999 commitments – above and beyond its estimates in the business plan put to the criteria committee.

• The criteria – so deeply flawed – did not, unbelievably, reflect the area of junior development by clubs, did not take into account the number of international players nurtured by clubs or the part any club had played in making rugby league one of Australia's premier sports.

• The indication that Ernst & Young had initially given the nod to the Juniors' $1.5 million per year being accepted as 'sponsorship', but that the NRL criteria committee had hit it on the head. I can tell you this: that right up to and including the night before we were kicked out of the competition, the NRL was still checking our financial figures. My understanding is that the last call to Mark Colley at the club came late in the evening of October 14. There is no doubt that the NRL went over Souths with an especially fine-tooth comb while accepting without question Ernst & Young's assessments on the other clubs.

The case turned into a gruelling slog which demanded a great deal from all involved. Nick Pappas and his team worked to the point of exhaustion for us. One afternoon when he got back from the court there were 27 faxes waiting from this battalion of legal opponents, each requiring an immediate and complex reply. The solicitors worked through the night on quite a few occasions. Even the other side wondered how our team hadn't drowned in a sea of paper. There was no enjoyment during the case, although I admit to occasionally sneaking a second helping of the delicious Portuguese tarts during the daily lunch breaks in the 14th floor cafeteria. The Souths' support group were given free coffee daily. I'm sure all of us were glad when our turn in the witness box was done – me, Neil Whittaker, Ian Frykberg, Ed Farish, Peter Macourt and the rest. The interrogation throughout was icy and tough. It was 'nothing personal', the other side said, but it was bruising stuff. In a comment to the media at one stage when my turn was finally done, I said: 'It's the toughest fight I've ever had.' Nolene was with me all the way, every day, encouraging and supporting.

In court they tore us down whenever they could. They accused us of falsely inflating crowd figures via cut-price tickets (something other clubs did, but not us). And they trotted out a letter from Complete Marketing which attacked the running of the club, claiming we lacked 'leadership, direction, systems, processes and energy'.

Details of Complete Marketing reports were leaked to the Murdoch press (*The Australian*) later in the year, no doubt to twist the knife a little more firmly. This was in line with tactics right throughout. Two separate and negative reports, apparently casting serious doubts over Souths' viability – one written by Bernie Lange, one by Mark Colley – were quoted in a lengthy article. At least the newspaper had the good grace to publish this paragraph: 'It is a picture steadfastly rejected by Souths chairman George Piggins who accuses the consultants once hired of working to undermine, rather than preserve, the club's future.'

Six weeks into the hearing, in early August, there was a dramatic new twist. We were asked to provide tangible proof of the fair dinkumness of Souths' Millennium Management Plan, about which I had expressed personal, honest concerns at both court hearings. The plan, covering the Rabbitohs' entire operations for the next five years, included a proposed sponsorship base of $20 million. Prove that you can raise half that amount, said Justice Finn on August 2, produce signed affidavits from sponsors to that effect. Finn was effectively saying that any Souths readmission to the NRL must not be a wasted exercise, with a talentless team without long-term financial backing. Our deputy chairman, Mike Whitney, told the media that the club already had $6.5 million, via sponsorships from the likes of Souths Juniors, Able Printing, telecommunications company RSL COM, clothing maker ISC and Express Glass. Said Whitney, 'We need someone to say, "We'll give you $3 million over a three-year option."'

Well, through the efforts of Andrew Denton and Whitney, that 'someone' arrived in the shape of Channel 7 boss Kerry Stokes. In a great gesture, based on his belief in the principles involved in the Souths' fight, Stokes pledged $3 million through one of his companies – a million a year for three years. The Stokes deal ambushed the 'futility' argument pleaded by our opponents, that there was no point putting Souths back in because we didn't have the required cash. A spokesman for Stokes, Tim Allerton, told the media that the Channel 7 chairman empathised with

Souths' battler image and believed the history of rugby league was being undermined by the Rabbitohs' exclusion. Meanwhile there was talk of Seven producing a 'Rabbitohs' rival to *The Footy Show*. On Helen Grasswill's excellent *Australian Story* shown in August 2001, Kerry Stokes revealed his side of the story. Stokes said, 'They [Denton and Whitney] came up to see me and told me the full story of the Rabbitohs. Their passion . . . I've never met two more committed people than they were to this cause. I was given to understand they [News Limited] weren't particularly happy with us making the commitment we did. But as I said at the time . . . when we make a commitment, the commitment is sound. And I won't be swayed into breaking a commitment by anybody.' South Sydney will always be grateful for what Kerry Stokes did.

The other mob were desperate to get Stokes into court to quiz him on his support for us, but mainly, I suspect, on his business operations. Being no mug, Stokes was understandably not keen. Why would he want to give another media organisation (News Limited) a free kick? The newspapers described him as the 'missing link' in the case. After much debate Justice Finn refused to allow Stokes's affidavit in which he confirmed his $3 million commitment, but did agree to allow a bank guarantee and security search of Stokes's many companies to be tendered. So the Stokes money was 'on board' and Souths had the required $10 million. Stories reached us that Rupert Murdoch was 'ballistic' about Stokes's entry into the fray.

At the start of September, after 40 long days (the case became known as 'the 40 days and nights'), it was at last over, following final submissions and slow dreary sessions weighed down in technical argument. We reckoned we had done as much as we could and all that was left to do now was to wait. In the final days of the court case, Souths had played a match against Sydney's Lebanon team at Redfern, and I invited the new NRL chief executive David Moffett along. Moffett turned up in a red-and-green jacket and was given polite applause by our crowd. At fulltime, when enthusiastic kids invaded the field to chase autographs and kick footballs around where the battle had just been fought (Souths 34–22), I turned to Moffett and said: 'I know how to fix rugby league. Just bottle what you see out there.'

The Lebanon game had been a spontaneous reaction to a brilliantly successful promotion – a match we played against a visiting American team, 'the Tomahawks', at Redfern. We drew a crowd of 20,000 for the US match and quickly organised the game against Lebanon for the following week.

On the eve of Justice Finn's judgment, in early October 2000, former Souths player and Origin coach Phil Gould wrote a powerful piece for the *Sun-Herald*. Previewing the next day's verdict, he declared, 'While I respect Justice Finn's education and qualifications I would prefer to go with the esteemed judge in such matters, Blind Freddie. Good ole Blind Freddie can see that Souths should be back in the NRL competition. In fact Freddie believes it was a gross injustice that Souths were excluded in the first place. The people who presided over this decision should hang their heads in shame.'

Gould pointed to the situation of the Auckland Warriors who, shortly before, had collapsed financially, leaving players and officials unpaid. In a major scandal given less attention than it warranted, players eventually received some money – but nowhere near their entitlements. He wrote: 'The handling of the Warriors' situation has been an absolute disgrace. Remember the Warriors supposedly passed the same criteria examination that expelled Souths and forced Wests, Balmain, Manly and Norths to merge . . . Good one boys!'

'Souths hoping for the best, ready for the worst,' read one newspaper headline on the big day, Friday, October 3. The club was ready for its biggest party, or 'one hell of a wake', said the *Daily Telegraph*. My personal 'preparation' had been some time down at the farm painting fences.

In his 181-page judgment, Justice Paul Desmond Finn went the other way. He rejected our claims that the NRL's selection criteria breached the *Trade Practices Act* and contractual law by excluding Souths from the competition. In a document which someone described as being 'mired in ponderous legal argument', he wrote: 'Souths' view . . . was that rugby league is an icon to be preserved for the people who love and support it, not a product to be carved up to the media for their own financial gratification. It is usually only fortuitous that some legal principle could be found that could provide such preservation sought. I have not been able to arrive at the conclusion in the present proceedings that such a principle is available to Souths.'

Justice Finn indicated that he had mined the law in search of such a principle. If he had found it, probably we would have got the nod. That was our strong feeling, giving further hope that the judge felt that Souths had proved their case, but couldn't find a law to hook that feeling up to. *Morally* he seemed to be saying we should be there, which of course was in tune with 95 per cent of the population, but the sad thing was that ultimately he couldn't see behind the legal argument.

Finn found that with no terms of fairness implied in the contract with the NRL (the one signed before the first-round game of 1998) that the 14-team arrangement was not exclusionary. He also found against Souths on the question of whether there was a class of people affected by our exclusion from the competition. He found in our favour on a third point, throwing out the other side's contention that 'the NRL' was an independent contractor. The bottom line was that we'd lost.

Stunned and upset, I struggled to find the words to indicate how I felt. How *we* felt. It was 10.35 on a Friday morning and I felt like I had been run over by a bus. But there was a huge media army to be faced, and our fans back at the club. And I knew very clearly what had to be done; that we had to take the fight one final step, and appeal to the full bench of the Federal Court. Back at the club I quickly sensed the air of defiance, an attitude of 'stuff 'em, let's keep fighting!' Before long there was advice from our legal team that there may be a case for overturning Finn's judgment on trade practices grounds. 'We will only stop fighting when we have exhausted every legal avenue,' I told our fans back at the leagues club. 'Hang in there. We're not beaten yet . . . we will march again!' The newspaper headlines and photos the next day were becoming sadly familiar now. The photos were of crying, distraught people – images of great sadness and loss and grief. But our determination to fight on was as strong as ever. 'For the NRL and News Limited they must feel as though they're living through a Dracula movie,' I said. 'Every time the bludgers think they've killed us we re-emerge to fight on.'

Men such as Alan Jones, Andrew Denton and Phil Gould spat out their anger. Jones said: 'You can't build history by destroying history. To argue that Souths, the most successful club in Australia, doesn't belong in rugby league is laughable.' Gould witnessed the grief-stricken scenes that followed the verdict: 'I am embarrassed that this can happen in the sport to which I have devoted the whole of my adult life. More than that I feel embarrassed as an Australian that this can happen in my country. Removing South Sydney from rugby league is like knocking down the Town Hall to put up a hamburger joint.'

Tucked away in the judgment were words that confirmed something that I firmly believed: if the ARL clubs had had the guts to tough it out after 1997 and keep going as a separate competition, Super League would have withered and died, and the News Limited grip on the game would have been cut loose. On page 75 mention was made of 1997 meetings between the likes of Ian Frykberg, Peter Macourt, Lachlan Murdoch and Ken Cowley. Justice Finn wrote: 'Mr Frykberg indicated at a number of those meetings that he did not consider Super League sustainable as a separate competition in the medium to long term.' Frykberg was gone from rugby league within a week of the court decision, stepping down as a League director and NRL committee man. He had done his job, I suppose.

I learned only later of a telephone hook-up on the day of the judgment, involving chief executives of the 14 NRL clubs. The question was put to them whether there was any support out there for Souths. The answer was a deathly silence. No surprises there in view of the previous 'loyalty' shown by them to a fellow club under the hammer.

You could feel the anger and the passion growing in the community in the days following Paul Finn's decision. We had failed some bodgie criteria put up by the NRL. Well my message to them was that they had failed the *people's* criteria, having been entrusted with the safeguarding, promotion and propagation of the beautiful game of rugby league. We would march again in downtown Sydney on November 12, and this time we wanted 'gridlock'.

And we got it, on a magnificent, emotional Sunday on which we drew 80,000 people to the heart of the city. Remarkably, the march had been put together in just eight days. That day the loss in the courtroom became a triumph of the people in the streets. And they came from all over – the union movement, the bush, the other clubs, from supporters groups who believed a great injustice had been done – to join the red-and-green army. I have no doubt there were many people there who had no interest in rugby league. They were there because what had happened to us was a symbol of what was happening elsewhere in Australia and especially in the bush as giant corporations cut and closed, downsized and played havoc with the lives of ordinary people. NSW Labor Council secretary Michael Costa called the rally 'a response to another example of corporate bullies beating up on the working class'. The Labor member for Sydney, Tanya Plibersek, continued the theme: 'If you look at an area like Waterloo, they've lost their Commonwealth Bank, they've lost their post office and now they've lost the most important recreational focus in their lives in losing the club.'

The big march was a wonderful example of anger channelled into something positive and worthwhile. And I can tell you there was a very deep collective anger within the club, and no shortage of suggestions such as that the march should go past Fox Studios and News Limited. A truckload of eggs donated to the club and destined for throwing at News's Surry Hills headquarters was quickly passed on to charity. All through the struggle we maintained a firm policy of non-violence, and the point was reinforced via the Internet and fliers. I'm sure News Limited would have loved to present us as a violent rabble. In fact all we were was a close-knit community.

The march went as before, from Redfern Oval, down past the Central Railway, and up George Street to the Town Hall. And what a line-up it was, with blokes like Frank Hyde, Mick Cronin, Bob O'Reilly, Alan Clarkson, Jack Gibson, Peter Wynn, Mikey Robins, Benny Elias, John Sattler, Alan Jones, Lisle Munro, Andrew Denton, Phil Gould, Bernie Purcell, Jack Rayner, Ian Heads, Clem Kennedy, Albert Clift and actor John Jarratt joining politicians, other media personalities, a solid Newcastle contingent headed by Barbara Davis and the Souths faithful. The view from the Town Hall steps was just amazing as people arrived from every conceivable angle to swell the crowd. In the midst of the huge throng the colours of other clubs were dotted in amongst the predominant red and green. CFMEU representatives, with their experience at large gatherings, did a mighty job at this rally as they had at the first.

Only one other club was there 'officially'; neighbours Easts had sent a strong representation. There were messages of support from John Howard, Kim Beazley and Paul Harragon, and a letter from Laurie Daley, who had been touring the bush. Daley described the game in the country areas as 'under seige', before offering words of encouragement: 'But one thing that hasn't changed since my last trip to the bush is the spirit and love for South Sydney that your fellow supporters continue to show. The red and green is still proudly worn by your fans, young and old, and I am certain they are there with you in spirit today.' The Roman Catholic bishop of Canberra, Geoffrey Maine, also wrote: 'Rugby league without Souths is like saying my church can exist without the Pope.' Henry Morris waved a big stick: the Juniors would take their 3500 players to rugby union if Souths were not reinstated to the NRL competition. 'Our blokes don't want to be Roosters, they don't want to be Eagles, they don't want to be Eels, they want to be Rabbitohs!' said Henry. Alan Jones called Souths 'a heritage club'. He stormed, 'We're saying to the league, you can't touch us!'

I was last at the rostrum, at the tail end of a long list of speakers. 'The fight's not over until you people walk away,' I told them. 'I promise you, if you don't walk away, if you want to fight, I'll come back every year and stay and fight with you.'

On that memorable day the die was cast, as Sydney and the bush came together to declare what they felt about what had been done to the South Sydney Rabbitohs. We would go on, to the full-time whistle, and into extra time if need be. On November 24 we lodged our appeal against Paul Finn's decision and served copies of the notice on the four respondents – News Limited, National Rugby League Investments, the NRL and the Australian Rugby League.

17. The Longest Wait

Those who know sport, who appreciate its values, its history and its traditions, know that replacing values, history and traditions with unsubstantiated, undefended and unargued theory about 14 teams will leave a scar on the game and its supporters which will not be easily, if ever, repaired. There are people running the game who don't understand the emotion and the passion that reside in putting on the jumper. And that includes the Souths jumper. Rugby league without emotion and passion betrays its history.

Alan Jones

AFTER JUSTICE PAUL FINN uttered his dry, unemotional verdict in the Federal Court, driving another nail into the coffin of the South Sydney Rabbitohs, we maintained the rage, taking our team to the country districts where the support for the Souths cause has been so strong. We filled the Roundhouse at the University of New South Wales with another bumper crowd for our Red & Green Ball. We raised more money in the endless chase. And we boxed three rounds or so in another short court hearing which provided hope that all was not lost. Then we waited for yet another verdict – as a team, a club, a community in limbo.

I filled the mark-time period with the other things in my life: keeping an eye on business in the city, and beating a regular path to the two places Nolene and I have out in the bush, south of the city. Now and then I pore over maps trying to figure if there is a back country route, via bushtracks and fire trails, from the stud at Burrawang in the Southern Highlands to Lake Conjola. Even via horseback it looks tricky, with the Shoalhaven River to be forded at some point . . . but not impossible.

And, you know, tackling the 'impossible' and trying to make it possible has become a way of life at South Sydney. I would like a dollar for every time we have been told via some 'expert' advice or a newspaper headline that we were 'dead in the water'. I read a quote recently about the unlimited possibilities that exist when people are passionate and totally committed to a cause. That theme is in tune with South Sydney, with the central core group of people who refused to flinch and who steered the ship, and with our supporters, from all stratas of society, from all walks of life, who stayed so solid.

The letters and faxes of support fill many boxes at home. Here, representative of the feelings of ordinary people at what was done to South Sydney, are excerpts from just four of them: Letter from Darrell Edwards, November 30, 1999:

> I am one of many Souths supporters currently serving in the Australian Army and posted in the Darwin region.
>
> I am proud to be a member of South Sydney Leagues Club and proud of the stance the club has taken and of your personal efforts. The Club of the Century is still there fighting for all that it is good in Rugby League and Mr Average Aussie, Mr Battler and Mr Sports Fan are all behind you 100%. Fight On.

Fax from Bob Arnold, managing director, HI-TORQUE, October 15, 1999:

> I have already taken a stance and cancelled advertising in any Murdoch related company.
>
> I have cancelled my Gold Ansett Golden Wings with 1.8 million miles credit. No-one in my company will ever fly Ansett again. We spent approximately $300,000 in air fares last year. I have advised Ansett that all company corporate cards have been cancelled.
>
> In relation to Diners credit cards, 21 credit cards have just been cancelled and the management of all the above companies have been informed of my disgust at the sacking of South Sydney Football Club.
>
> More people should take the same stance as I have done with my company. I employ 75 people.

Letter from Noel H.K. Lewis, managing director, Yellow Express, November 13, 2000:

> Please find enclosed my cheque to join the club and a donation of $1000. I also threw in $100.00 at the rally. Put me down for more if needed in the battle with the bastards.
>
> I was wiping the tears away from my eyes for most of the rally. A combination of remembering my roots and being among the 'unfashionable' working-class people for the first time in 30 years.

Copy of letter to NRL from Mark Berg, sports organiser, Maroubra Bay Public School, October 18, 1999:

> I am deeply disturbed by the decision taken on Friday, 15th October, in which the NRL elected to remove South Sydney DRLFC from the premiership competition.

The NRL decision is reckless and foolhardy. The teachers that I have consulted in this zone PSSA feel offended and hurt. All we have tried to achieve now appears lost.

Unfortunately as the NRL has removed South Sydney I feel you have removed our students' aspirations and their ability to represent their District Team. Our parent bodies and the broader school communities are devastated.

I shall be moving at our next sports association meeting a recommendation to the effect that our strong Friday afternoon League competition be suspended. Further, that ESPSSA affiliated schools boycott involvement in the 2000 Westmont Shield Knockout Competition. Also we will not select a zone or contribute representatives to a combined zone team to attend the area PSSA League Trials in 2000. This boycott will stay in place until such time as the South Sydney DRLFC is returned to its rightful place in the premier rugby league competition.

AFL development officers have already begun active campaigns to attract new players and will run a program over the next four weeks in our area at Latham Park. It looks like a very attractive option.

And so it went, day after day, people moved to put pen to paper to express how they felt.

Along the way, via the big rallies and the awareness of the injustice done to the South Sydney District Football Club by big business, we recruited many, many people to our cause. Not always rugby league fans, they joined the fight because they saw us as representative of a bigger canvas – of a world in which, increasingly, huge corporations such as News Limited roll brutally over the 'little people' in chasing their own business ambitions. People in Australia, and other countries too, are suddenly saying 'enough', and at South Sydney, we were in the middle of all that, fighting for something that is good and right and important.

As I discussed way back in Chapter 1, the fight took its toll. People from afar perhaps saw me standing staunchly and unaffected by all the conflict, but my health suffered. There were casualties of a different kind too, some of them stemming from the continuing stress and pressure that this decision by Rupert Murdoch and the football code he owns created for everyone involved at South Sydney.

One such instance came in early December 2000 when Souths deputy chairman Mike Whitney and I clashed heatedly at a board meeting, an incident that led to Whitney resigning from the board. It is something that would have been better off not happening, and I have my regrets.

I'm sure he does too.

The story of what happened has never been made public, but probably should be told here. It is, after all, part of what went on over these years at Souths. The fight for survival had been such a long hard one, and I'd been in the thick of it since late 1994 and I'd said to our board that when it was done – whatever the outcome once we had taken it to the very last possibility – that my inclination was to step down, to move on to a few of the things I had started in my life and enjoyed, like breeding racehorses.

During the Justice Finn Federal Court hearing, at a get-together between three of our people – Mike Whitney, Deirdre Grusovin and Laurie Brereton – and members of the Juniors board, Whitney made some reference to how he intended things would be between the two clubs when I stepped down and he became chairman. There was ongoing tension between the clubs at the time over the 'grant'/'sponsorship' argument that was going on in court, and over the unexplained appearance of a piece of paper on a Juniors letterhead, referring to the $1.5 million as a 'grant'. Whitney apparently talked about 'festering wounds' between the clubs and of his belief they should be 'like brothers'.

News of what Michael had said got back to me. Not long afterwards I invited Michael and his partner Natalie over for dinner. In a private conversation between the pair of us I told him I thought it would have been better if he hadn't taken that line. At that time we were still in the Federal Court case and the other mob would feed off any rumours of a crack in solidarity at our club. In Whitney's presence I called Juniors' chairman Henry Morris, who had not been at the meeting in question, but who had been briefed by a third party on what Mike Whitney had said. The thing was that I was not offended by anything said, because I had told Whitney privately that I *would* be going when the timing was right. But the fact was that back at that time, I just didn't like the clique that existed on our board. The call to Morris made, we had dinner.

Anyhow it didn't seem to be any sort of continuing worry until a Saturday morning a couple of months later, early December 2000, when Frank Cookson, who had taken over from Henry Morris as chairman of the Juniors football club, called for a meeting between the two boards to discuss where we were taking Souths, why we weren't putting a first division side in the comp and so on. Frank was on his way back from holidays on the north coast that morning and was running late. But most of the Juniors board were gathered outside our boardroom waiting for the meeting to start. I spoke to them briefly and they all seemed to be of the opinion that we shouldn't run a first division team in 2001 – and that it was the district club's call anyway.

In the process of waiting for the meeting Michael Whitney said something along the lines of 'I hope Barry Dunn (Juniors director) doesn't open his mouth today. If he does I'm going to give it to him.' I told him I didn't think it was too smart, bawling out a bloke in front of everyone, and especially so considering the Juniors were $1.5 million per year backers of ours. Barry Dunn was supporting our cause and I didn't want Michael arguing the point with him over something that I felt we had sorted out between ourselves. I said that Barry Dunn wasn't the person who had told me what Michael had said (that day at the

Juniors), and that I had heard it second-hand from another (Juniors) director. My understanding was Michael knew it had been Henry Morris who told me and not Barry; Henry told that to Michael on the phone, on the night he and Natalie came to my house for dinner.

Things became heated within the boardroom when Deirdre Grusovin got involved, saying something along the lines of: 'Well, did he say it or didn't he say it? You can't have it both ways.' That's when I blew up. I thought it questioned my integrity and I just snapped my brain. 'Who the friggin' hell do you think you're talking to?' I said. And I went on with it. Then Whitney intervened and said I had no right to talk to her (Deirdre) like that. And I thought to myself – Michael, you've really put me in a position. I said something like this to him: 'She's a politician sitting on a football board, and she gives as good as she gets. You can suit yourself – we can go out to the back office or we can go over to the park and settle it. But you won't stand over me.' I told them I was sick and tired of the clique that existed on the board and that I had been fed up with it all for some time. In the wake of what took place Whitney packed his briefcase and left the meeting.

Things quietened down and the meeting finally got going, and business got done. A week or so later at a CFMEU-hosted fundraising dinner (which raised more than $50,000 for our fight), Nicholas Pappas suggested to me that I owed Whitney an apology. And I told him, well, I probably owe half an apology . . . I shouldn't have challenged him to go over to the park. I subsequently tried to ring Michael, but couldn't get through, so I left a message on his mobile. Unbeknown to me he had gone to Bali for 10 days, and he didn't ring back. Nothing further was said.

At the next board meeting in early December 2000, Michael was there and as I walked in he stuck out his hand and said, 'G'day champ.' We shook hands. The board members mingled around for a time and then when I opened the meeting, he interrupted me. 'Mr Chairman,' he said, 'can I say something before we go any further?' And I said, 'Yes Michael, go ahead.' And he said, 'I resign,' and handed me a letter of resignation. He wished us well with the court case. There was a silence as I took the letter and put it down in front of me. 'Well, Michael,' I said, 'thank you for these last 18 months.' Whitney said his farewells to the other board members and left the room. No-one felt good about it.

I had nothing, and have nothing, against Michael Whitney. I like the bloke. He's a genuine Souths supporter, and I guess he'll always be that. The incident could probably be seen as some sort of reflection on the discomfort I had always felt being on the 'new' board. I had never been as comfortable with the changed board as with the old group at Souths, blokes like Bernie O'Neill, Ray Furse, Tony Henderson, Bob Byrne, Les Bell, Darryl Reilly, Merv Neave and Stan Browne, who had worked hard to keep the club active and alive in difficult times and all of whom had been selfless in their action in giving up their seats when we decided on a new direction as the threat to the club from the game's new leaders grew. When they stepped down our net asset position was a positive $1.8 million, which contributed a great deal towards our fight and gave us a platform on which to mount our campaign. When the old board took control the football club had been more than $1 million in debt. Subsequently, I felt there was some 'tag-teaming' on the new board, and said that when I opened up on the day Whitney and I clashed. I mentioned 'cliques' and that I felt there were forces working against me.

But having said that, the board that served throughout the court case was united behind the principle of Souths standing alone, and certainly, the board's commitment to the club and the principle of fighting on in the quest for justice could not be questioned. Look, to be very honest, maybe it *is* getting close to time for me to go. But it won't happen until I'm absolutely satisfied with the structure of both the board and the 'front office'. There may be new horizons that they can open up, and if it reaches a stage where I am hindering that, I'll know what to do. I am aware that a number of people have put their working lives on the line to a fair extent with some of the pro-Souths, anti-Murdoch things they have said publicly, undoubtedly angering what is probably the toughest and most influential corporation in Australia.

The 2001 premiership arrived in the heat of February, kicking off once again with no Souths.

To me, it had the smell of a game in steady decline. The much-hyped opening double-header at the Olympic Stadium drew only 54,000 (and how many thousands of 'freebies' were involved in this?), way down on previous crowds. From very early on, the merged teams were looking like dead weights in the competition, unable to draw crowds. Around Souths the inevitable 'merger' rumours circulated once again. This time it was both Canberra and Cronulla. Did anyone by now *really* believe that mergers were the future of rugby league?

Anyway, people had not given us a couple of million bucks for us to go that far and then buckle and merge. In the *Sydney Morning Herald*, Roy Masters had his say on the mergers when he wrote: 'The joint ventures are financial disasters.' Other clubs were bleeding red ink.

I am not alone in my concerns for the game, and the damage done by the dumping of South Sydney. Australian and the Storm coach Chris Anderson called the cutting of Souths 'sad' and said: 'I think there are decisions being made for other than football reasons. I thought Souths had a better case for being in the competition than, say, Eastern Suburbs. But money talks . . . and that's sad.'

There was still some smart thinking going on in the game, but regrettably not much of it seemed to come from the blokes pulling the strings. For example Wayne Bennett, a football man I respect and like, backed the sensible, simple idea of a 'two-tier' competition structure with some form of promotion and relegation between them each year – the right of the second-tier premiers to challenge the premier competition bottom team, or whatever. As Bennett said, such a system would have preserved the traditional clubs, and, most importantly, provided the priceless quality of hope to rugby league. A Wests or a Balmain or a Souths playing in the second tier would have been driven by the annual dream of winning selection to the top competition. How much better would something like that be than what we have now, with the killing-off of clubs who have been the game's lifeblood, and the creation of contrived merged teams which no-one cares about?

By 2001 match kick-off times were geared specifically to suit the wishes of pay TV programmers, not to the needs of the fans – another dumb decision made by the blokes running the game. They have taken away regular programming of matches. Once, fans of a particular club knew that their team would be at home every second Sunday at 3 pm, and away the other weeks. Now matches are all over the place, and at different kick-off times, at the whim of the TV decision makers. What happens is that people get out of the habit of going to the football, and all of a sudden they find that they don't miss it too much and that there are other, probably cheaper, things to do. The blokes running the game now have changed our way of life, and I don't think they can change it back. They have created a breed of people who watch their football on television, or worse, don't watch at all because the habit has died. The shattering of certainty and regularity in programming matches is just one of many tragic decisions made, just another to make you wonder about the calibre of the people holding the reins.

I don't care what any of the spin doctors try to make us believe. If anyone reckons there is anything like the same passion for rugby league as there once was, in either Queensland or New South Wales, they're kidding. The game from 1995 onwards has progressively dumped its grassroots and its tradition, and thrown away the things that made it strong. People abandoned it in droves. Many will never come back. The percentage of over-16s who have walked away from the game in our district, a growing trend on the wider scale I'm sure, is a real worry. Have a look at Balmain, Cronulla and Easts, the signs are there of a game disintegrating at the bottom end. And the drop-off in the bush is alarming. In the first half of 2001, as we continued to work and promote to raise funds for the ongoing court case, we took a Souths team to several bush centres – to Maitland, Dubbo and Wagga – to play matches against the locals. Even for us, so well supported in the bush, the crowds were poor. Rank-and-file sympathy was with us, but we were flat out drawing enough people to pay our way. It was a reflection of the way things were going for rugby league in NSW country districts.

The sweet irony of the whole thing for blokes like me was that Murdoch and his company by then had long since become captives of the new sporting 'vision' they had tried to establish after a battle that was purely and simply about pay TV rights, and one that had got right out of hand. In the *Australian Financial Review* in late 1999, journalist Ivor Ries summed it up when he wrote: 'News Corp's continuing need to pump new cash into the NRL serves as a lesson to media moguls all over the world about the dangers of trying to "own" a sport in order to obtain the media rights.'

We went back to court 21A in the Federal Court building in May 2001 to ask the full bench of the court to overturn Justice Paul Finn's verdict of the previous year. Our claim was that Finn had erred nine times in his November judgment. Our QC, David Jackson, asked Justices Heerey, Moore and Merkel to order that Souths be reinstated to the NRL and have its legal fees paid by the defendants. The claim was that the 14-team competition was discriminatory and breached the *Trade Practices Act* because it curtailed competition. The scenario we hoped for, the best result, would be a permanent injunction restraining the NRL from excluding Souths on the basis of the 14-team term. The hope was that such a judgment would come with substantial damages awarded to us. Even with such a result there were no guarantees of readmission. And we knew that.

The case, argued in dense legal terms over three days, seemed to go well for our side. David Jackson was particularly impressive when he summed up Souths' case. Our blokes reckoned it was 50–50, and there was speculation that they might have been erring on the side of caution in that assessment. But the law being what it is, who would know? A group of 60 or so of us stuck it out for the duration, and it was heavy going. We walked away none the wiser. And settled back, as autumn turned to winter, for a verdict. There were no guarantees. A victory for us would not absolutely ensure us a place in the premiership although it would certainly enhance the chances. A further step, into the High Court, was not impossible.

I found myself thinking a lot about the future, mine and the game's. I knew I would be okay if I got cut off from rugby league. I would almost certainly be a healthier person and free to concentrate on things that I had set aside in my life. Of the game, I was not so sure.

Stories suggesting that one day there would only be one rugby code appeared from time to time in the papers. And when you look at football on a dollar-and-cents basis – and that's about the only way it's looked at today – you've gotta think that one day News Limited, or someone, might drive the two rugby codes together. After all, it'd be cheaper to finance one game than two. And the lines between the games are blurred, not what they used to be. Union has drawn closer to league in the way it's played on the field and with the damage done to league, union has made considerable inroads too at schools level, where once it was just an upper-crust GPS game. I honestly never thought that rugby union would ever get on top of league, but the indications are now that it's doing that, and especially so as rugby is now such a genuinely international game, played in so many countries, and drawing huge TV audiences. At the same time rugby league's international platform, which has always been small, has just about collapsed. I doubt that rugby union needs much from the game itself when it comes to rugby league. But there are two things within the game it would love to have: the players and the revenue base provided by the successful leagues clubs. Keep an eye on it. Anything's possible in a day and age when the people running sports prefer to classify them as 'businesses'.

From every possible way you look at the period since 1995, it's been a shocker for rugby league, such a bloody tragedy that it was our game that was caught in the middle of all the greed and self-interest. A great sport has been changed forever. And the damage done in city and country is beyond measuring. I hope all of that is sinking in with the people responsible, but considering their qualities, I doubt it. How do they feel, I wonder, when they learn of country towns that no longer play rugby league? Of junior clubs that have crumbled and died? Of the countless people who don't give a bloody damn about the game anymore? I know what they *should* feel. A deep shame.

It is all so sad. The game has been such a part of Australian sporting life, especially so on the eastern seaboard, for so many years. Its rawness and toughness forged a special link with the Aussie character from the first time it was played, all those seasons ago. That rugged appeal of the game still exists today, and remains the only hope. There are terrific athletes playing league in 2001, as there always have been, and the pure 80 minutes on the paddock can still be something very special. But the Murdoch raiders and their fellow travellers ripped something right from the very deepest roots of it when they arrived with their cheque books and promises. At vast expense they created a game which has all but lost its soul. It is now much closer to 'product', and far less appealing.

South Sydney, my club, is right at the heart of all that. I am fortunate. I am able to draw on the memories I have of a time when rugby league was pretty much as it should be and you played alongside your mates on a Saturday arvo, proud of the red-and-green jumper you were wearing and revelling in the opportunity. With the style, the unmatched success, wonderful traditions and tight community spirit, Souths stood for the very best of rugby league. The Rabbitohs at the end of the 20th century represented the heritage of sport in Australia. They offered priceless links with a game which had been so special. Yet, in trying to turn this wonderful sport into a business the corporate mob did their darnedest to kill us.

But, as I wrote many, many pages ago, the rugby league world turned on July 6, 2001 when Justices Moore and Merkel delivered their Federal Court judgments in favour of the Rabbitohs. This book therefore is no traditional Agatha Christie–style thriller, with the big revelation at the end. Instead I chose to start it with the great and good news of Souths winning their long fight, of justice being done, and of the game of rugby league being given hope for its future. For me it represents both a perfect beginning and ending to this story. Even though the NRL and News Limited are seeking leave to appeal to the High Court against the Federal Court decision, South Sydney, Pride of the League, are back in the competition in 2002. But against all the odds in this grim tale, we have a happy ending, and rugby league is, perhaps, back in with a chance. As has happened many times in the game's past, rugby league's fortunes will once more be hitched to the most famous colours in football: the cardinal and myrtle. If there is to be a revival for this fallen game, it will be a red and green–driven revival. But all that is for another season . . . and another storyteller . . .

But, by the last month of winter 2001, it was clear that I would have to stay in fighting mode and so would the club. My problems with sections of the Souths board re-emerged. When I attempted to nominate an excellent candidate (Jim Hatfield) to the board, I couldn't even get a seconder! Jim eventually got on when Sean Garlick stepped away from the board after being appointed football manager of the club, but that didn't change the total lack of support the board had afforded the club chairman. I decided then and there that I would take a 'ticket' to the members – putting forward a board comprised of people I knew I could work with – and let the rank and file members decide.

In the wider picture, the conciliatory words that News Limited had offered when we won the Federal Court case initially appeared to count for little when, in early August, they announced they would be seeking leave to appeal to the High Court on *all* the trade practices aspects of the Federal Court decision. A week or so before I had been invited to lunch in the News boardroom by company heavies John Hartigan and Peter Macourt. It was an affable enough affair, and at least there was final confirmation that Souths were safely back in the competition for 2002 with a guaranteed spot until the end of the 2005 season, whatever else happened. During 2005 all clubs would be subjected to assessment via 'benchmarks' established by the NRL. The word 'criteria' had apparently been dropped from the language of the game. Just a few days later the papers were served, confirming the News Limited decision to seek leave to appeal. They indicated that News were seeking costs, which could amount to several million dollars.

At face value it seemed we were going to have to fight on two fronts: defend against this legal move by News Limited, while at the same time trying to put together a professional and successful side for the 2002 premiership. I went public, via the *Sun-Herald* of August 5, expressing my concerns. I told the paper's Danny Weidler that we were sick and tired of fighting News and now the bloody thing was on again with the chance they could bankrupt us. The responses were quick and positive. In the car on my way back from a country trip to Gunnedah, after a day on which grandstands at the local ground had been named after famous footballing sons of the town – John O'Neill, John 'Dallas' Donnelly and Ron Turner – John Hartigan rang me with reassuring words. Soon afterwards a letter from News arrived confirming that it would not press the issue of costs, and would pay Souths' costs covering the High Court hearing, or hearings. In essence, they would pick up the tab. This was welcome news, and we refocused on building a football team we hoped would do us proud.

I suspect Murdoch himself was probably behind the decision for News to go in hard with the appeal. I'm sure he wouldn't have liked it one bit that the little bloke had climbed off the canvas and thumped the big bloke. Perhaps the News Limited view was that the Federal Court decision – which deemed them to be running an illegal 14-team competition in breach of the *Trade*

Practices Act – was a black mark against the name of the company, and they felt they were obliged to fight it to the limit. And so it was they would bid to challenge the finding of the Full Bench.

Meanwhile there was agitation elsewhere. The Wests Tigers – comprising two foundation clubs which had played alongside Souths since 1908 – made mumbled threats about suing over the fact that it was to be a 15-team competition, instead of the 14 they were promised. St George continued to be disappointing in their attitude towards us, even trying to muscle in on the initially suggested 2002 opening round game – Rabbitohs v. Dragons – and claim it as their home gate. I didn't want us to play St George; I have nothing against their members, but I reckon their officials are ordinary, as you may have gathered. But if I was going to let my feelings towards Saints' officials interfere with my capacity to run South Sydney professionally, then I didn't deserve to be chairman. The fact was, St George were the best financial prospect. So a compromise was arrived at: we would resurrect the annual Charity Shield game and play St George in that. But our bumper opening round premiership game, at the SCG in mid-March, would be against old rivals Easts (Sydney Roosters).

The euphoria that followed the Federal Court decision of July 6 didn't last long for me. Within days I was battling against a Souths board that I believed contained unsupportive members. One thing was for sure: I wasn't going to be a puppet chairman for any board. As far as I was concerned, there had to be changes. It was them or me. So there eventuated a short, sharp election campaign, and when it came to the vote, I got 93 per cent support – and three businessmen who had my confidence and who I knew could do the job joined the board: Peter Hodge, Chris Wilson and David Wilson. The Lissing brothers, Martin and Jerry, were voted off, along with Steve McDermott.

My feeling now is we have a board to carry us into the future – but also that until we get a major leagues club backer, it will always be a struggle. I think of Parramatta and the $70 million they have boasted of pouring in (without winning a premiership!). The plus is that we can be very strong in merchandising and marketing because of what we have achieved, and the support that has rallied behind us. As I write these final words of my story, the dual challenge to build the best possible 'new' Rabbitohs and to find the ideal future for our leagues club at Redfern was continuing. In November 2001, the Juniors made a move to take over the running of the Redfern club. But their offer was nowhere near what I believed it needed to be. They offered to pay AMP off ($6 million) then give the club a two-year trial. If it wasn't profitable at that stage, they would have the right to sell the lot – building, land etc. – and grab the cash and the poker machine licences. Within their offer there was no provision for ongoing support of the football club. It was simply not acceptable to me, or to plenty of others. I had put 10 years of my life into that place (the leagues club) and no way was I going to allow someone to come in and walk away with the whole kaboodle after a couple of years. As far as I was concerned there were other, better options. A special meeting in late November knocked back the Juniors bid – and the battle continued. I felt strongly about the issue and decided to challenge again for the chairmanship of the leagues club. I was elected at November's meeting, knowing there was still unfinished business to complete.

Progressively our management team for the future fell into place, headed by Paul Dunn as chief executive. And the quartet of Dunn, Sean Garlick (football manager), Craig Coleman and Phil Gould cast a wide net to gather the mix of young and more experienced players who would comprise the new Souths team – and take us into 2002 and beyond. I didn't have much input; I knew I could identify a footballer, but the fact was I hadn't watched the game for two years. For the administrative team the challenge was to balance the sport, the club and its tradition with the business side of the operation. A successful club these days has to be able to manage both those strands well. As Alan Jones said in his speech at a 400-head gala luncheon we hosted at the Sydney Cricket Ground at the end of the 2001 season, the point Souths have arrived at now is not an ending. It is a beginning. We have our chance to lay down a model of responsible financial management which can show the way to all clubs.

In the wake of the July Federal Court decision, I found myself in demand, invited all over the place as a guest speaker. And you know, that's not really my go. But when the Ansett collapse happened in September 2001 and I was asked to go and talk to some of the workers, I did that, along with coach Craig Coleman. The flavour of what we said at the airport was what Souths had managed to achieve as a club by sticking together. I urged the Ansett people to do the same. What happened to that company was a disgrace – the fact that it was allowed to happen. The company and what it has been and should be in Australian life is such an enormous part of our community, and if it doesn't climb back off the floor, the government really has got something to answer for.

Among the invitations I received was one to the Newcastle–Parramatta grand final. I didn't go, because I had no interest in it. And to tell you the truth, I didn't feel like heading back to my first game of football with a team of blokes I didn't have much time for. I'll see them on level ground in 2002, when I'm there with my officials. That'll be soon enough. They won't be outgunned, and I won't be outgunned. I'll be there with my blokes – looking down on some of them and thinking how bloody weak they were.

So I watched the 2001 grand final at home, and I've gotta say it wasn't much like the grand finals I remembered. One mob scoring 24 points in one half . . . and the other mob getting 24 points in the second half – that's not grand final football! What happened to the wars of attrition that grand finals used to be, of sides defending their line for 20 minutes, of games that were real tests of stamina and character? I suppose though you could say the match was a fair example of modern football – all quickness and razzle dazzle, but without the toughness and the impact that was always in rugby league. I take nothing away from Newcastle. With Andrew Johns, the maestro, their maturity showed through. The first half reminded me of an older dog dealing with a pup, with the older dog now and then going whack! and the pup retreating and lying in a corner for a while, wondering what to do. The young Parramatta blokes were like that; they got flustered, and couldn't adjust. Bill Harrigan didn't add much of value. I think he's an arrogant ref and an ordinary one, and his display on grand final day was a long way short of great.

Rugby league is still a strong game, and a good game. But I think the blokes running it have gone a fair way towards ruining it by the way they've opened it up for the demands of TV, via the 10 metres rule and other changes. They have taken it too far. The game at its highest level now reminds me of the President's Cup football I was playing as a 19-year-old kid back in the '60s: athletic and fast, but lacking an essential quality.

By the end of 2001, we were heading towards 20,000 members on the books of the South Sydney RLFC – a number unprecedented in the history of the game. Responding to our recruitment drive, people came from far and wide to join, reflecting just how much Souths' win had meant to ordinary Australians. People do not want to see big business take over sport – that message couldn't have been any clearer. Souths' pending return raised the spirits of the game. And even though News Limited were taking us back to court, I suspected that deep down they were happy to see the Rabbitohs back too.

As the dust settled after the long fight, the other side of my life progressively looked more appealing: the thought of working down on the farm far away from it all, working with the horses, something I loved doing a whole lot more than arguing with people at board meetings. But as the season neared I made up my mind too that I wasn't going anywhere just yet. We had fought a hell of a battle because we knew we were right. No way was I going to walk away until Souths were 'bedded down', safely installed in the competition as we should be, and with the right people firmly in charge.

My aim – our aim at Souths – was to get back to where we once were: to being the Pride of the League. My personal hope is we're going to be in the competition for another 100 years and win another 20 premierships, and that no-one will ever again try to take all that away. And, whatever happens in rugby league's uncertain future, I'll always be a South Sydney football supporter. I look forward to the day when I'll just be a face in the crowd, relaxing and enjoying the game.

One football afternoon before too long, I'll be just that. There'll come a day pretty soon when I can look out over a stadium dotted with red and green and say to myself at last that we really had won, that we had fought a great and good fight against huge odds, and that justice had finally been delivered. And, best of all, that the proudest club in the League was truly going to live on because of that fight, for the enjoyment of football's future generations.

Ian Heads has written about the game of rugby league for more than 35 years for various publications including the *Daily* and *Sunday Telegraph*, *Rugby League Week*, the *Sydney Morning Herald* and the *Sun-Herald*. He was a league writer through the entire period of George Piggins's playing career. Since 1988 Heads has authored or co-authored 30 books, many of them on rugby league, including definitive histories of the game – *True Blue* and *The Kangaroos*, a history of the South Sydney Rabbitohs, and a best-selling pictorial history of the club, *Pride of the League*.